Modelling with Generalized
Stochastic Petri Nets

(W) WILEY SERIES IN PARALLEL COMPUTING

SERIES EDITORS:

R.G. Babb II, *Oregon Graduate Institute, USA*
J.W. de Bakker, *Centrum voor Wiskunde en Informatica, The Netherlands*
M. Hennessy, *University of Sussex, UK*
R. Oldehoeft, *Colorado State University, USA*
D. Simpson, *Brighton University, UK*

Modelling with Generalized Stochastic Petri Nets

M. Ajmone Marsan, *Politecnico di Torino, Italy*
G. Balbo, *Università di Torino, Italy*
G. Conte, *Università di Parma, Italy*
S. Donatelli, *Università di Torino, Italy*
G. Franceschinis, *Università di Torino, Italy*

JOHN WILEY & SONS
Chichester · New York · Brisbane · Toronto · Singapore

Copyright © 1995 by John Wiley & Sons Ltd.
           Baffins Lane, Chichester
           West Sussex PO19 1UD, England

           National Chichester (01243) 779777
           International (+44) 1243 779777

Other Wiley Editorial Offices

John Wiley & Sons, Inc., 605 Third Avenue,
New York, NY 10158-0012, USA

Jacaranda Wiley Ltd, 33 Park Road, Milton,
Queensland 4064, Australia

John Wiley & Sons (Canada) Ltd, 22 Worcester Road,
Rexdale, Ontario M9W 1L1, Canada

John Wiley & Sons (SEA) Pte Ltd, 37 Jalan Pemimpin #05-04,
Block B, Union Industrial Building, Singapore 2057

Library of Congress Cataloging-in-Publication Data

Modelling with generalized stochastic Petri nets / M. Ajmone Marsan
   ...[et al.].
      p.   cm. — (Wiley series in parallel computing)
   Includes bibliographical references and index.
   ISBN 0 471 93059 8
      1. Electronic data processing—Distributed processing.   2. Petri
nets.   I. Ajmone Marsan, M.   II. Series.
   QA76.9.D5M64   1995
   004′.36—dc20   94-20916
                                                                  CIP

British Library Cataloguing in Publication Data

A catalogue record for this book is available from the British Library

ISBN 0 471 93059 8

Produced from camera-ready copy supplied by the authors using LaTeX
Printed and bound in Great Britain by Bookcraft (Bath) Ltd

This book is printed on acid-free paper responsibly manufactured
from sustainable forestation, for which at least two trees are planted
for each one used for paper production.

Contents

List of Figures

List of Tables

Preface

The goal of this book is to introduce readers to the use of Generalized Stochastic Petri Nets (GSPNs) for the performance analysis of distributed systems of different natures. We hope that a unified presentation of GSPN theory, together with a set of illustrative examples from different application fields, will further extend the success that GSPNs have obtained in recent years as a modelling paradigm for the quantitative analysis of distributed systems.

The book is addressed to beginners, rather than experts in the field of Petri Net applications to performance analysis, and aims to be a useful tool for a first approach to the GSPN field, and a support for a graduate course on modelling and performance evaluation of computer and communication systems.

For this reason, the book is written in an informal style, trying to always explain concepts in plain language before giving a formal definition (often even omitting formal definitions that are not strictly necessary), and including as many examples as possible, to visualize the concepts being explained.

Before a short outlook on the book's content, some historical remarks and acknowledgments are necessary.

The origin of GSPNs goes back to the early 80s, and is due to the cooperation of three of the authors, who participated in the research group that was organized in the city of Torino to join a national research project on the design, implementation and performance evaluation of multiprocessor systems.

Gianni Conte was the initiator of the group: he was the one with the most experience in multiprocessor architectures, and he had known about the possibility of adopting the Petri net paradigm for the description and analysis of such systems from the papers of L. Dadda. Gianfranco Balbo was the one with the most experience in the performance analysis field: he had just obtained his PhD in Computer Science from Purdue University with a thesis on queuing networks and their applications to the performance analysis of computer systems. Marco Ajmone Marsan had recently returned from UCLA, where he had met Mike Molloy, and had learnt about stochastic Petri nets (SPNs), and their usefulness. Actually, the idea of introducing immediate transitions into the SPN paradigm was discussed several times along the corridors of Boelter Hall at UCLA between the two.

The original description of GSPNs was submitted to the 1982 European Workshop on Petri Net Applications and Theory in Varenna, but was rejected with the longest list of negative comments that we ever saw! In fact, the original version of the theory was not quite clean, but after a number of changes, a revised GSPN presentation was submitted to SIGMETRICS'83, and selected as one of the two best papers of the conference, deserving publication in the ACM Transactions on Computer Systems. The official birth date for GSPNs is thus the May 1984 issue of the ACM TOCS.

The first students to write a thesis on GSPN theory and applications were Giovanni Chiola at the Electronics Department of Politecnico di Torino and Gianfranco Ciardo at the Computer Science Department of the University of Torino. They were also the first to implement the software for a GSPN analysis tool. G. Ciardo, after his graduation, went to the USA for a PhD at Duke University with Professor Kishor S. Trivedi. G. Chiola, instead, remained in Torino, first at Politecnico, then at the University, where he made some very significant contributions to the development of GSPN theory, he applied GSPNs to the performance analysis of many different types of systems, and he developed the GreatSPN software tool for the analysis of GSPN models. We all deeply regret the choice of Giovanni to participate only in the early discussions about the contents of this book. Many of the ideas and results presented in the chapters on GSPN theory are his own, and he surely is today one of the most active and creative researchers in the field of GSPNs.

The presence of G. Ciardo at Duke helped make the GSPN paradigm known, and one of the first groups in the USA to adopt GSPNs was indeed the one led by Professor Trivedi. In particular, when the idea arose of organizing a first workshop to bring together the researchers active in the development and application of GSPNs and similar modelling paradigms, the support of Professor Trivedi was the key factor to give us sufficient confidence to organize the International Workshop on Timed Petri Nets in July 1985 in Torino. The name of the workshop was originally meant to be the International Workshop on Stochastic Petri Nets, but the fear of characterizing the topic too narrowly suggested the actual name. However, given the success of the Workshop in Torino, the subsequent editions adopted a different name: International Workshops on Petri Nets and Performance Models were held in Madison, Wisconsin, in 1987; in Kyoto, Japan, in 1989; in Melbourne, Australia, in 1991; in Toulouse, France, in 1993; and the next one will be hosted by Duke University in Durham, North Carolina, in October 1995.

Susanna Donatelli and Giuliana Franceschinis were the first students to choose GSPN theory and applications as a subject for their doctoral theses at the Computer Science Department of the University of Torino. S. Donatelli studied techniques for

the analysis of large GSPNs. G. Franceschinis developed coloured extensions of the
GSPN paradigm, to exploit symmetries in the GSPN model definition and analysis.
After the completion of their doctoral studies, both Susanna and Giuliana continued
their research on GSPNs at the Computer Science Department of the University of
Torino.

The continuing success of GSPNs, and the growing number of researchers interested
in them, suggested the collection of the main results of more than ten years of research
in this book, with the intent of providing newcomers to the GSPN field with a useful
tool for their first approach with the formalism.

The book is divided into two parts. Part 1 comprises Chapters 1–6, and summarizes
the main results in GSPN theory. Part 2 is made up of Chapters 7–11, which present
examples of application of the GSPN methodology.

Chapter 1 contains an informal introduction to Petri nets, mainly intended for
those readers who have had no previous experience with them. This chapter, however,
is also useful for a first presentation of some Petri net models that will be used in later
chapters.

Chapter 2 provides a formal definition of Petri nets, Petri net systems, and Petri
net models, and contains a summary of some of the definitions and results of classical
Petri net theory that are most useful for the development of the theory in the rest of
the book.

Chapter 3 contains a first discussion about the introduction of temporal concepts
into Petri nets, and provides an intuitive justification for the importance of priority
in timed Petri nets. This discussion naturally leads to the problem of priority in Petri
nets, which is addressed in Chapter 4, where formal definitions and theoretical results
for Petri nets with priority are presented, extending the results of Chapter 2 to this
environment.

After these four introductory chapters, the reader is ready to enter the GSPN arena.
Chapter 5 provides the definitions of SPN (stochastic Petri net) and GSPN, as well
as a description of the dynamic behaviour of these models. Chapter 6 illustrates
the techniques for the analysis of SPN and GSPN models. Both chapters contain
illustrative examples, to help the reader understand the concepts that are explained
in the text.

The second part of the book is entirely devoted to application examples, to show
how the GSPN methodology can be used in different fields.

Chapter 7 shows how GSPN models can account for activities with generally
distributed durations, using as an example the classical central server model. In
particular, the chapter shows how it is possible to develop a central server model
in which the execution times are characterized with an Erlang-2 distribution, rather
than with the usual negative exponential distribution adopted in SPNs and GSPNs.

The possibility of generalizing the approach to any phase-type distribution is also discussed.

Chapter 8 provides examples of the application of the GSPN approach to the performance analysis of flexible manufacturing systems. A model of the classical "Kanban" system, and two models of a push production system fed by either a continuous transport system or an automated guided vehicle are presented.

Chapter 9 illustrates the construction of GSPN models of polling systems, which find a variety of applications in the fields of telecommunications, manufacturing, and computer engineering. Rather than looking at the classical cyclic polling systems, we study *random* polling systems, since this choice allows the discussion of the approaches that can often be followed for the construction of *compact* GSPN models, with the advantage of a significant reduction in the cost of the model solution. An example of the reduction process that transforms a GSPN model into an SPN model is also contained in this chapter.

Chapter 10 provides an example of how GSPNs can be used to validate and evaluate concurrent programs. An automatic translation from the software to a GSPN is illustrated, and the techniques for the identification of faults in the software are outlined.

Chapter 11 provides examples of the application of the GSPN approach to the analysis of massively parallel computer architectures.

All the numerical results presented in the examples are obtained with the GreatSPN software package [Chi91a].

The book is completed by two appendices. Appendix A collects some of the results of the theory of stochastic processes that are necessary in the development of GSPN theory. Appendix B contains a glossary with most of the notation used throughout the book.

It should be noted that prerequisites for the study of GSPNs are the knowledge of some simple results of the theory of stochastic processes, and of the theory of Petri nets. Whereas the latter are presented in Chapter 2, the former are discussed in Appendix A. The reason for giving more space to the theory of Petri nets in Chapter 2, and for extracting the presentation of the basic results of the theory of stochastic processes from the main body of the book, lies in the fact that we imagine that a majority of the readers may already be familiar with the material in Appendix A, and in the wide variety of good books devoted to the theory of stochastic processes.

Before leaving the reader to the technical discussions, we wish to acknowledge the support and patience of Gaynor Redvers-Mutton, our Editor at John Wiley in England, and of her staff, and to thank all of our colleagues who read the early versions of the manuscript and provided useful comments and suggestion; in particular we wish to thank Giovanni Chiola and Gianfranco Ciardo for their very constructive remarks.

We also wish to thank L. Brino for providing some of the figures. We acknowledge the financial support of several agencies, which over the years have sponsored our research in the field of GSPNs. In particular, we are grateful to the Italian National Research Council, to the Italian Ministry for University and Research, and to the European Economic Community for their support.

Torino, Italy
June 1995

M.A.M.

G.B.

G.C.

S.D.

G.F.

1

INTRODUCTION

The recent rapid advances in different technological fields have led to remarkable increases in system complexity in several application areas. A representative example of this process is provided by the area of computer engineering, where the advances in the fields of VLSI and software design have led to complex distributed computing systems whose capabilities largely surpass those of traditional computers.

The effective exploitation of the possibilities offered by technological innovations requires adequate tools to describe, to model, and to analyse the various design alternatives. In particular, since system performance is often the ultimate goal behind increased system complexity, tools that allow the relative merits and the intrinsic quality of the possible solutions to be quantified are badly needed.

Many different paradigms for the description of complex systems heve recently been developed, but only a few of these allow the integration of performance analysis concepts within the description itself. Petri nets are one of the few paradigms allowing this integration.

Petri Nets (PNs) are a graphical tool for the formal description of systems whose dynamics are characterized by concurrency, synchronization, mutual exclusion, and conflict, which are typical features of distributed environments. PNs incorporate a notion of (distributed) state and a rule for state change that allow them to capture both the static and the dynamic characteristics of real systems.

PNs can be fruitfully applied in quite a diverse variety of fields, ranging from distributed computing — in its architectural, algorithmic, hardware, and software components — to flexible manufacturing, communication protocols, control systems, transportation, banking, and organization of work.

In this book we are mainly interested in the application of PNs for performance evaluation of distributed systems, with examples taken from the computing, communications, and manufacturing fields, using either simulation or numerical methods. However, it is important to mention that PNs can be successfully employed to support many aspects of the development of complex systems, such as:

- formal specification
- verification of correctness
- rapid prototyping
- documentation

This means that PNs can play a very important role in the life cycle of a distributed system, starting from the initial phases of the design, on to the system development, and to the maintenance during its operational phase.

PNs were originally introduced by Carl Adam Petri in his doctoral thesis [Pet66] to describe concurrent systems in terms of cause/effect relations without explicit time considerations. The introduction of temporal concepts into PN models was proposed several years later by C.Ramchandani [Ram74], P.M.Merlin and D.J.Farber [MF76], and J.Sifakis [Sif78], with different approaches. A variety of different proposals followed, mostly based on the use of deterministic timing. The first definitions of PNs with stochastic timing are due to F.Symons [Sym78], G.Florin and S.Natkin [FN85], and M.Molloy [Mol82]. These proposals opened the possibility of linking PNs to the field of performance evaluation, traditionally based on a stochastic modelling approach. Such models, and their offsprings, are today collectively named Stochastic PNs (SPNs). An extension of the approach proposed by Molloy was provided in [AMBC84], where stochastic timing is mixed with deterministic null delays, so that both the temporal and the logic evolution of a system can be described within one model. The resulting modelling paradigm, named Generalized SPNs (GSPNs), is the subject of this book.

PNs will be formally introduced and defined in the next chapter. In the rest of this chapter we shall instead provide an informal description of PNs, to help the reader intuitively understand what they are, and what they can be used for. This will be done with the aid of some very simple examples of the use of PNs for the description of a few basic elementary behaviours of distributed systems.

A PN comprises *places*, *transitions*, and *arcs*, which define its structural component. Places are used to describe possible local system states (named conditions or situations[1]). Transitions are used to describe events that may modify the system state. Arcs specify the relation between local states and events in two ways: they indicate the local state in which the event can occur, and the local state transformations induced by the event.

Tokens are indistinguishable markers that reside in places, and are used to specify the PN state (usually called the PN *marking*). If a place describes a condition, and

---

[1] The term "condition" actually stands for "boolean condition", in the sense that conditions can be associated with boolean variables. On the contrary, situations can be associated with nonnegative integer variables.

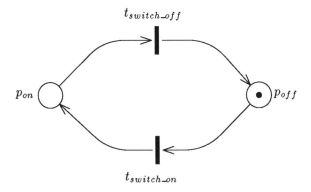

t_{switch_off}

p_{on}

p_{off}

t_{switch_on}

Figure 1   PN description of a switch

thus can contain either zero or one token, the condition is true if a token is present in the place, and false otherwise. If a place defines a situation, the number of tokens contained in the place is used to specify the situation.

A PN model[2] is graphically represented by a *directed bipartite graph* in which places are drawn as circles, and transitions are drawn as either bars or boxes. Tokens are drawn as black dots within places. A very simple first example of a PN model is given in Fig. 1, where two places p_{on} and p_{off}, and two transitions t_{switch_on} and t_{switch_off} are connected with four arcs. Both places define conditions (that we may call the "on condition" and "off condition"). The state depicted in the drawing is such that place p_{off} contains one token; thus the "off condition" is true; instead, since place p_{on} is empty, the "on condition" is false.

The dynamic behaviour of the PN is governed by the *firing rule*. A transition can fire (an event takes place) if all the transition *input places* (i.e., those places connected to the transition with an arc whose direction is from the place to the transition), contain at least one token. In this case the transition is said to be *enabled*. The firing of an enabled transition removes one token from all of its input places, and generates one token in each of its *output places* (i.e., those places connected to the transition with an arc whose direction is from the transition to the place). When arc weights larger than one are used, the number of tokens required in each input place for the transition enabling and the number of tokens generated in each output place by the

---

[2] In this chapter, with the term "PN model" we indicate a model of a real system that uses PNs as the description paradigm. In the rest of the book, starting with the next chapter, the term "PN model" will be used in a formal manner, to indicate a Petri net with a parametric marking. The term "PN system" will indicate a Petri net with a numeric marking, and the term "Petri net" will be used for the cases in which the marking is not considered.

transition firing are determined by the weight of the arc connecting the place and the transition. The firing of a transition is an atomic operation. Tokens are removed from input places, and deposited into output places with one indivisible action.

In the simple example of a PN model given in Fig. 1, transition t_{switch_on} is enabled, and it can fire, removing one token from p_{off} and depositing one token in p_{on}, so that the new state is such that the "on condition" is true and the "off condition" is false. In the new state, transition t_{switch_off} is enabled, and it can fire, restoring the state shown in Fig. 1. The simple PN model in Fig. 1 can obviously be interpreted as the PN description of the behaviour of a switch.

Typically, the firing of a transition describes the result of either a logical condition becoming true in the system, or the completion of an activity. The latter interpretation is the reason for associating timing with transitions, as many authors did in their proposals for the definition of temporal concepts in PNs.

It should be noted that the PN state transformation is local, in the sense that it involves only the places connected to a transition by input and/or output arcs (this will be visible in the forthcoming examples; the PN model of a switch is so simple that local and global states coincide). This is one of the key features of PNs, which allows the easy description of distributed systems.

In order to familiarize the reader with the PN notation, with some elementary PN concepts, and before giving a formal definition of PNs (in the next chapter), we now illustrate a few simple examples of PN descriptions of some typical behaviours of distributed systems.

1.1   Shared Resources

Suppose it is necessary to describe the orderly access to a shared resource. This may result, for example, because a CPU must address a memory location, or a part must be worked by a machine, or a packet must be processed by a protocol. We can consider the individual states of the resource and of its user separately. The resource can be in either an idle or a busy condition, and it obviously alternates between these two states. We can describe the behaviour of the resource with the PN in Fig. 2(b), where two places describe the two possible resource conditions (p_{idle} and p_{busy}), and two transitions (t_{start} and t_{end}) describe the two events that modify such resource condition, from idle to busy, and from busy back to idle. One token is present in the PN, and we can assume that it is initially in place p_{idle}.

The user can be in one of three possible conditions: active (doing something that does not involve the shared resource), requesting, and accessing. The behaviour of the user corresponds to cycling through these three conditions. We can describe

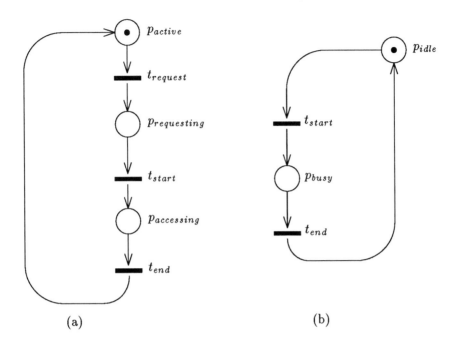

(a)   (b)

Figure 2   PN description of the user (a), and of the resource (b)

the user behaviour with the PN in Fig 2(a), where three places describe the three user conditions (p_{active}, $p_{requesting}$, and $p_{accessing}$), and three transitions describe the three events that modify the user condition, from active to requesting ($t_{request}$), from requesting to accessing (t_{start}), and from accessing back to active (t_{end}).

The combined description of one user and one resource is obtained by merging the two PNs in Fig. 2 via the superposition of the transitions named t_{start} and t_{end}, so as to obtain the PN in Fig. 3. The description can be immediately extended to the case of two users competing for the access to the same resource, that now becomes *shared*. In this case the transitions named t_{start} and t_{end} in the resource model are superposed to the transitions t_{start_1} and t_{end_1} in the model of the first user, as well as to the transitions t_{start_2} and t_{end_2} in the model of the second user, as shown in Fig. 4.

It is interesting to observe that the PN descriptions of the user and resource are equivalent to their state machine representations. Indeed, the two PNs in Fig. 2 contain only one token that "moves"[3] from place to place when transitions fire, and that

---

[3] Actually, tokens do not move; the one in the input place is destroyed, and a new one is created in the output place at every transition firing. However, in this case we can visualize the model behaviour as that of a token cycling around the chain of places.

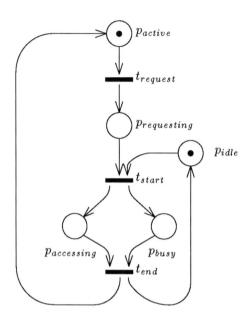

Figure 3   PN description of the user access to a resource

defines the global state of the system. In our example, the combination of the two PN submodels is not equivalent to the independent combination of the state machines, in the sense that the state space is not the Cartesian product of the state spaces of the two components. Instead, the PN description in Fig. 4 is equivalent to a queuing model where two customers request service from one server.

It is easy to see that in the PN in Fig. 4, the place p_{busy} is redundant (the same is also true for the place with the same name in Fig. 3). Indeed, when it contains one token, also one of the two places $p_{accessing\_1}$ and $p_{accessing\_2}$ must contain one token. The number of tokens in p_{busy} can be expressed as the sum of the numbers of tokens in $p_{accessing\_1}$ and in $p_{accessing\_2}$. Furthermore, the net structure is such that the number of tokens in p_{busy} does not condition the model dynamics. We can thus simplify the PN by removing place p_{busy}, as shown in Fig. 5. This is very simple evidence of the fact that PN models can be *reduced*. Much research effort was devoted to the identification of PN reduction rules [Ber87, Sil85], but this topic will be only marginally addressed in this book.

When several identical users exist with similar characteristics, a different representation is also possible. Indeed, we may collectively describe the users' behaviour by placing as many tokens as there are users in the PN in Fig. 2(a). By

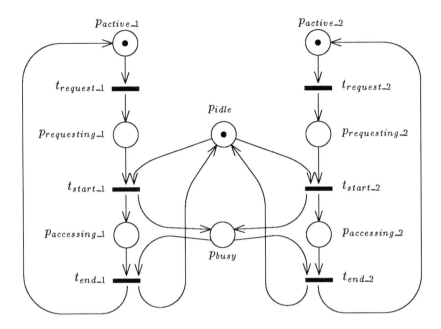

Figure 4 PN description of two users accessing a shared resource

so doing, the identity of users is lost, and the firing of transitions corresponds to the change of state of one of the users; which one is not specified. For example, if N users exist, N tokens may be initially allocated to place p_{active}. The firing of $t_{request}$ indicates that one user (which one is not known) has generated an access request to the resource. The same can also be done for the resources, if several of them (say M) exist. The combination of the descriptions then leads to the PN model in Fig. 6, where N tokens are allocated to p_{active}, and M to p_{idle} (note that the PN in Fig. 6 is reduced, i.e., place p_{busy} has been removed).

It should be observed that, by taking $N = 2$ and $M = 1$, the PN model in Fig. 6 becomes equivalent to the one in Fig. 5, except for the fact that now the user identity is lost. It is interesting to note that this new model for the case of two users sharing one resource actually corresponds to a folding of the PN in Fig. 5, where the two user subnets have been overlaid. The model folding entails a reduction in the number of states of the model, corresponding to the loss of information about the user identity.

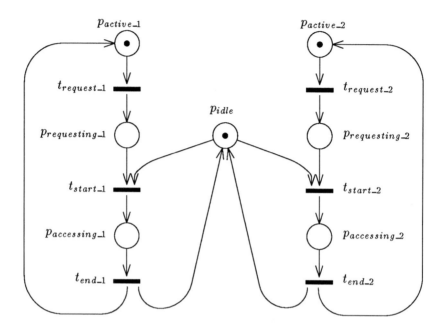

Figure 5   Reduced PN description of two users accessing a shared resource

1.2   Fork and Join

Consider next a fork and join behaviour that is typically found in both manufacturing and distributed systems. In its simplest form, such behaviour can be described with the PN of Fig. 7, where transition t_{fork} represents the fork operation, the three transitions t_{exec_1}, t_{exec_2}, and t_{exec_3} represent the three parallel branches of either the manufacturing process or the distributed program, and transition t_{join} represents the synchronization at the end of the parallel part. Finally, the whole process is restarted by transition $t_{restart}$.

In this case, due to the presence of more than one token in p_{start}, places represent situations, rather than boolean conditions. Note that this also means that the join operation is not necessarily performed with the three tokens generated by the fork: tokens in the triplets may be shuffled, because no specific queuing discipline is enforced among tokens within places.

Observe that the fork and join behaviour, unlike the resource access, is impossible to capture with a classical queuing description. On the other hand, queuing disciplines, such as the FIFO strategy that is often assumed as a default in queuing systems, may

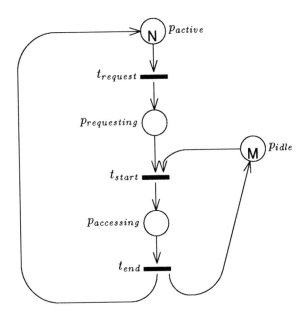

Figure 6   PN description of a system with N users and M resources

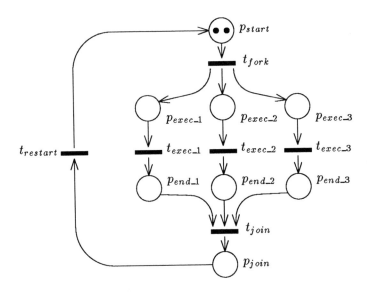

Figure 7   PN description of a fork and join behaviour

be difficult to represent with PNs.[4]

Using the fork and join submodel, it is possible to construct models of the behaviours of interesting parallel systems. For example, Fig. 8 depicts a PN model of a simple parallel computation.[5] The system operations are modelled as follows. A set of new data is read (firing of transition $t_{newdata}$), and two processes are started in parallel with the same set of data (the fork operation — firing of t_{start}). When both processes complete (firing of t_{par1}, and t_{par2}, respectively), a synchronization takes place (the join operation — firing of transition t_{syn}). The consistency of the two results is then controlled, and one of the two transitions t_{OK} or t_{KO} fires, indicating whether the results are acceptable, or not. If the results are not consistent, the whole computation is repeated on the same data, after a further control (firing of t_{check}); otherwise, the results are output (firing of transition $t_{I/O}$), and a new set of data is considered.

It must be observed that the PN in Fig. 8 contains a new construct, formed by the two transitions t_{OK} and t_{KO}. These two transitions, together with their input place, model a choice, and form what in PN terms is called a *free-choice conflict*. The name conflict indicates the presence of a choice and the fact that if the input place that is common to t_{OK} and t_{KO} contains only one token, the firing of one of the two transitions prevents the other from doing the same. The conflict is free-choice because the two transitions are always enabled together: the choice of which one to fire does not depend on the marking of the net.

1.3   Kanban Process

Consider next a simple manufacturing process called Kanban, consisting of a scheme for the coordination of production cells fed by parts. A very simple description of the Kanban behaviour is represented by the PN in Fig. 9. Incoming parts are deposited in place p_{input} through the firing of transition t_{arrive}. These parts can enter the first Kanban cell by firing transition t_{enter_1} only if free cards are available in place p_{cards_1}. After entering the cell, parts waiting for processing are stored in place p_{wait_1}, where they remain until they are worked upon, and transition t_{work_1} fires, placing them in p_{out_1}. Parts processed by the first cell can enter the second cell only when cards from this new cell are available. While waiting for this situation to occur, cards of the first cell are held by the parts. Whenever there are cards for the second cell available (place p_{cards_2} contains tokens) one card is removed from place p_{cards_2} and simultaneously one card is returned to place p_{cards_1}. At the end of the processing in the second cell, transition t_{exit} fires, releasing one card, and placing a part in the output buffer

---

[4] The representation of the FIFO discipline is possible for finite waiting lines, but quite cumbersome.
[5] The model in Fig. 8 has a parallelism degree of 2, but the extension to higher levels of parallelism is trivial.

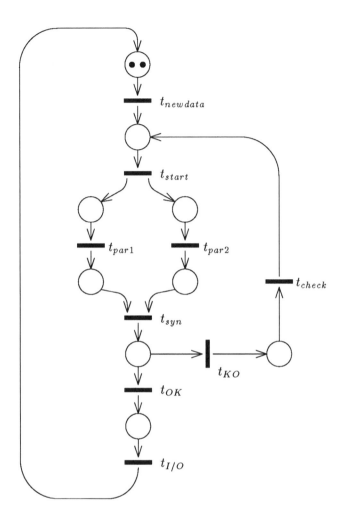

Figure 8   PN description of a parallel system

modelled by place p_{output}. Finally, worked parts are removed from the model through the firing of transition t_{leave}.

Observe that, unlike the previous models, this one is such that an arbitrarily large number of tokens can accumulate in p_{input} and p_{output}. In other words, and with a terminology borrowed from the queuing jargon, this is an *open* model.

Also in this case it is possible to observe that the PN formalism allows a precise representation of all the important details of the behaviour of the Kanban system, while a queuing network model of this same manufacturing system would only convey the general idea, but would be forced to describe the details with the help of additional

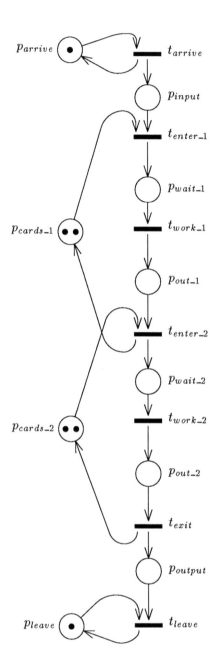

Figure 9   PN description of a Kanban system

informal specification sentences.

1.4 Token Ring LAN

As a final introductory example, consider a token[6] ring local area network (LAN) with three users. An abstract description of the LAN behaviour is represented by the PN in Fig. 10. The token "cycles" around the network through transitions t_{move_1-2}, t_{move_2-3}, and t_{move_3-1}, and polls the three stations when it reaches places p_{poll_1}, p_{poll_2}, and p_{poll_3}, respectively. The three users are described with similar subnets, comprising places p_{idle_i}, p_{wait_i}, and $p_{transmit\_i}$, with $i = 1, 2, 3$. The three triplets of places model conditions that represent the current state of each user: either idle, with no message to transmit, or waiting for the token because a message is ready for transmission, or transmitting the message. We assume that each user handles one message at a time. The three transitions $t_{arrival\_i}$, $t_{start\_tx\_i}$, and $t_{end\_tx\_i}$ model the events that modify the state of the individual user.

Of particular interest in this case is to describe the *if-then-else* behaviour when the token reaches a user. Indeed, when a user is polled, *if* a message is waiting, *then* it must be transmitted; *else* the token must proceed to the next user. The two alternatives are described with transitions $t_{start\_tx\_i}$, and $t_{proceed\_i}$. The former is enabled when both places p_{poll_i} and p_{wait_i} are marked with one token. The second must be enabled when one token is in place p_{poll_i}, but p_{wait_i} contains zero tokens. The test for zero is implemented with a new construct: the *inhibitor arc*, which is represented as a circle-headed arc originating from the place that must be tested for the zero marking condition. Implementing the test for zero with normal arcs is not possible in general. The addition of inhibitor arcs is an important extension of the modelling power of PNs, which gives them the same computational power as Turing machines [Pet81].

The reader is encouraged to play with the examples presented in this chapter for a while before moving on to the next one. In particular, it may be helpful to use markers to execute the networks by playing the so-called token game (pushpins are the normal choice – do not hurt yourself! – but headache pills may become a multipurpose instrument if you plan to play for a longer time).

The main purpose of this chapter was to introduce PNs and their notation informally, and to show that PNs can be an adequate tool for the development of models of a wide variety of real systems. The next chapter will provide a formal

---

[6] The protocol token should not be confused with the PN tokens — unfortunately, the terminologies in the two fields use the same word with quite different meanings.

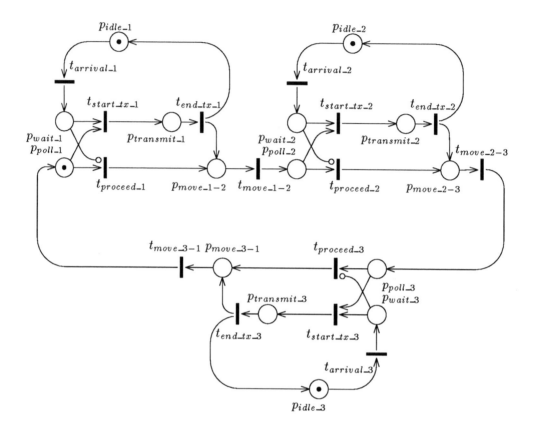

Figure 10   PN description of a token ring LAN with three users

introduction to the same concepts, and will also show what sort of results can be obtained with the analysis of PN models. Further chapters will discuss the introduction of priorities and temporal concepts into PN models, leading to the definition of GSPNs, the modelling paradigm adopted for the PN-based stochastic analysis of the application examples described in the second part of the book.

2

PETRI NETS AND THEIR PROPERTIES

In this chapter we introduce all the definitions, concepts and analysis methods for untimed Petri nets that are used in the later chapters of the book. The choice of the topics included in this chapter is mainly guided by the desire to present in a formal setting all the definitions and properties to be used later, without trying to be complete with respect to the Petri net literature.

We start this chapter emphasizing the difference between a Petri net (a set of places, transitions and weighted arcs), a PN system (a Petri net with a fixed initial marking), and a PN model (a Petri net with a parametric initial marking). Following this distinction, we discuss the analysis methods that can be applied to each class.

The definitions and properties are introduced by means of a formal notation, with the help of an example derived from a variation of the well-known model of the readers & writers algorithm.

2.1 Petri Net Models

A *PN model* is graphically represented by a *directed bipartite graph* in which the two types of nodes (places and transitions) are drawn as circles, and either bars or boxes, respectively.

The arcs of the graph are classified (with respect to transitions) as:

- *input* arcs: arrow-headed arcs from places to transitions
- *output* arcs: arrow-headed arcs from transitions to places
- *inhibitor* arcs: circle-headed arcs from places to transitions

Multiple (input, output, or inhibitor) arcs between places and transitions are permitted and annotated with a number specifying their multiplicities.

Places can contain *tokens*, that are drawn as black dots within places. The state of a PN is called *marking*, and is defined by the number of tokens in each place. As in classical automata theory, in PN there is a notion of initial state (*initial marking*).

The number of tokens initially found in the PN places can be conveniently represented by symbols that are parameters of the model. An initial marking with one or more parameters represents the family of markings that can be obtained by assigning different legal values to the parameters.

A Petri net model can be formally defined in the following way:

Definition 2.1.1 *A PN model is an 8-tuple*

$$\mathcal{M} = \{P, T, I, O, H, PAR, PRED, MP\} \tag{2.1}$$

where

P is the set of places;

T is the set of transitions, $T \cap P = \emptyset$;

$I, O, H : T \to Bag(P)$, are the input, output and inhibition functions, respectively, where $Bag(P)$ is the multiset on P;

PAR is a set of parameters;

PRED is a set of predicates restricting parameter ranges;

$MP : P \to \mathbb{N} \cup PAR$ is the function that associates with each place either a natural number or a parameter ranging on the set of natural numbers.

Functions I, O, and H describe the input, output, and inhibitor arcs of transitions, respectively. Given a transition $t \in T$, we denote with $^\bullet t = \{\, p \in P \ : \ I(t, p) > 0 \,\}$ and with $t^\bullet = \{\, p \in P \ : \ O(t, p) > 0 \,\}$ the input and output sets of transition t, and with $^\circ t = \{\, p \in P \ : \ H(t, p) > 0 \,\}$ the inhibition set of transition t. Since $Bag(P)$ can be seen as a function from P to $\mathbb{N}$, then both the following are syntactically correct:

- $I(t)$, representing the multiset of input places of transition t
- $I(t, p)$ denoting the multiplicity of element p in the multiset $I(t)$

For convenience, I, O, and H can also be represented by $|T| \times |P|$ matrices of natural numbers.

Formally, a marking is a function $M : P \to \mathbb{N}$ and we refer to $M(p)$, for $p \in P$, as the number of tokens in place p in marking M. For convenience, the marking can also be viewed either as a $|P|$-component vector, or as an element of $Bag(P)$.

MP is to be interpreted as the *parametric initial marking* of the PN model: by instantiating to actual values all the parameters (in the set PAR), we obtain a class of models that have a fully specified initial marking. Predicates allow the specification of restrictions over the set of admissible parameter values, and/or the relations among the model parameters.

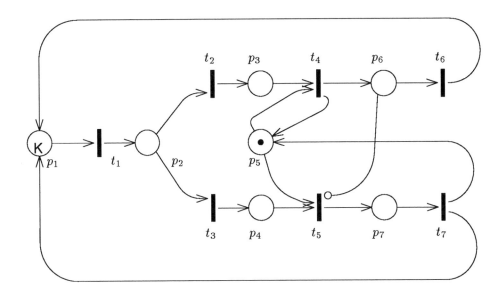

Figure 11   A Petri net model

As an example, in Fig. 11 the graphical representation of a PN model is shown. It comprises seven places ($P = \{p_1, p_2, p_3, p_4, p_5, p_6, p_7\}$) and seven transitions ($T = \{t_1, t_2, t_3, t_4, t_5, t_6, t_7\}$). Transition t_1 is connected to p_1 through an input arc, and to p_2 through an output arc. Place p_5 is both input and output for transition t_4. Only one inhibitor arc exists in the net, connecting p_6 to t_5. Only two places are initially marked: p_1 and p_5. The former contains a parametric number of tokens, defined by the parameter K (restricted by the predicate $K \geq 1$), while the latter contains one token. According to the definition of parametric initial marking, this initial situation can be expressed with the vector $[K, 0, 0, 0, 1, 0, 0]$; a more convenient notation (that will be often used throughout the book) for expressing this same situation is however $Kp_1 + p_5$ (a formal sum denoting the multiset on P defined by the marking).

The PN model in Fig. 11 is a description of the well-known readers & writers system, where a set of processes may access a common database for either reading or writing. Any number of readers may access the database concurrently; instead, a writer requires exclusive access to the resource. This example will be used throughout the chapter for illustrative purposes since it comprises three interesting aspects of parallel systems: concurrency of events (two processes may be concurrently accessing the database for reading), mutual exclusion (only one process at a time may access the database for writing) and choice (an access can either be a read or a write). The detailed explanation of the net is delayed after the definition of the system dynamics.

According to our PN definition, the model in Fig. 11 can be described by the 8-tuple $\mathcal{M}$, where P and T are as given earlier, $PAR = \{K\}$, $PRED = \{K \geq 1\}$, MP associates the parameter K with p_1, the value 1 with p_5 and the value 0 with all other places. Examples of the input, output, and inhibition functions are the following: $I(t_1) = \{p_1\}$, $O(t_1) = \{p_2\}$, $H(t_1) = \emptyset$ and, for example, $I(t_5) = \{p_4, p_5\}$, $I(t_5, p_4) = 1$, $O(t_5) = \{p_7\}$ and $H(t_5) = \{p_6\}$.

2.2 Models, Systems, and Nets

PN models are characterized by a basic structure and by a parametric initial marking. Therefore, a PN model describes a set of real systems, whose precise model can be obtained by assigning a value to each parameter comprised in the initial marking. A PN model in which the initial marking is completely specified is called a *PN system*, and can be formally defined as follows:

Definition 2.2.1 *A* PN system *is the 6-tuple*

$$S = \{P, T, I, O, H, M_0\} \tag{2.2}$$

where

P is the set of places;

T is the set of transitions, $T \cap P = \emptyset$;

I, O, H : $T \rightarrow Bag(P)$, are the input, output and inhibition functions, respectively, where $Bag(P)$ is the multiset on P,

M_0 : $P \rightarrow \mathbb{N}$ is the initial marking:*, a function that associates with each place a natural number.*

A PN system can be obtained from a PN model by appropriately assigning a value to the parameters of the model. Given a PN model $\mathcal{M} = \{P, T, I, O, H, PAR, PRED, MP\}$ we can define the *PN system derived from model* $\mathcal{M}$ under the substitution function $sub : PAR \rightarrow \mathbb{N}$ as

$$S = \{P', T', I', O', H', M_0'\} \tag{2.3}$$

where $P' = P$, $T' = T$, $I' = I$, $O' = O$, $H' = H$ and M_0' is defined as

$$M_0'(p) = \begin{cases} M(p) & \text{if } M(p) \in \mathbb{N} \\ sub(MP(p)) & \text{if } M(p) \in PAR \end{cases}$$

and the substitution function sub must satisfy the set of predicates $PRED$.

PN systems are obtained from PN models by specializing the initial marking. Moving in the opposite direction, it is possible to generalize from a Petri net model by not considering the initial marking at all. This is equivalent to considering only the underlying structure of the model as a weighted bipartite graph. This structure is simply called a *net* (or a *Petri net*), and it is formally defined as follows:

Definition 2.2.2 *A net (or a Petri net) is the 5-tuple*

$$\mathcal{N} = \{P, T, I, O, H\} \tag{2.4}$$

where

P is the set of places;

T is the set of transitions, $T \cap P = \emptyset$;

$I, O, H : T \rightarrow Bag(P)$, are the input, output and inhibition functions, respectively, where $Bag(P)$ is the multiset on P.

Given a PN model $\mathcal{M} = \{P, T, I, O, H, PAR, PRED, MP\}$ we can define the *net derived from model $\mathcal{M}$* as

$$\mathcal{N} = \{P', T', I', O', H'\} \tag{2.5}$$

where $P' = P$, $T' = T$, $I' = I$, $O' = O$, $H' = H$.

Observe that, in general, properties derived for a PN system are valid only for the selected instance of the initial marking, whereas assertions proved for the PN model are valid *for all* PN systems obtained from the model by specializing the initial marking. Moreover, any property proved on a Petri net holds true *for all* PN models obtained from that net by selecting a parametric initial marking, and hence *for all* PN systems obtained from such models by instantiation of the marking parameters. Properties derived from a Petri net are usually termed "structural properties".

From a modelling point of view, the main interest is on PN models: indeed, PN systems may be too specific (for example, in order to study the behaviour of a given computer system as a function of the number of tasks circulating in it, different PN systems must be set up and analysed, all with the same structure, but with different initial markings), while Petri nets may be too abstract (the behaviour of two identical nets may differ significantly if no restriction is imposed on the possible initial markings).

2.3   System Dynamics

So far we have dealt with the static component of a PN model. We now turn our attention to the dynamic evolution of the PN marking that is governed by transition firings which destroy and create tokens.

2.3.1   Enabling and firing rules

An "enabling rule" and a "firing rule" are associated with transitions. The enabling rule states the conditions under which transitions are allowed to fire. The firing rule defines the marking modification induced by the transition firing. Informally, we can say that the enabling rule defines the *conditions* that allow a transition t to fire, and the firing rule specifies the *change* of state produced by the transition.

Both the enabling and the firing rule are specified through arcs. In particular, the enabling rule involves input and inhibitor arcs, while the firing rule depends on input and output arcs. Note that input arcs play a double role, since they are involved both in enabling and in firing.

A transition t is *enabled* if and only if (i) each input place contains a number of tokens *greater or equal* than a given threshold, and (ii) each inhibitor place contains a number of tokens *strictly smaller* than a given threshold. These thresholds are defined by the multiplicities of arcs. In the example in Fig. 12, t is enabled if the number of tokens in place p_1 is greater than or equal to n and the number of tokens in place p_2 is less than m.

We can now give the following definition:

Definition 2.3.1 (Enabling) *Transition t is enabled in marking M if and only if*

- $\forall p \in \, {}^\bullet t, M(p) \geq O(t, p)$ **and**
- $\forall p \in \, {}^\circ t, M(p) < H(t, p)$

When transition t fires, it *deletes* from each place in its input set ${}^\bullet t$ as many tokens as the multiplicity of the arc connecting that place to t, and *adds* to each place in its output set $t^\bullet$ as many tokens as the multiplicity of the arc connecting t to that place.

Definition 2.3.2 (Firing) *The firing of transition t, enabled in marking M produces marking M' such that*

$$M' \;\; = \;\; M \;\; + \;\; O(t) \;\; - \;\; I(t)$$

This statement is usually indicated in a compact way as $M[t\rangle M'$, and we say that M' is *directly reachable* from M. Referring to Fig. 12, we may observe that the firing of t changes the marking by deleting n tokens from p_1 and by adding k tokens to p_3; place p_2 is unaffected by the firing of t. Of course, for t to remove n tokens from p_1, at least n need to be there, and this is precisely part of the condition tested by the enabling rule.

It is interesting to interpret the enabling conditions and the effect of firing for some of the transitions of the readers & writers model of Fig. 11. Transitions t_4 and t_5 represent the beginning of a read and a write access, respectively. Several processes may access simultaneously the database for reading, as long as no write is under way.

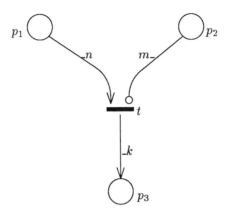

Figure 12 The enabling and firing rules

Indeed, the enabling condition of t_4 requires a token in input place p_5 (that represents the condition "no write is in progress"). Observe that the firing of t_4 does not change the condition "no write is in progress", since it does not alter the content of p_5. A process may get exclusive access for a write whenever no read is under way *and* no other write is in progress. The "and" of the two conditions is obtained by the enabling condition of t_5 that requires zero tokens in inhibitor place p_6 (whose marking represents the number of processes currently performing a read access), and one token in input place p_5 (representing the condition "no write is in progress"). Observe also that the firing of t_5 changes the condition "no write is in progress" by removing the token from p_5. The condition is re-established at the end of the write access, when transition t_7 fires by putting a token back into place p_5.

The natural extension of the concept of transition firing is the firing of a *transition sequence* (or execution sequence). A transition sequence[1] $\sigma = t_{(1)}, \cdots, t_{(k)}$ can fire starting from marking M if and only if there exists a sequence of markings $M = M_{(1)}, \cdots, M_{(k+1)} = M'$ such that $\forall i = (1, \cdots, k), M_{(i)}[t_{(i)}\rangle M_{(i+1)}$. We denote by $M[\sigma\rangle M'$ the firing of a transition sequence, and we say that M' is *reachable* from M.

An important final consideration is that the enabling and firing rules for a generic transition t are "local": indeed, only the numbers of tokens in the input and inhibitor places of t, and the weights of the arcs connected to t need to be considered to establish whether t can fire and to compute the change of marking induced by the firing of t. This justifies the assertion that the PN marking is intrinsically "distributed".

---

[1] We write $t_{(1)}$ rather than t_1 because we want to indicate the first transition in the sequence, that may not be the one named t_1.

2.3.2   Reachability set and reachability graph

The firing rule defines the dynamics of PN models. Starting from the initial marking it is possible to compute the set of all markings reachable from it (the state space of the PN system) and all the paths that the system may follow to move from state to state. Observe that only when the initial state is completely specified (specific values should be assigned to all parameters) it is possible to compute the set of reachable markings, and therefore this computation is possible only for PN systems.

Definition 2.3.3 *The Reachability Set of a PN system with initial marking M_0 is denoted $RS(M_0)$, and it is defined as the smallest set of markings such that*

- $M_0 \in RS(M_0)$
- $M_1 \in RS(M_0) \land \exists t \in T : M_1[t\rangle M_2 \Rightarrow M_2 \in RS(M_0)$

When there is no possibility of confusion we indicate with RS the set $RS(M_0)$. We also indicate with $RS(M)$ the set of markings reachable from a generic marking M.

The structure of the algorithm for the computation of the RS of a given PN system is simple: the RS is built incrementally starting from the set containing only M_0. New markings are then iteratively added into the RS by selecting a marking M that is already present in the RS and by inserting all the new markings that are directly reachable from M. Once a marking M has been considered in an iteration, it must not be considered in successive iterations. Moreover, if a marking is reachable by many markings it is obviously added only once in the RS. The algorithm does terminate only if the reachability set is finite.

Fig. 13 shows the RS of the readers & writers PN system obtained from the PN model in Fig. 11 by setting $K = 2$.

The RS contains no information about the transition sequences fired to reach each marking. This information is contained in the reachability graph, where each node represents a reachable state, and there is an arc from M_1 to M_2 if the marking M_2 is directly reachable from M_1. If $M_1[t\rangle M_2$, the arc is labelled with t. Note that more than one arc can connect two nodes (it is indeed possible for two transitions to be enabled in the same marking and to produce the same state change), so that the reachability graph is actually a multigraph.

Definition 2.3.4 *Given a PN system and its reachability set RS, we call Reachability Graph $RG(M_0)$ the labelled directed multigraph whose set of nodes is RS, and whose set of arcs A is defined as follows:*

$$\begin{aligned} &\bullet A \subseteq RS \times RS \times T \\ &\bullet \langle M_i, M_j, t \rangle \in A \Leftrightarrow M_i[t\rangle M_j \end{aligned} \qquad (2.6)$$

M_0 is taken as the initial node of the graph.

$M_0 =$	$2p_1 +$				p_5		
$M_1 =$	$p_1 +$	$p_2 +$			p_5		
$M_2 =$		$2p_2 +$			p_5		
$M_3 =$	$p_1 +$		$p_3 +$		p_5		
$M_4 =$	$p_1 +$			$p_4 +$	p_5		
$M_5 =$		$p_2 +$	$p_3 +$		p_5		
$M_6 =$		$p_2 +$		$p_4 +$	p_5		
$M_7 =$	$p_1 +$				$p_5 +$	p_6	
$M_8 =$	$p_1 +$						p_7
$M_9 =$			$2p_3 +$		p_5		
$M_{10} =$			$p_3 +$	$p_4 +$	p_5		
$M_{11} =$		$p_2 +$			$p_5 +$	p_6	
$M_{12} =$				$2p_4 +$	p_5		
$M_{13} =$		$p_2 +$					p_7
$M_{14} =$			$p_3 +$		$p_5 +$	p_6	
$M_{15} =$				$p_4 +$	$p_5 +$	p_6	
$M_{16} =$			$p_3 +$				p_7
$M_{17} =$				$p_4 +$			p_7
$M_{18} =$					$p_5 +$	$2p_6$	

Figure 13 The reachability set of the readers & writers PN system obtained from the PN model in Fig. 11 by letting $K = 2$

We use the notation $\langle M_i, M_j, t \rangle$ to indicate that a directed arc connects the node corresponding to marking M_i to the node corresponding to marking M_j, and a label t is associated with the arc. Fig. 14 shows the RG of the readers & writers PN system corresponding to the RS of Fig. 13.

The algorithm for the construction of the RG is quite similar to that for the computation of the RS. The only difference is that, in the construction of the RG, the arcs connecting the markings must be stored. At each iteration, and for each reached marking, besides adding the marking (if new) to the RS, the algorithm also adds one arc labelled with the proper transition name to the set A.

When the RS is not finite, the RG is not finite as well. This happens when some place in the PN system can contain an unlimited number of tokens[2].

---

[2] A finite representation for infinite RG can be given, by providing only partial information with the *coverability tree*. A description of this structure and of an algorithm for constructing it can be found in [Pet81]. The PN systems considered in the following chapters are all bounded, so that we

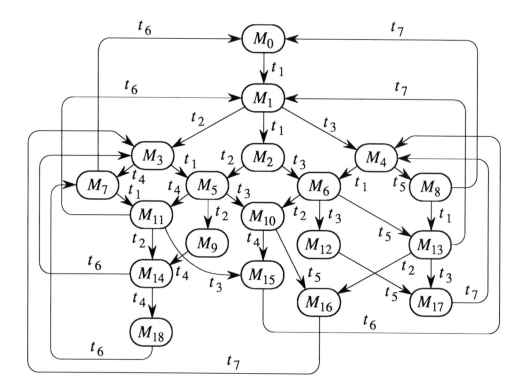

Figure 14   The reachability graph of the readers & writers PN system obtained from the PN model in Fig. 11 by letting $K = 2$

2.3.3 Modelling issues

Let's now come back to our readers & writers example. The readers & writers PN model in Fig. 11 refers to a system with K active processes. The PN places define the local situations of the system components:

- p_1 may contain tokens modelling processes performing activities that are not related to the database access;
- p_2 may contain tokens modelling processes that need the database, but that have not yet specified whether their access implies a write or a read;
- p_3 may contain tokens modelling processes that need the database for a read;
- p_4 may contain tokens modelling processes that need the database for a write;
- p_5 may contain one token that specifies the condition "no write in progress";

always use the classical reachability graph construction.

- p_6 may contain tokens modelling processes that are accessing the database for a read;
- p_7 may contain a token modelling the process that is accessing the database for a write.

Note that, since a token in p_5 expresses the condition that no process is performing a write, if the model has to represent a readers & writers model, then an obvious restriction on the initial marking is that if p_5 is marked, p_7 is not, and viceversa.

In general, as we already noted in Chapter 1, places in PN models can be used to describe either (boolean) conditions (e.g., no user is performing a write access), or physical locations that can contain objects (e.g., a buffer), or logical situations for some object (e.g., reading). Places of the first kind can contain either one or zero tokens, corresponding to the possible truth values of the modelled conditions. In our example, place p_5 belongs to this category: it represents the condition "no write is in progress". Places of the other kinds in general may contain several tokens representing the objects at a physical location, or in a logical situation. In our example, all places but p_5 belong to this category: for example, place p_6 is used to describe the logical situation "accessing the database for a read"; and place p_7 to describe "accessing the database for a write".

Transitions in PN models are in general used to represent either events or logical choices. In our example, the two transitions t_2 and t_3 form a conflict that describes the selection of the access type; all other transitions describe events. Actually, also the choice can be viewed as an event, so that we can state that the transitions in the model of Fig. 11 describe the following events:

- a database access request is generated (transition t_1);
- the access request is for a read (transition t_2), or for a write (transition t_3) action;
- the database read (transition t_4), or write (transition t_5) starts;
- the database read (transition t_6), or write (transition t_7) terminates.

Once more, the reader should note the difference between the static nature of places, that are instrumental for the definition of the PN marking, and the dynamic nature of transitions, that specify the rules for the change of marking.

Modelling logical conditions — The PN formalism provides ways for testing the marking of a place p. Different types of tests are possible, such as $>$, $\leq$ or $=$; they can be implemented by carefully combining input and inhibitor arcs, and by adjusting their associated weights (multiplicities). If transition t must be enabled only when the number of tokens in p is $> n$ (we shall write simply $M(p) > n$), an input arc of weight $n + 1$ is sufficient; instead, to check if $M(p) = n$ we connect p to t with an input arc of multiplicity n *and* an inhibitor arc of weight $n + 1$ (indeed $M(p) = n$ is equivalent

$$M(p) > n \qquad\qquad\qquad M(p) = n$$

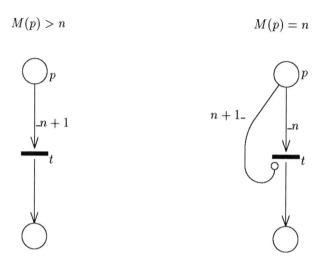

Figure 15   Implementation of tests

to $M(p) \geq n \wedge M(p) < n + 1$), as shown in Fig 15.

Another useful test consists in checking whether a place contains more than n tokens, without modifying the token count in the place. The implementation of this test is tricky. Indeed, avoiding the removal of the n tokens through the firing of t is not possible, but tokens can be put back into the place with an output arc, exploiting the fact that firing is an atomic action. The resulting pair of arcs is usually called a "test arc". As a further generalization, Fig. 16 is an example of a transition that tests if there are $\geq n$ tokens in p_1, and produces a new marking with $n - m$ less tokens in p_1, if $n \geq m$, or $m - n$ more tokens, if $m \geq n$.

The enabling rule of PN transitions is basically an *and* rule, and it is very well suited to express conditions such as "$p_1 \geq n$ and $p_2 < n$". Conditions of type *or* can also be expressed with the PN paradigm, but in a more complex manner. Suppose we want transition t to delete three tokens from p_1 and add one to p_4 when $p_2 \geq 1$ or p_3 is empty. This can be described by means of *two* transitions t_1 and t_2, both changing the marking in the same way, depending however on which of the two alternative preconditions holds true. This situation is depicted in Fig. 17.

2.3.4   *Typical situations in the PN system evolution*

Conflicts —   In the previous section we stated that PNs are well suited to the description of conflicts and concurrency. Indeed, a conflict entails a choice which can be

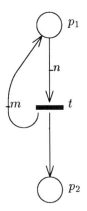

Figure 16 Implementation of a test

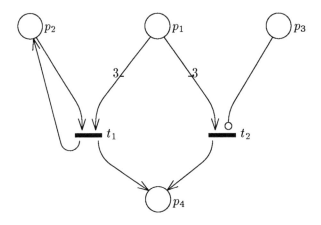

Figure 17 Implementation of an or

naturally described with the PN notation as in Fig. 18. When transition t fires, a token is deposited in place p, and both t_1 and t_2 become enabled. However, as soon as any one of them fires, it removes the token from p, thus disabling the other one. Consider now the case of two tokens in p. If t_1 fires first then t_2 is still enabled: nevertheless something has changed since now t_2 can fire at most once in a row. We want our definition of conflict to capture also these situations, and we therefore distinguish how many times a transition is enabled in a given marking with the following definition.

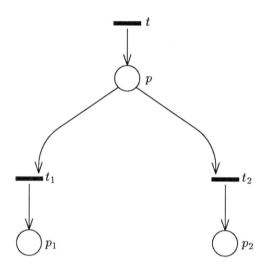

Figure 18   Modelling conflict

Definition 2.3.5 (Enabling degree) *For any PN system, the enabling degree is a function ED : $T \times [P \to \mathbb{N}] \to \mathbb{N}$ such that $\forall t \in T, \ \forall M : P \to \mathbb{N}, ED(t, M) = k$ iff*

- $\forall p \in {}^{\bullet}t, \quad M(p) \geq k \cdot I(p, t),$ **and**
- $\forall p \in {}^{\circ}t, \quad M(p) < H(p, t),$ **and**
- $\exists p \in {}^{\bullet}t : \quad M(p) < (k + 1) \cdot I(p, t)$

We therefore indicate with $ED(t, M)$ the number of times that transition t is enabled in marking M. We indicate with $E(M)$ the multiset of transitions enabled in marking M. We denote by $t \in E(M)$ the condition "t enabled in M", and with $T' \subseteq E(M)$, where $T' \subseteq T$, a set of transitions enabled in M.

In general, a conflict is any situation in which the firing of a transition reduces the enabling degree of another transition (note that we disregard conflicts of transitions with themselves). If the enabling degree is reduced to zero, then the firing of a transition has disabled another transition that was previously enabled.

If we go back to the example of Fig. 11, then we see that t_2 and t_3 are in conflict and in any marking where place p_2 is marked with only one token, the firing of t_2 also causes the disabling of t_3. This conflict represents the choice made by a process when it decides to require either a read or a write access to the database. Also transitions t_4 and t_5 form a conflict, which is however less obvious. Indeed, t_4 and t_5 share an input place (p_5), but this is not the reason why the firing of t_4 disables t_5 (it is however

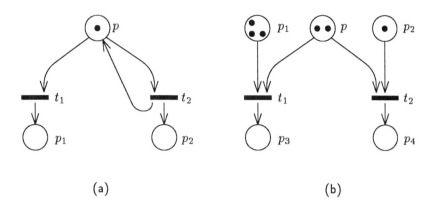

Figure 19   Two cases of asymmetric conflict

the reason why the firing of t_5 disables t_4). Transition t_4 only tests the number of tokens in p_5 (note the output arc from t_4 to p_5). The reason why the firing of t_4 disables t_5 is the existence of the inhibitor arc from p_6 to t_5. Since p_6 is an output of t_4, the firing of t_4 marks p_6, and t_5 becomes disabled. In general, a test for zero on an output place of a transition is a condition for conflict. It is worth observing that in our readers & writers example conflicts are always symmetric: whenever the firing of t decreases the enabling degree of t', it is also true that the firing of t' decreases the enabling degree of t. This indeed happens for t_2 and t_3, and for t_4 and t_5. However, this is not always the case. *Asymmetric* conflicts can be easily constructed as shown in Fig. 19. In the net of Fig. 19(a) the asymmetry is due to the structure (the firing of t_2 does not decrease the enabling degree of t_1, but the converse is clearly false) while in Fig. 19(b) it is due to the particular marking. In the marking depicted in the figure, $M = 3p_1 + 2p + p_2$, we have $ED(t_1, M) = 2$, $ED(t_2, M) = 1$, and the firing of t_1 does not decrease the enabling degree of t_2, while the converse is false. A specular situation arises when $M = 2p_1 + 3p + p_1$. Notice the similarities between the net in Fig. 19(a) and the portion of the readers & writers example that comprises transitions t_4 and t_5: the only difference is the absence of the inhibitor arc.

Formally, we state that transition t_l is in effective conflict with transition t_m in marking M, and we write $t_l EC(M) t_m$, *if and only if* t_l and t_m are both enabled in M, but the enabling degree of t_m in the marking M', produced by the firing of t_l, is strictly smaller than the enabling degree of t_m in M. In formulae:

Definition 2.3.6 (Effective conflict) *For any Petri net system, $\forall t_l, t_m \in T$ such that $t_l \neq t_m$, $\forall M : P \to \mathbb{N}$, transition t_l is in effective conflict with t_m in marking M*

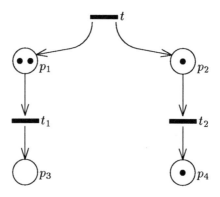

Figure 20   Modelling concurrency

(denoted $t_l EC(M)t_m$) iff

$$M[t_l\rangle M' \quad and \quad ED(t_m, M) < ED(t_m, M')$$

Observe the use of the qualifier "effective" to the term conflict: historically the term "conflict" has been reserved to the situation in which two transitions have a common input place: we shall instead call such situation *structural conflict*.

A case of particular interest are *free-choice* conflicts: two transitions form a free-choice conflict if they are in effective conflict, they are always enabled together and their effective conflict is symmetric.

Concurrency — Contrarily to conflict, concurrency is characterized by the parallelism of activities; therefore two transitions t_l and t_m are said to be concurrent in marking M if they are both enabled in M, and they are not in conflict. In formulae:

Definition 2.3.7 (Concurrency) *For any Petri net system, transitions t_l and t_m are concurrent in marking M iff*

$$t_m, t_l \in E(M) \quad \Rightarrow \quad not(t_l EC(M)t_m) \ and \ not(t_m EC(M)t_l)$$

Figure 20 shows an example of concurrency: t_1 and t_2 are concurrent in the depicted marking $(2p_1 + p_2 + p_4)$, since $t_1 \in E(M), t_2 \in E(M), t_1$ is not in effective conflict with t_2 and t_2 is not in effective conflict with t_1.

Confusion — An intriguing situation arises if concurrency and conflict are mixed, thus invalidating the naive interpretation that concurrency stands for "independency". Observe the net in Fig. 21: if we consider the marking M in which only places p_1 and

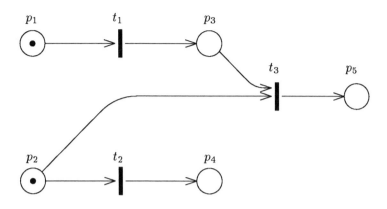

Figure 21   Confusion

p_2 are marked, then t_1 and t_2 are concurrent. However, if t_1 fires first, then t_2 is in conflict with t_3, whereas if t_2 fires first, no conflict is generated. What actually happens is that, although t_1 and t_2 are concurrent, their firing order is not irrelevant from the point of view of conflict resolution, as one ordering may implicitly resolve the conflict ahead of time. In particular, if we start from marking $p_1 + p_2$ and we end up in marking $p_4 + p_3$, then we are not able to tell whether it was necessary to solve a conflict, because this depends on the firing order of the two concurrent transitions t_1 and t_2. This situation is called *confusion*, and it may be particularly annoying if we are modelling a system where conflicts are not resolved non-deterministically, but with the intervention of an external oracle (or through some metrics): the firing order of two non-conflicting transitions as t_1 and t_2 is thus going to decide whether the oracle is called or not (the metrics are used or not) to resolve the potential conflict between t_2 and t_3. As we shall see in the next chapters, the solution of a conflict due to the firing order can cause very subtle problems in the stochastic definition of GSPNs.

Causal connection — Another possible relation among transitions is *causality*. Two transitions t_l and t_m are in causal relation in M if t_l is enabled in M, t_m has enabling degree k in M (possibly $k = 0$, that is to say t_m is not enabled in M), and the firing of t_l generates a marking where the enabling degree of t_m is strictly greater than k. In formulae:

Definition 2.3.8 (Causal connection) *For any PN system $\mathcal{S}$, transitions t_l and t_m are in causal relation in marking M, and we write $t_l CC(M) t_m$ iff*

$$M[t_l\rangle M' \;\Rightarrow\; ED(t_m, M') > ED(t_m, M) \tag{2.7}$$

An example of causal connection can be seen in Fig. 21. In marking $M = p_1 + 2p_2 + p_3$, $t_1\ CC(M)\ t_3$ since the enabling degree of t_3 in marking M is 1, while after the firing of t_1 the enabling degree of t_3 is 2. Observe that in marking $M = p_1 + p_2 + p_3$ transition t_1 is not in causal connection with t_3 since the enabling degree of t_3 is bounded to one by the marking of the input place p_2.

Mutual exclusion — When PN models are used for the validation or verification of systems, it is important to know whether two transitions can never be enabled in the same marking, i.e., whether two transitions are *mutually exclusive*. In formulae:

Definition 2.3.9 (Mutual exclusion) *For any PN system $\mathcal{S}$, transitions t_l and t_m are mutually exclusive iff*

$$\nexists M \in RS(M_0) : t_l \in E(M) \text{ and } t_m \in E(M) \tag{2.8}$$

Observe that while conflict, concurrency, confusion and causal connection are properties of a single marking, mutual exclusion is a property of two transitions in a given system, and needs therefore to be proved by cheking every reachable marking, at least in principle.

2.4   Properties of Petri Nets

Several important properties of PN models, PN systems and Petri nets, can be defined and proved with suitable analysis tools. Proving properties is a key step in the analysis of PN models, since it allows statements to be made about the modelled system behaviour in an objective manner.

We introduce several of the most useful properties below, and we comment on their usefulness with respect to the modelling and analysis process. We discuss in the next section what analysis methods can be used to prove these properties, while we shall present examples of proofs in the chapters devoted to applications.

Reachability and reversibility — As defined in the previous sections, a marking M' is *reachable* from M if there exists a sequence σ_M such that $M[\sigma_M\rangle M'$. For example, consider again the PN model of Fig. 11, with initial marking $M = 2p_1 + p_5$; the transition sequence $\sigma_M = t_1, t_1, t_2, t_3, t_4$ is fireable in M and $M[\sigma_M\rangle M'$ where $M' = p_4 + p_5 + p_6$. Observe that also the following holds: $M[\sigma'_M\rangle M'$ where $\sigma'_M = t_1, t_3, t_1, t_2, t_4$; we can thus conclude that there are at least two different sequences fireable in M that lead to the same marking M'.

Reachability can be used to answer questions concerning the possibility for the modelled system of being in a given marking M. Returning to our basic example in Fig. 11, suppose we want to know whether it is possible for all the processes to execute a read at the same time. In terms of reachability analysis this is equivalent to asking whether the marking M' with K tokens in place p_6 is reachable from the initial marking. If the number of markings in the reachability set is finite, and a maximum value for K is fixed, this question can be answered in finite time by inspecting the different reachability sets (one for each value of K). The parametric proof valid for arbitrary values of K may instead be nontrivial to carry out.

An important reachability property is *reversibility*: a PN system is said to be *reversible* if and only if from any state reachable from M_0, it is possible to come back to M_0 itself. In more formal terms, a PN system with initial marking M_0 is reversible if and only if $\forall M \in RS(M_0), M_0 \in RS(M)$. Reversibility expresses the possibility for a PN system to come back infinitely often to its initial marking.

It is however possible that the state to which we want to be always able to come back is not the initial marking of the PN system. We say that $M \in RS(M_0)$ is a *home state* for the PN system if and only if $\forall M' \in RS(M_0), M \in RS(M')$.

Absence of deadlock — A PN system contains a deadlock if it can reach a state in which no transition can be fired. A PN model is deadlock-free if all PN systems that can be obtained by instantiation of its parametric initial marking are deadlock-free.

There is no definition of deadlock-freeness for Petri nets. As we shall see in a later section it is instead possible to determine whether a Petri net can potentially have a deadlock, depending on its graph structure.

Liveness — A transition t is said to be *live* in a PN system if and only if, for each marking M reachable from M_0, there exists a marking M', reachable from M, such that $t \in E(M')$. A transition t is said to be live in a PN model if it is live in *all* PN systems obtained from the PN model by instantiating the parametric initial marking MP to an initial marking M_0. A PN system is said to be live if all $t \in T$ are live in it. A PN model is said to be live if *every* PN system, obtained by instantiating the parametric initial marking, is live. Finally, a Petri net is live if *there exists* a live PN system obtained from the net. Liveness of a Petri net is an existential property since in most cases it is possible to build a corresponding PN system that is not live: just take as initial marking one for which no transition is enabled.

The PN model of our readers & writers example in Fig. 11 is live for any $K \geq 1$. This means for example that from any possible marking there is at least one evolution that allows another read or another write to take place.

A transition that is not live is said to be *dead*. For each dead transition t, it is possible to find a marking M such that none of the markings in $RS(M)$ enables t.

A very important consequence of liveness is that, if at least one transition is live, then the PN system cannot deadlock. However, the absence of deadlock is not a sufficient condition for a PN system to be live: a system without deadlock states and with some dead transitions is *partially live*.

Liveness defines the possibility for a transition to be enabled (and to fire) infinitely often. If instead we are interested in more detailed information, that is whether the transition may be enabled infinitely often with enabling degree k, then we are interested in the so-called *k-liveness* of a transition. A transition t in a PN system is k-live if and only if from every reachable marking M it is possible to reach a marking M' such that $ED(t, M') \geq k$.

Boundedness — A place p of a PN system is said to be *k-bounded* if and only if, for each reachable marking M, the number of tokens in that place is less than or equal to k. A PN system is said to be *k-bounded* if and only if all places $p \in P$ are k-bounded.

A PN model is said to be *k-bounded* if every PN system obtainable through a suitable instantiation of the parametric initial marking is k-bounded.

PN models and PN systems that are 1-bounded are said to be *safe*.

PN models and PN systems that are K-bounded for some k are said to be *bounded*.

A very important consequence of boundedness is that it implies the finiteness of the state space. In particular, if a PN model comprising N places is *k-bounded*, the number of states cannot exceed $(k + 1)^N$.

Boundedness can also be defined at the net level (*structural boundedness*) as we shall see in the next section. A Petri net is said to be *bounded* if and only if for every finite initial marking M_0 the resulting PN system is bounded.

It is interesting to note that boundedness, liveness and reversibility are independent properties. The interested reader can find in [Mur89] eight examples of nets that present all possible combinations of these three properties.

Mutual exclusion — Two mutual exclusion properties are of interest: one among places and one among transitions. Two places p and q are mutually exclusive in a PN system if their token counts cannot be both positive in the same marking, i.e., $\forall M \in RS \;\; M(p) \cdot M(q) = 0$. Two transitions in a PN system are mutually exclusive if they cannot be both enabled in any marking. Two places (or two transitions) are mutually exclusive in a PN model if they are mutually exclusive in any PN system that can be obtained by instantiating the model parameters.

The properties introduced so far are generic. Their interpretation heavily depends on the specific system being studied. For example, if a PN system describes the behaviour of a distributed program, it is important for the correctness of the program that the PN system has no deadlock states. Viceversa, if the model describes a program that is supposed to terminate, then it is not only desirable to have a deadlock in the system, but the deadlock state must also be reachable from all markings, thus ensuring that the program will eventually terminate.

2.5 Structural Analysis Techniques

PN models (and systems) in which the initial marking is disregarded, simply become bipartite graphs that define the *structural* or *static* component of the models. This structural component of a PN model is what we called Petri net. Many studies were devoted in recent years to the investigation of the properties of Petri nets that may be proved directly from their structure. The interest in this topic is due to the fact that any property proved using only the PN structure is valid for each possible PN system (or model) obtained from the Petri net by superposing an arbitrary marking to it.

We now illustrate some techniques used to investigate structural properties: they are called *structural techniques*[3]. We divide them into two classes: (1) linear algebraic techniques, that work on a matrix description of the Petri net called *incidence matrix*, and (2) graph analysis techniques, that work directly on the bipartite graph description of the net.

2.5.1 Linear algebraic techniques

Definition 2.5.1 *The incidence matrix C of a PN with m places and n transitions is an $m \times n$ matrix whose entries are defined as*

$$C(p,t) = O(t,p) - I(t,p) \tag{2.9}$$

The entry $C(p,t)$ of the incidence matrix C represents the (negative or positive) change in the number of tokens in place p due to the firing of transition t. In other words, the columns of C correspond to transitions, and the rows of C correspond to places; the column corresponding to transition t, $C(\cdot, t)$ defines the state change in all places induced by the firing of t; similarly the row corresponding to place p, $C(p, \cdot)$ defines the change in the marking of p induced by the firing of all transitions of the net.

If we consider the functions O and I as matrices of natural integers, then we can simply write

$$C = O^{\mathrm{T}} - I^{\mathrm{T}} \tag{2.10}$$

where O^{T} (I^{T}) denotes the transpose of matrix O (I).

Observe that inhibitor and test arcs do not influence the entries of C. This is because inhibitor and test arcs do not induce changes in the token count of places. Note also

---

[3] As opposed to *state space* or *reachability* techniques that will be considered later in this chapter.

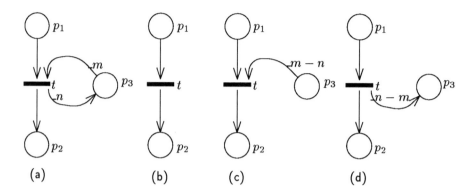

Figure 22   Petri nets with equal incidence matrix

that, in the computation of $C(p,t)$, input arcs from p to t, and output arcs from p to t, "cancel out". For example, the net in Fig. 22(a) has the same incidence matrix as that in Fig. 22(b) if $m = n$, as that in Fig. 22(c) if $m > n$, and as that in Fig. 22(d) if $m < n$. This incidence matrix is always given by:

$$C = \begin{array}{c|c} & t \\ \hline p_1 & -1 \\ p_2 & +1 \\ p_3 & (m-n) \end{array}$$

It follows that during the construction of the incidence matrix, some information is lost with respect to that contained in the Petri net, both because of inhibitor arcs, and because of places that belong to the input and output sets of the same transition.

The loss of information due to the fact that the incidence matrix does not capture the effect of inhibitor and test arcs is due to the decision of disregarding any information on the marking. Indeed, when the marking is neglected, we can no longer rely on the enabling aspects (that in general depend on the particular initial marking), but only on the state transformation aspects, that are marking independent (a transition either fires or not, but its firing always causes the same state change).

Referring again to our basic example in Fig. 11, we can observe that its incidence matrix is the following:

$$C = \begin{array}{c|ccccccc} & t_1 & t_2 & t_3 & t_4 & t_5 & t_6 & t_7 \,. \\ \hline p_1 & -1 & 0 & 0 & 0 & 0 & +1 & +1 \\ p_2 & +1 & -1 & -1 & 0 & 0 & 0 & 0 \\ p_3 & 0 & +1 & 0 & -1 & 0 & 0 & 0 \\ p_4 & 0 & 0 & +1 & 0 & -1 & 0 & 0 \\ p_5 & 0 & 0 & 0 & 0 & -1 & 0 & +1 \\ p_6 & 0 & 0 & 0 & +1 & 0 & -1 & 0 \\ p_7 & 0 & 0 & 0 & 0 & +1 & 0 & -1 \end{array}$$

Neither the inhibitor arc from p_6 to t_5 nor the test arc from p_5 to t_4 are represented in the matrix.

The relevance of the incidence matrix is due to the fact that it allows the net dynamics to be expressed by means of linear algebraic equations. In particular, we can observe that *for any marking M*, the firing of a transition t enabled in M produces the new marking

$$M' = M + C(.,t)^{\mathrm{T}} \tag{2.11}$$

where M and M' are row vectors, and $C(.,t)$ is the column vector of C corresponding to transition t.

A similar relation holds for transition sequences. Given a transition sequence $\sigma = t_{(1)}, \cdots, t_{(k)}$, we define the transition count vector V_σ whose ith entry indicates how many times transition t_i appears in the transition sequence. V_σ is a $|T|$-component column vector. The marking M'' obtained by firing the transition sequence σ from marking M ($M[\sigma)M''$) can be obtained using the following equation:

$$M'' = M + [CV_\sigma]^{\mathrm{T}} \tag{2.12}$$

Observe that only the number of times a transition fires is important: the order in which transitions appear in σ is irrelevant. The order is important for the definition of the transition sequence, and for checking whether the sequence can be fired, but it plays no role in the computation of the marking reached by that sequence. This remark leads to important consequences related to the definition of invariant relations for PN models.

In our readers & writers example, starting from the initial marking we can fire the sequence t_1, t_2, t_1, t_4; we can thus define a firing count vector $V_\sigma = [2, 1, 0, 1, 0, 0, 0]^{\mathrm{T}}$, whose firing leads to the new marking

$$\begin{aligned} & [K, 0, 0, 0, 1, 0, 0] + [CV_\sigma]^{\mathrm{T}} \\ = \; & [K, 0, 0, 0, 1, 0, 0] + 2C(.,t_1)^{\mathrm{T}} + C(.,t_2)^{\mathrm{T}} + C(.,t_4)^{\mathrm{T}} \\ = \; & [K - 2, 1, 0, 0, 1, 1, 0] \end{aligned}$$

where the second equation is obtained by writing the vector V_σ as the sum of seven vectors: each vector has all elements equal to zero but the ith one, which is equal to $V_\sigma[i]$.

The same result can be computed by repeatedly applying (2.11):

$$
\begin{aligned}
& [K, 0, 0, 0, 1, 0, 0] + C(., t_1)^{\mathrm{T}} + C(., t_2)^{\mathrm{T}} + C(., t_1)^{\mathrm{T}} + C(., t_4)^{\mathrm{T}} \\
= \ & [K, 0, 0, 0, 1, 0, 0] + 2C(., t_1)^{\mathrm{T}} + C(., t_2)^{\mathrm{T}} + C(., t_4)^{\mathrm{T}} \\
= \ & [K - 2, 1, 0, 0, 1, 1, 0]
\end{aligned}
$$

P-semiflows and P-invariant relations — Let us define a $|P|$-component weight column vector $Y = [y_1, y_2, \cdots, y_{|P|}]^{\mathrm{T}}$, whose entries are natural numbers. Consider the scalar product between the row vector representing an arbitrary marking M', and Y (denoted $M' \cdot Y$). If $M[t\rangle M'$, then using (2.11) we can rewrite $M' \cdot Y$ as:

$$M' \cdot Y = M \cdot Y + C(., t)^{\mathrm{T}} \cdot Y \tag{2.13}$$

Obviously, if $C(., t)^{\mathrm{T}} \cdot Y = 0$, the weighted token count in the Petri net (using the entries of Y as weights) is the same for M and M'. This means that the weighted token count is *invariant* with respect to the firing of t.

More generally, if

$$C^{\mathrm{T}} \cdot Y = 0 \tag{2.14}$$

i.e., vector Y is an integer solution of the set of linear equations

$$\forall t \in T: \quad C(., t)^{\mathrm{T}} \cdot Y = 0 \tag{2.15}$$

then, no matter what sequence of transitions fires, the weighted token count does not change, and remains the same for any marking reachable from any given initial marking M. The positive vectors Y that satisfy equation (2.14) are called the *P-semiflows* of the Petri net. Note that P-semiflows are computed from the incidence matrix, and are thus independent of any notion of (parametric) initial marking. Markings are only instrumental for the interpretation of P-semiflows.

In the special case in which Y is a vector of all 1's, then the following relation holds:

$$\forall t \in T: \quad \sum_{p \in P} C(p, t) = 0 \tag{2.16}$$

This implies that the total number of tokens in a marking is not affected by the firing of a transition t: since this is true for all transitions t, the total number of tokens is not affected by any firing sequence. We can thus conclude that in this net, given any initial marking M_0, all markings reachable from M_0 have the same total number of tokens.

If Y is an arbitrary vector of natural numbers, it can be visualized as a bag of places in which p_i appears with multiplicity y_i. This leads to the expression

$$\forall t \in T : \quad \sum_{p_i \in P} C(p_i, t) \cdot y_i = 0 \qquad (2.17)$$

which identifies an invariant relation, stating that the sum of tokens in all places, weighted by Y, is constant for any reachable marking, and equal to $M_0 \cdot Y$, for any choice of the initial marking M_0. This invariant relation is called a place invariant, or simply P-invariant.

As a consequence, if in a PN model all places are covered by P-semiflows[4], then for any reachable marking in any PN system obtained by instantiation of the parametric initial marking, the maximum number of tokens in any place is finite (since the initial marking is finite) and the net is said to be *structurally bounded*.

All P-semiflows of a PN can be obtained as linear combinations of the P-semiflows that are elements of a minimal set PS. Algorithms for the computation of P-semiflows can be found in [Lau87, MS81, AM82, AT85].

For example, the set PS for the readers & writers PN model in Fig. 11 contains two P-semiflows:

- $\boldsymbol{PS}_1 = [1, 1, 1, 1, 0, 1, 1]$
- $\boldsymbol{PS}_2 = [0, 0, 0, 0, 1, 0, 1]$

We can also write the P-semiflows as bags of places as follows:

- $PS_1 = p_1 + p_2 + p_3 + p_4 + p_6 + p_7$
- $PS_2 = p_5 + p_7$

It is possible to visualize the P-semiflows above as (possibly cyclic) paths in the representation of the Petri net, as shown in Fig. 23, where we have drawn with dotted lines the part of the Petri net that is *not* related to the P-semiflow. With the usual parametric initial marking MP that assigns K tokens to p_1 and one token to p_5, the two P-semiflows define the following P-invariants:

- $M(p_1) + M(p_2) + M(p_3) + M(p_4) + M(p_6) + M(p_7) = K$
- $M(p_5) + M(p_7) = 1$

As a consequence, places p_5 and p_7 are 1-bounded, while all other places are K-bounded. Moreover, since the marking is an integer vector, it can never happen that places p_5 and p_7 are marked together.

Observe that any linear combination of the two P-semiflows PS_1 and PS_2 is also a P-semiflow: for example $\boldsymbol{PS}_1 + \boldsymbol{PS}_2 = [1, 1, 1, 1, 1, 1, 2]$ is a solution of (2.14).

---

[4] A place p is covered by P-semiflows if there is at least one vector of Y with a non null entry for p

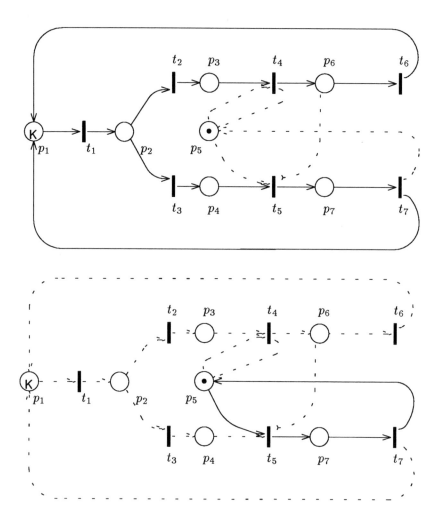

Figure 23   Visualization of the two minimal P-semiflows of the readers & writers example

T-semiflows and T-invariant relations — As observed in Equation (2.12), if V_σ is a firing count vector of a transition sequence σ, then

$$M' = M + [CV_\sigma]^{\mathrm{T}} \tag{2.18}$$

Obviously, if $[CV_\sigma]^{\mathrm{T}} = 0$, we obtain that $M' = M$ and we can observe that the firing sequence σ brings the PN back to the same marking M. The vectors X, that are integer solutions of the matrix equation

$$C \cdot X = 0 \tag{2.19}$$

are called T-semiflows of the net. This matrix equation is equivalent to the set of linear
equations

$$\forall p \in P : \quad \boldsymbol{C}(p,.) \cdot \boldsymbol{X} = 0 \qquad (2.20)$$

In general, the invariant relation (called transition invariant or T-invariant)
produced by a T-semiflow is the following:

$$\forall p \in P : \quad \sum_{t \in T} C(p,t) \cdot X(t) = 0 \qquad (2.21)$$

This invariant relation states that, by firing from marking M any transition sequence
σ whose transition count vector is a T-semiflow, the marking obtained at the end of
the transition sequence is equal to the starting one, provided that σ can actually be
fired from marking M $(M[\sigma)M)$.

Note again that the T-semiflows computation is independent of any notion of
(parametric) marking, so that T-semiflows are identical for all PN models and systems
with the same structure.

Observe the intrinsic difference between P- and T-semiflows. The fact that all places
in a Petri net are covered by P-semiflows is a sufficient condition for boundedness,
whereas the existence of T-semiflows is only a necessary condition for a PN model to
be able to return to its starting state, because there is no guarantee that a transition
sequence with transition count vector equal to the T-semiflow can actually be fired.

Like P-semiflows, all T-semiflows can be obtained as linear combinations of the
elements of a minimal set TS.

The reader can easily verify that the set TS for our readers & writers model is:

- $\boldsymbol{TS}_1 = [1, 1, 0, 1, 0, 1, 0]$
- $\boldsymbol{TS}_2 = [1, 0, 1, 0, 1, 0, 1]$

We can also write the T-semiflows as bags of transitions as follows:

- $TS_1 = t_1 + t_2 + t_4 + t_6$
- $TS_2 = t_1 + t_3 + t_5 + t_7$

These two T-semiflows correspond to a whole cycle through the system made
respectively by a reader and by a writer. In this case, both TS_1 and TS_2 correspond
to transition sequences that are fireable from the initial marking.

It is possible to visualize the T-semiflows above as paths in the graph representation
of the net, as shown in Fig. 24.

It may be possible in some cases to prove that a PN system (or model) is *not live*
using structural techniques: since the covering by T-semiflows is a necessary condition
for liveness of bounded nets, if at least one transition is not included in any T-semiflow,
while the net is covered by P-semiflows (hence being structurally bounded), the net
is not live (as well as any PN system or model with that same structure).

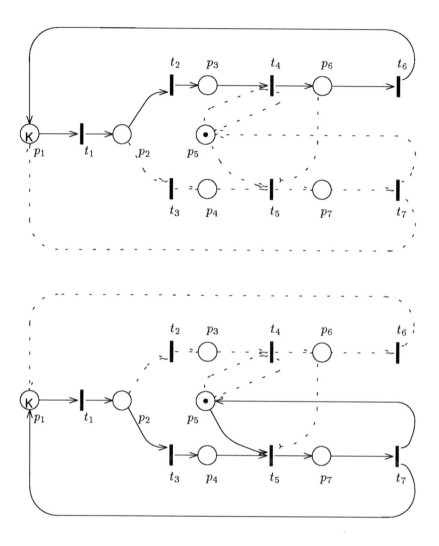

Figure 24 Visualization of the two T-semiflows of the readers & writers example

2.5.2 Graph-based structural techniques

In this section we define *deadlocks* and *traps* [BL89, ESB89] which are particular configurations of a Petri net useful to study the liveness of PN systems. Furthermore, some structural relations between transitions are defined, that allow the derivation of necessary conditions for the occurrence of situations such as conflict, mutual exclusion and confusion in PN systems.

Deadlocks and traps — The following definitions of deadlocks and traps are restricted to PNs without inhibitor arcs and in which all arc weights are either zero or one (ordinary nets).

Definition 2.5.2 *A* deadlock *is a subset of places $P_D \subseteq P$ such that the set of its input transitions is a subset of the set of its output transitions; that is:*

$$\bigcup_{p \in P_D} \{^\bullet p\} \subseteq \bigcup_{p \in P_D} \{p^\bullet\}$$

Definition 2.5.3 *A* trap *is a subset of places $P_T \subseteq P$ such that the set of its output transitions is a subset of the set of its input transitions; that is:*

$$\bigcup_{p \in P_T} \{p^\bullet\} \subseteq \bigcup_{p \in P_T} \{^\bullet p\}$$

Deadlocks and traps can be used to study the liveness of systems by exploiting the following properties:

- there is no way of increasing the total marking of an empty deadlock P_D: once a deadlock has lost all its tokens, all transitions that have an input place in P_D cannot fire; as a consequence the system is not live.
- if a trap is marked in the initial marking, then it will never lose all its tokens; hence a good way to ensure that a deadlock will not lose all its tokens is to make sure that it contains a trap marked in the initial marking.

As a consequence we can state the following property [Sil85]: if in a PN system every deadlock contains a trap marked in the initial marking then the system is partially live (there is always at least one transition fireable in every reachable marking) and therefore it will not block. Notice that a P-semiflow is both a deadlock and a trap. Since deadlocks and traps have been defined only for ordinary nets, then also the above property holds only on this subclass. In the particular case of ordinary free-choice nets the property is even stronger: indeed the presence of a marked trap into each deadlock is a sufficient condition for the system to be live.

Structural relations between transitions — In section 2.3.4 we introduced the concepts of *conflict, confusion, mutual exclusion,* and *causal connection.* We now define some properties that characterize from a structural point of view the corresponding behavioural properties.

The structural conflict relation between transitions is a necessary condition for the existence of an effective conflict relation.

Definition 2.5.4 *Transition t_i is in* structural conflict *relation with transition t_j (denoted $t_i \ SC \ t_j$) iff*

- $\bullet t_i \cap \bullet t_j \neq \emptyset$ **or**
- $t_i^\bullet \cap {}^\circ t_j \neq \emptyset$

Indeed, a transition t_i that fires can affect the enabling degree of another transition t_j only if it changes the marking of either the input or the inhibition set of t_j.

We can similarly define a necessary condition for a conflict to be free-choice by defining a free-choice structural conflict as follows:

Definition 2.5.5 *Transition t_i is in* free-choice structural conflict *relation with transition t_j iff*

- $I(t_i) = I(t_j)$ **and**
- $H(t_i) = H(t_j)$

It is clear from the definition that this conflict is symmetric and that if two transitions are in free-choice structural conflict then they are always enabled together in any possible marking, with the same enabling degree.

It is also possible to find necessary conditions for mutual exclusion of transitions: one is based on inhibitor arcs and one on invariants. Mutual exclusion due to inhibitor arcs is called HME, and we can intuitively say that t_l HME t_m if there are places that are at the same time part of the input set of t_l and of the inhibition set of t_m with arc multiplicities such that if one is enabled the other one is not, and viceversa; an example is shown in Fig. 25. More precisely:

Definition 2.5.6 *Transition t_l is mutually exclusive with t_m due to inhibitor arcs (t_l HME t_m) if and only if $\exists p_k \in P$:*

- $0 < H(t_l, p_k) \leq I(t_m, p_k)$ **or**
- $0 < H(t_m, p_k) \leq I(t_l, p_k)$

Mutual exclusion due to invariants is called MME and it is based on the observation that the token count of a P-invariant may prevent t_l and t_m from being simultaneously enabled in any reachable marking due to a lack of tokens in their input places; an example is shown in Fig. 26.

Definition 2.5.7 *Transition t_l is mutually exclusive with transition t_m due to P-invariants, t_l MME t_m iff $\exists \mathbf{Y} \in PS$ (the set of minimal P-semiflows) such that:*

$$\left(\sum_{p_j \in P} y_j \cdot \max(I(t_l, p_j), I(t_m, p_j)) \right) > \left(\sum_{p_j \in P} y_j \cdot M_0(p_j) \right) \qquad (2.22)$$

Also for causal connection it is possible to define a structural counterpart that is a necessary condition for causality, and that we shall call structural causal connection (SCC).

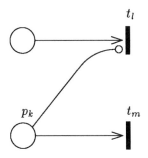

Figure 25   An example of HME relation: t_l HME t_m

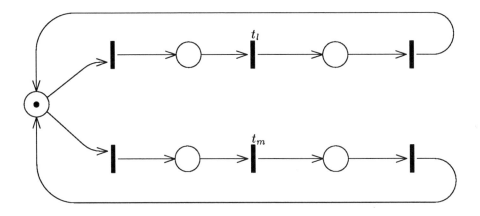

Figure 26   An example of MME relation: t_l MME t_m

Definition 2.5.8 *Transition t_m is structurally causally connected to t_l (denoted by t_l SCC t_m) iff:*

$$I(t_m) \ \cdot \ C^+(t_l) \ + \ H(t_m) \ \cdot \ C^-(t_l) \ > \ 0 \qquad (2.23)$$

where C^+ is the matrix containing the positive elements of the incidence matrix C, while C^- contains the absolute values of the negative elements of C.

Structural causal connection between two transitions exists when the firing of the first transition either increments the marking of some input place, or decrements the marking of some inhibition place of the second one. The structural relation of causal connection is a necessary, but not sufficient condition for the firing of a transition to cause the enabling of another transition.

2.6   State Space Analysis Techniques

As we mentioned before, there exist properties of PN systems that depend on the initial marking, and that can thus be studied only by taking this information into account. The techniques used to prove these properties are called state space (or reachability) analysis techniques. State space analysis techniques are inherently non parametric with respect to the initial marking, since they require its complete instantiation. Thus state space techniques refer to PN systems, not to PN models or Petri nets.

The reachability analysis is based on the construction of the RG of the PN system, and it is feasible only when the RS and the RG are finite. Even if the RS and RG are finite, their size can vary widely with the PN structure and the number of tokens in M_0. In many cases, the growth in the number of markings can be combinatorial both in the number of places and in the number of tokens in M_0. Reachability analysis techniques are very powerful, since they allow the proof of most properties of interest by inspection, as the RS and RG contain all possible evolutions of the PN system. However, it often happens that the space and time complexity of the RG construction algorithm exceeds any acceptable limit.

Once the RG has been built, properties may be checked using classical graph analysis algorithms, as explained in the following. Let us consider separately each property discussed in section 2.4.

Reachability —   To check whether a marking M' is reachable from a marking M in a given PN system, it is only necessary to check if RG comprises a directed path connecting M to M'. The concatenation of the labels of the arcs forming the path gives the transition sequence σ such that $M[\sigma\rangle M'$.

Reversibility —   To check whether a given marking M is a home state, it is sufficient to build the set of all the markings that can be reached by following backwards in the RG any path entering M, and to verify that this set is $RS(M)$.

A PN system is *reversible* if and only if its initial marking is a home state. This is true if and only if the RG has a unique strongly connected component that contains M_0.

Absence of deadlock —   The presence of a deadlock can be checked on the RG by looking for a dead marking, i.e. a node with no output arcs. The absence of such a node is sufficient to guarantee the absence of deadlock.

Liveness —   Transition t of a PN system is live if and only if from every marking $M \in RS$ it is possible to reach a new marking M' such that $t \in E(M')$. In [Sil85] the following characterization of the liveness property in terms of the RG structure is given:

t is live if and only if

- the RG contains no dead marking;
- t labels some arc of every strongly connected component of RG.

It is easy to check on the RG of Fig. 14 that t_5 is live: the RG has no dead marking, it has a unique strongly connected component, and t_5 labels, for example, the arc connecting M_4 and M_8.

Boundedness — A place $p \in P$ of a PN system is k-bounded iff

$$k = \max_{M \in RS} M(p)$$

Of course this can be computed only for finite reachability sets.

Mutual exclusion — Mutual exclusion between places p and p' in a given PN system is checked by verifying that

$$\forall M \in RS: \ M(p) \cdot M(p') = 0$$

Mutual exclusion between transitions t and t' in a given PN system is checked by verifying that
$$\nexists M \in RS \text{ such that } \{t, t'\} \subseteq E(M)$$

In the readers & writers PN system with two customers, places p_6 and p_7 are mutually exclusive: this property ensures that the mutual exclusion requirement between readers and writers in the modelled system is satisfied. In the same PN system, transitions t_6 and t_7 are mutually exclusive, again due to the impossibility for read and write accesses to be concurrently active.

Effective conflict and confusion — By inspection of the RG, using the definition of EC, it is possible to identify all markings in which an effective conflict arises among transitions; this requires the knowledge of the multiset $E(M)$ for each marking $M \in RS$.

Some effective conflicts that can be identified on the RG in Fig. 14 are: $t_2 \ EC(M_1) \ t_3$, $t_3 \ EC(M_1) \ t_2$, $t_4 \ EC(M_{10}) \ t_5$. Notice that in this PN system every effective conflict is symmetric.

Given a sequence of non-conflicting transition firings that cause the system to move from marking M to M', all the permutations of the sequence are present in the RG

between the same two markings. An example of this situation can be observed in Fig. 14, where M_5 can reach M_{15} either by firing t_3 and t_4 or by firing t_4 and t_3.

It is important to notice that the EC relation does not capture every situation where a conflict between activities is solved, because of the possibility of confusion. Confusion can be easily recognized on the RG by looking for sets of transition sequences connecting the same two markings (containing the same transitions although in different order) such that the patterns of EC relations along the sequences are not the same. For example, there is confusion in the sequences connecting M_5 and M_{15}, since in the first sequence the EC relations between t_2 and t_3 at the first step, and between t_4 and t_5 at the second step, can be observed, while in the second sequence only the effective conflict between t_2 and t_3 occurs. It can thus be deduced that the conflict between t_4 and t_5 is hidden in the second sequence.

3

TIME IN PETRI NETS

In this chapter we discuss the issues related to the introduction of *temporal concepts* into PN models and systems. The goal of the chapter is not to provide an exhaustive overview of the field of timed PN, that is out of the scope of this book, but instead to discuss the temporal semantics peculiar to stochastic PNs (SPNs) and generalized SPNs (GSPNs). For this reason we shall always assume that timed transitions are associated with temporal specifications such that the simultaneous firing of two or more timed transitions can be neglected (this event has probability zero in SPNs and GSPNs).

3.1   The Motivations for Timing

The PN models and systems that were considered in the previous chapter include no notion of time. The concept of time was intentionally avoided in the original work by C.A.Petri [Pet66], because of the effect that timing may have on the behaviour of PNs. In fact, the association of timing constraints with the activities represented in PN models or systems may prevent certain transitions from firing, thus destroying the important assumption that all possible behaviours of a real system are represented by the structure of the PN.

In [Pet81], the first book on PNs that dealt extensively with applications, the only remark about timed PNs was the following: "*The addition of timing information might provide a powerful new feature for PNs, but may not be possible in a manner consistent with the basic philosophy of PNs*". This attitude towards timing in PN models is due to the fact that PNs were originally considered as automata and investigated in their theoretical properties. Most of the early questions raised by researchers thus looked into the fundamental properties of PN models and systems, into their analysis techniques and the associated computational complexity, and into the equivalence between PNs and other models of parallel computation. When dealing with these problems, timing is indeed not relevant.

Very soon PNs were however recognized as possible models of real concurrent systems, capable of coping with all aspects of parallelism and conflict in asynchronous activities with multiple actors. In this case, timing is not important when considering only the logical relationships between the entities that are part of the real system. The concept of time becomes instead of paramount importance when the interest is driven by real applications whose efficiency is always a relevant design goal. Indeed, in areas like hardware and computer architecture design, communication protocols, and software system analysis, timing is crucial even to define the logical aspects of the dynamic operations.

The pioneering works in the area of timed PNs were performed by P.M.Merlin and D.J.Farber [MF76], and by J.D.Noe and G.J.Nutt [NN73]. In the former work, the authors applied PNs augmented with timing to communication protocol modelling; in the latter case, a new type of timed nets was used for modelling a computer architecture. In both cases, PNs were not viewed as a formalism to statically model the logical relationships among the various entities that form a real system, but as a tool for the description of the global behaviour of complex structures. PNs were used to *narrate* all the possible stories that the system can experience, and the temporal specifications were an essential part of the picture.

Different ways of incorporating timing information into PN systems and models were proposed by many researchers during the last two decades; the different proposals are strongly influenced by the specific application fields. In this chapter we do not discuss and compare the different approaches, but only the temporal semantics used in SPNs and GSPNs. The reader interested in other approaches to timed PNs is referred to the original papers [Ram74, Zub80, HV85, RH80, MF76, Sif78, CR85, WDF85] with a warning: the differences among the various models are sometimes subtle and often not easy to identify at a first glance.

When introducing time into PN models and systems, it would be extremely useful not to modify the basic behaviour of the underlying untimed model. By so doing, in the study of timed PNs it is possible to exploit the properties of the basic untimed model as well as the available theoretical results. The addition of temporal specifications therefore must not modify the unique and original way of expressing synchronization and parallelism that is peculiar to PNs. This requirement obviously conflicts with the user' wishes for extensions of the basic PN formalism to allow a direct and easy representation of specific phenomena of interest. SPNs satisfy the first of these two requirements and provide a formalism that allows the construction of models that can be used both for behavioural analyses based on classic PN theory, and for performance studies based on temporal specifications and probabilistic models. GSPNs represent instead a sort of compromise between the two needs, since they include extensions that are very useful in practical modelling, without losing, except for some special cases, the possibility of performing quantitative and qualitative studies.

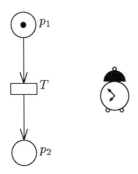

Figure 27   A timed transition

3.2   Timed Transitions

The firing of a transition in a PN model corresponds to the event that changes the state of the real system. This change of state can be due to one of two reasons: it may either result from the verification of some logical condition in the system, or be induced by the completion of some activity. Considering the second case, we note that transitions can be used to model activities, so that transition enabling periods correspond to activity executions and transition firings correspond to activity completions. Hence, time can be naturally associated with transitions.

We now look in some detail at the semantics of transitions with associated temporal specifications that are called *timed* transitions; they are graphically represented by boxes or thick bars and are denoted with names that usually start with T.

Consider, as the simplest possible example, the timed transition T in Fig. 27. Transition T can be associated with a local clock or timer. When a token is generated in place p_1, T becomes enabled, and the associated timer is set to an initial value. The timer is then decremented at constant speed, and the transition fires when the timer reaches the value zero. The timer associated with the transition can thus be used to model the duration of an activity whose completion induces the state change that is represented by the change of marking produced by the firing of T. The type of activity associated with the transition, whose duration is measured by the timer, depends on the modelled real system: it may correspond to the execution of a task by a processor, or to the transmission of a message in a communication network, or to the work performed on a part by a machine tool in a manufacturing system. It is important to note that the activity is assumed to be in progress while the transition is enabled. This means that in the evolution of more complex nets, an interruption

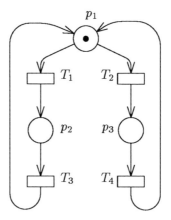

Figure 28 A timed PN system

of the activity may take place if the transition loses its enabling condition before it can actually fire. The activity may be resumed later on, during the evolution of the system in the case of a new enabling of the associated transition. This may happen several times until the timer goes down to zero and the transition finally fires. As an example of this type of behaviour, consider the timed PN system depicted in Fig. 28, where transitions T_3 and T_4 behave exactly as transition T in Fig. 27. Transitions T_1 and T_2 have however a more complex dynamic behaviour since they belong to a free-choice conflict, and the firing of either one of them disables the other (with the notation introduced in the previous chapter, T_1 SC T_2, and T_3 MME T_4). In fact, if the initial marking is that shown in the figure, the timers of T_1 and T_2 are set to their initial values, say θ_1 and θ_2, with $\theta_1 < \theta_2$; after a time θ_1, transition T_1 fires, and the timer of T_2 is stopped. Now the timer of T_3 is started and decremented at constant speed until it reaches the zero value. After T_3 fires, the conflict comprising T_1 and T_2 is enabled again. The timer of T_1 must be set again to an initial value (possibly, again θ_1), whereas the timer of T_2 can either resume from the point at which it was previously interrupted, i.e., from $\theta_2 - \theta_1$, or be reset to a new initial value. The choice depends on the behaviour of the modelled system, and defines the transition *memory* that will be discussed in detail in a following section.

It is possible to define a *timed transition sequence* or *timed execution* of a timed PN system as a transition sequence (as defined in 2.3.1) augmented with a set of nondecreasing real values describing the epochs of firing of each transition. Such a

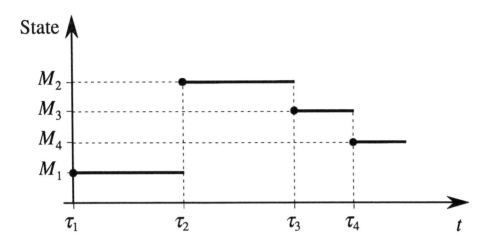

Figure 29   Pictorial representation of a timed execution

timed transition sequence is denoted as follows:

$$[(\tau_{(1)}, T_{(1)}); \cdots; (\tau_{(j)}, T_{(j)}); \cdots]$$

The time intervals $[\tau_{(i)}, \tau_{(i+1)})$ between consecutive epochs represent the periods during which the timed PN system sojourns in marking $M_{(i)}$. This sojourn time corresponds to a period in which the execution of one or more activities is in progress and the state of the system does not change. A simple pictorial representation of a timed execution is given in Fig. 29.

3.2.1   Immediate transitions

As we noted before, not all the events that occur in a model of a real system correspond to the end of time-consuming activities (or to activities that are considered time-consuming at the level of detail at which the model is developed). For instance, a model of a multiprocessor system described at a high level of abstraction often neglects the durations of task switchings, since these operations require a very small amount of time, compared with the durations of task executions. The same can be true for bus arbitration compared with bus use. In other cases, the state change induced by a specific event may be quite complex, and thus difficult to obtain with the firing of a single transition. Moreover, the state change can depend on the present state in a complex manner. As a result, the correct evolution of the timed PN model can often be conveniently described with subnets of transitions that consume no time and describe

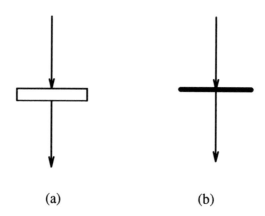

(a)   (b)

Figure 30   Timed (a) and immediate (b) transitions

the logics or the algorithm of state evolution induced by the complex event.

To cope with both these situations in timed PN models, it is convenient to introduce a second type of transition called *immediate*. Immediate transitions fire as soon as they become enabled (with a null delay), thus acquiring a sort of precedence over timed transitions and leading to the choice of giving priority to immediate transitions in the definition of GSPNs. In this book immediate transitions are depicted as thin bars, as shown in Fig. 30, whereas timed transitions are depicted as boxes or thick bars.

3.2.2   Two examples

The basic concepts deriving from the introduction of timed and immediate transitions are of paramount importance in understanding the definitions and the results presented in the later chapters of this book. To make sure that these concepts are clear to the reader, we present two simple examples of timed PN systems.

In Chapter 1, we described an example of a PN system with two users accessing a shared resource (see Fig. 5). We now revisit that model, adding temporal specifications to transitions. The timed PN system is shown in Fig. 31. Transitions $T_{request\_1}$ and $T_{request\_2}$ model the operations of the two users when they are not requesting or accessing the shared resource. Transitions T_{end_1} and T_{end_2} model the operations of the two users when accessing the shared resource. All these activities are time-consuming and thus the four transitions are timed. On the contrary, transitions t_{start_1} and t_{start_2} model the acquisition of the resource; this operation may be assumed to require a negligible amount of time, so that transitions t_{start_1} and t_{start_2} are immediate. The timed PN system in Fig. 31 may be interpreted as a simple model

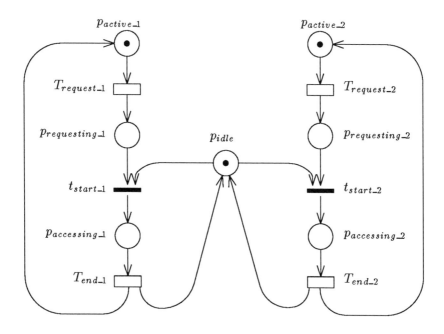

Figure 31   Timed version of the PN system in Fig. 5

of the behaviour of a two-processor system with two private memories (one for each processor), and one shared memory. Transitions $T_{request\_1}$ and $T_{request\_2}$ model the activities performed by the processors while accessing their private memories. The temporal characterization of these two transitions is based on either measurements or assumptions about the duration of such operations. Transitions T_{end_1} and T_{end_2} model the activities performed by the processors while accessing the shared memory. The temporal characterization of these two transitions is again derived by measurements or assumptions about the durations of shared memory accesses. Transitions t_{start_1} and t_{start_2} model the acquisition of the interconnection network and of the shared memory; the choice of using immediate transitions here amounts to neglecting the delays inherent in such operations.

As a second example of use of immediate transitions, consider now the following modelling problem: when a given event occurs, all the tokens that are present in place p_a must be removed and an equal number of tokens must be generated in place p_b. Informally, we may say that all the tokens contained in p_a are moved (or migrate) to place p_b. This is a typical problem that arises when several items are waiting for a synchronization before being allowed to proceed to an execution phase. Implementing this operation in one step is not possible, due to the fact that arc weights

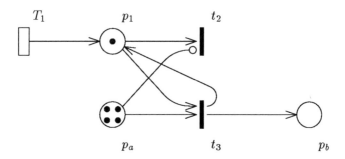

Figure 32   Subnet modelling the migration of tokens from p_a to p_b when a synchronizing event takes place

are assumed to be constant in the nets that we consider[1]. The same result can however be obtained with immediate transitions, as shown in Fig. 32. The firing of T_1 models the synchronizing event that generates the condition that induces the migration of all the tokens from p_a into p_b. The marking of the net in Fig. 32 models the state of the system just after the synchronizing event. Transition t_3 is enabled and fires as many times as the number of tokens in p_a, thus removing all the tokens from p_a and adding the same number of tokens to p_b. Then, the lack of tokens in p_a deactivates the inhibitor arc to t_2, so that t_2 becomes enabled and fires, removing the token from p_1. Tokens can now be again collected in place p_a, waiting for a new synchronization.

3.3   Parallelism and Conflict

The introduction of temporal specifications in PN models must not reduce the modelling capabilities with respect to the untimed case. Let us verify this condition as far as parallelism and conflict resolution are considered.

Pure parallelism can be modelled by two transitions that are independently enabled in the same marking. The evolution of the two activities is measured by the decrement of the clocks associated with the two transitions. Consider the net in Fig. 33: transitions T_1 and T_2 are not related and model two completely independent concurrent activities. When one of the timers (for example that associated with T_1) reaches zero, the transition fires and a new marking is produced. In the new marking, transition T_2 is still enabled and its timer can either be reset or not; different ways of managing this timer will be discussed in the next section.

---

[1] Some authors extended the formalism by introducing *marking-dependent* arc weights, mainly to be able to implement the flushing of all tokens from one place using a single action.

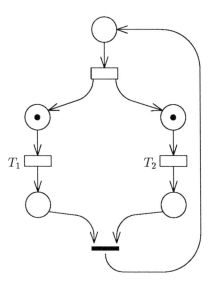

Figure 33   Non-conflicting concurrent transitions

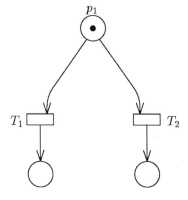

Figure 34   Conflicting transitions

Consider now transitions T_1 and T_2 in Fig. 34. In this case, the two transitions are in free-choice conflict. In untimed PN systems, the choice of which of the two transitions to fire is completely nondeterministic. In the case of timed PN systems, the conflict resolution depends on the delays associated with transitions and is obtained through the so-called *race* policy: when several timed transitions are enabled in a given

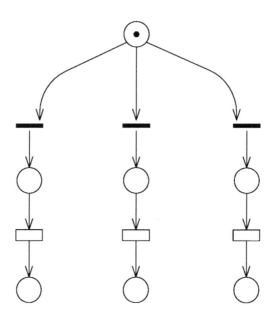

Figure 35   Using immediate transitions to separate conflict resolution from transition
timing specification

marking M, the transition with the shortest associated delay fires first (thus disabling
the possible conflicting transitions).

Having discussed the conflict resolution policy among timed transitions, it is
important to emphasize the fact that, when two or more immediate transitions are
enabled in the same marking, some rule must be specified to select the one to fire first,
thus ordering the firing of immediate transitions. Two types of rules will be used when
situations of this type occur in the following. The first one is based on a deterministic
choice of the transition to fire using the mechanism of *priority*, whose introduction in
PNs is discussed in the next chapter. A second mechanism consists in the association
of a discrete probability distribution function with the set of conflicting transitions.
In this case the conflicts among immediate transitions are randomly solved.

In some cases, however, it may be desirable to separate conflict resolution from
timing specification of transitions. Immediate transitions can be used to obtain this
separation. The conflict can be transferred to a barrier of conflicting immediate
transitions, followed by a set of timed transitions, as in Fig. 35. The extensive use
of this technique can eliminate from a net all conflicts among timed transitions that
are simultaneously enabled in a given marking. If this mechanism is consistently used
to prevent timed transitions from entering into conflict situations, a *preselection* policy

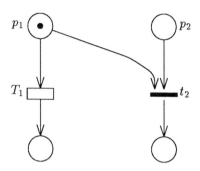

Figure 36   Interrupting an activity with an immediate transition

of the (timed) transition to fire next is said to be used.

Conflicts comprising timed and immediate transitions have an important use in timed PN systems: they allow the interruption (or preemption) of ongoing activities, when some special situation occurs. Consider for example the subnet in Fig. 36. A token in place p_1 starts the activity modelled by timed transition T_1. If a token arrives in p_2 before the firing of T_1, immediate transition t_2 becomes enabled and fires, thus disabling timed transition T_1. This behaviour again provides an example of the precedence of immediate over timed transitions.

The presence of immediate transitions induces a distinction among markings. Markings in which no immediate transitions are enabled are called *tangible*, whereas markings enabling at least one immediate transition are said to be *vanishing*. The timed PN system spends a positive amount of time in tangible markings, and a null time in vanishing markings.

3.4   Memory

An important issue that arises at every transition firing when timed transitions are used in a model is how to manage the timers of all the transitions that do not fire.

From the modeling point of view, the different policies that can be adopted link the past history of the systems to its future evolution considering various ways of retaining *memory* of the time already spent on activities. The question concerns the *memory policy* of transitions, and defines how to set the transition timers when a state change occurs, possibly modifying the enabling of transitions. Two basic mechanisms can be considered for a timed transition at each state change.

• **Continue.** The timer associated with the transition holds the present value and will *continue* later on the count-down.

- **Restart**. The timer associated with the transition is *restarted*, i.e., its present value is discarded and a new value will be generated when needed.

To model the different behaviours arising in real systems, different ways of keeping track of the past are possible by associating different continue or restart mechanisms with timed transitions. We discuss here three alternatives:

- **Resampling**. At each and every transition firing, the timers of all the timed transitions in the timed PN system are discarded (restart mechanism). No memory of the past is recorded. After discarding all the timers, new values of the timers are set for the transitions that are enabled in the new marking.

- **Enabling memory**. At each transition firing, the timers of all the timed transitions that are disabled are restarted whereas the timers of all the timed transitions that are not disabled hold their present value (continue mechanism). The memory of the past is recorded with an *enabling memory variable* associated with each transition. The enabling memory variable accounts for the work performed by the activity associated with the transition since the last instant of time its timer was set. In other words, the enabling memory variable measures the enabling time of the transition since the last instant of time it became enabled.

- **Age memory**. At each transition firing, the timers of all the timed transitions hold their present values (continue mechanism). The memory of the past is recorded with an *age memory variable* associated with each timed transition. The age memory variable accounts for the work performed by the activity associated with the transition since the time of its last firing. In other words, the age memory variable measures the *cumulative* enabling time of the transition since the last instant of time when it fired.

The three memory policies can be used in timed PN models for different modelling purposes. In the first case (resampling) the work performed by activities associated with transitions that do not fire is lost. This may be adequate for modelling, for example, competing activities of the type one may find in the case of the parallel execution of hypothesis tests. The process that terminates first is the one that verified the test; those hypotheses whose verification was not completed become useless, and the corresponding computations need not be saved. The practical and explicit use of this policy is very limited, but it must be considered because of its theoretical importance in the case of SPNs and GSPNs.

The other two policies are of greater importance from the application viewpoint. They can coexist within the same timed PN system, because of the different semantics that can be assigned to the different transitions of the model. For a detailed discussion on this topic the reader is referred to [AMBB[+]89, CL93].

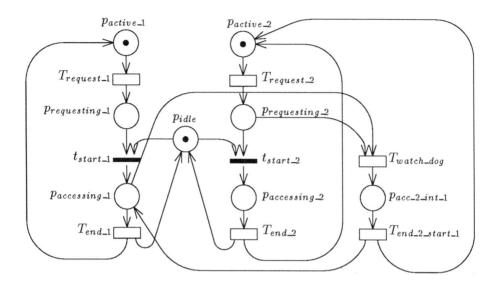

Figure 37   Timed PN system with an example of enabling memory policy

3.4.1   An example with the enabling memory policy

A possible application of the enabling memory policy is provided by transitions used
to model time-out or watch-dog mechanisms.

When the transition modelling the time-out mechanism is enabled, it can either fire,
or be disabled by some other conflicting event that takes place within the predefined
time-out interval. If the transition modelling the time-out is disabled because the
system evolves into its next natural state, the reading of the timer associated with the
time-out transition can be discarded, and the timer will be reset to a completely new
time-out delay when the transition becomes enabled again.

Let us consider for example the multiprocessor modelled by the timed PN system in
Fig. 31, augmented with the following further specification: one of the two processors
(say processor_2) has the privilege of interrupting the other one (say processor_1) when
the former has been waiting for the resource for an amount of time greater than a
given threshold $\tau_{watch-dog}$. This behaviour can be modelled by means of a transition
$T_{watch-dog}$ enabled when a request from processor_2 is pending and processor_1 is
using the resource. The PN system in Fig. 37 describes this behaviour by means of
the transition $T_{watch-dog}$ which is timed with enabling memory policy. This transition
models the time-out associated with the preemption privilege of processor_2 and the
timer associated with the transition is set to $\tau_{watch-dog}$ whenever it becomes enabled.
In fact, if the activity of processor_1 using the common resource ends while the timer

associated with $T_{watch-dog}$ has not yet reached zero, transition T_{end_1} fires moving a token to p_{idle} (the common resource is *naturally* released). This new marking enables the immediate transition t_{start_2} and disables $T_{watch-dog}$. When $T_{watch-dog}$ will be enabled again, its associated timer will again be set to $\tau_{watch-dog}$. It must be observed that the memory policies of the other timed transitions of the same PN system need not be the same.

3.4.2   An example with the age memory policy

As an example of the use of the age memory policy, consider the timed PN system depicted in Fig. 38. This net models the activity of a single processor in a MIMD (multiple instruction multiple data) computer architecture. The processor operates in a multitasking environment, executing a set of concurrent tasks performing cyclic activities. These activities include a local operation phase, followed by a request for service addressed to one of the neighbor processors. Each processor is available to provide service to requests coming from the neighbors. Requests coming from outside have priority over local activities, and thus preempt them. The external requests are modelled by the loop: p_{ext_req}, t_{req_start}, p_{req_exe}, T_{req_end}, p_{ext}, T_{ext}. Tokens in p_{local_ready} represent local ready tasks waiting for processor service, which starts (one process at a time) when transition t_{start} fires. The token in p_{exec} models the process activity and enables timed transition T_{end}. If a request for service arrives from a neighbor (firing of T_{ext}), one token moves to p_{ext_req}, the immediate transition t_{req_start} fires and removes the token from $p_{not\_ext\_req}$, thus disabling T_{end}. The active process is temporarily suspended (the timer associated with T_{end} is *halted*), but it will be restarted after the firing of T_{req_end}, when the processor resumes the interrupted activity. The age memory policy is necessary to capture the fact that the reading reached by the timer associated with T_{end} is kept to avoid forgetting the amount of work already performed on the local request. Obviously, when the timer associated with T_{end} expires, the transition fires. The timer associated with the transition will be reset at a new initial value when the transition becomes enabled again after firing.

As we observed before, there may be situations in which the enabling memory and age memory policies must coexist within a timed PN model. An example can be provided again by the multiprocessor system of Fig. 37 where the time-out mechanism is used to allow processor_2 to quickly access the common resource. If the interruption of the access of processor_1 can be implemented without losing the useful work already performed by processor_1 before the interruption, an age memory policy must be used for transition T_{end_1}. In this way, the activity performed by processor_1 on the common resource before the preemption by processor_2 can be resumed upon completion of the access of processor_2 without losing the work already carried on

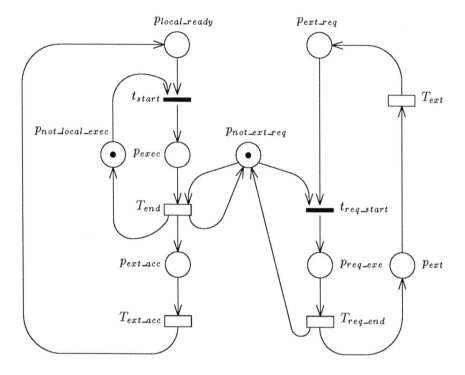

Figure 38   Timed PN system with age memory policy

before the interruption.

3.5   Multiple Enabling

Special attention must be paid to the timing semantics in the case of timed transitions with enabling degree larger than one. Consider transition T_1 in Fig. 39, which is enabled whenever one or more tokens are simultaneously in places p_1 and p_2. Different semantics are possible when several tokens are present in both input places. Borrowing from queueing network terminology, we can consider the following different situations.

1. **Single-server semantics**: a firing delay is set when the transition is first enabled, and new delays are generated upon transition firing if the transition is still enabled in the new marking. This means that enabling sets of tokens are processed serially and that the temporal specification associated with the transition is independent of the enabling degree, except for special marking dependency functions that will be discussed in Chapter 6.

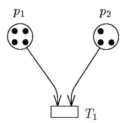

Figure 39   Timed transition with enabling degree 3

2. **Infinite-server semantics**: every enabling set of tokens is processed as soon as it forms in the input places of the (timed) transition. Its corresponding firing delay is generated at this time, and the timers associated with all these enabling sets run down to zero concurrently. Multiple enabling sets of tokens are thus processed in parallel. We can say that the overall temporal specifications of transitions with this semantics depend directly on their enabling degrees.

3. **Multiple-server semantics**: enabling sets of tokens are processed as soon as they form in the input places of the transition up to a maximum degree of parallelism (say K). For larger values of the enabling degree, the timers associated with new enabling sets of tokens are set only when the number of concurrently running timers decreases below the value K. The overall temporal specifications of transitions with this semantics depend directly on their enabling degrees up to a treshold value K,

   A simple example will help the reader understand the three semantics. Consider the timed transition T_1 in Fig. 39, with enabling degree 3. The three enablings are associated with three activities whose durations are 3, 2, and 4 time units, respectively. We describe next the detailed behaviour of the net, considering the three different semantics with reference to Fig. 40 that illustrates the firing epochs.

1. Single-server semantics: the serial execution of the activities induces the following sequence of events:

   - t = 0: T_1 is enabled and the first activity starts.
   - t = 3: the first activity (duration 3) ends, T_1 fires and the second activity starts.
   - t = 5: the second activity (duration 2) ends, T_1 fires and the third activity starts.
   - t = 9: the third activity (duration 4) ends and T_1 is disabled.

2. Infinite-server semantics: the parallel execution of the activities induces the following sequence of events:

   - t = 0: T_1 is enabled and all the activities start.

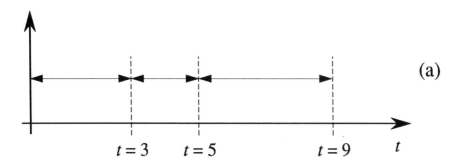

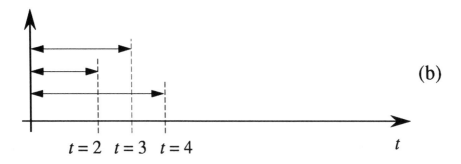

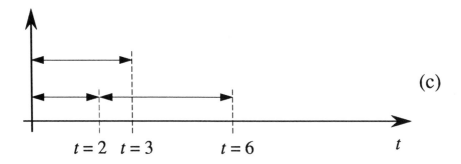

Figure 40   Firing epochs corresponding to the three different timing semantics

- $t = 2$: T_1 fires because of the completion of the second activity (duration 2).
- $t = 3$: T_1 fires because of the completion of the first activity (duration 3).
- $t = 4$: T_1 fires because of the completion of the third activity (duration 4) and it is disabled.

3. Multiple-server semantics: in this case we assume that the maximum parallelism is $K = 2$. This induces the following sequence of events:

- $t = 0$: T_1 is enabled and the first two activities start.
- $t = 2$: T_1 fires because of the completion of the second activity (duration 2) thus the third activity can start.
- $t = 3$: T_1 fires because of the completion of the first activity (duration 3).
- $t = 6$: T_1 fires because of the completion of the third activity (duration 4) and it is disabled.

The introduction of these different firing semantics permits the definition of PN systems that are graphically simple without losing any of the characteristics that allow the analysis of their underlying behaviours.

An example of this type of situation is represented by the well-known queueing network model of a timesharing computer system with a fixed number of users, shown in Fig. 41. It can be translated into a timed PN system as shown in Fig. 42, where the infinite-server station that models the terminal think time is represented by timed transition T_1 with infinite-server semantics, and the single-server station that models the CPU activity is represented by transition T_2 with single-server semantics.

This same example allows also to observe that service policies (like FIFO or LIFO) cannot be directly embedded into the enabling/firing mechanism of a single transition because tokens cannot be individually recognized. These policies must be described with the help of specific subnets that actually implement the selection algorithm of the specific queueing discipline.

The infinite-server and multiple-server semantics are just an example of the possibility for temporal specifications to depend on the marking of the PN system. With these semantics, only the places that determine the transition enabling degree influence the transition timing. More complex relationships can be envisioned, but an extensive exploitation of marking dependencies may introduce problems in the model specification and in its dynamic behaviour. We shall return to this point in Chapter 6.

3.6   A Timed PN Model Example

To conclude this chapter, we illustrate the timed PN model resulting from the introduction of temporal specifications in the readers & writers example discussed earlier in this book.

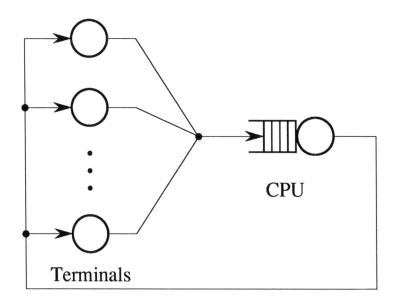

Figure 41 Queueing network model of a timesharing system

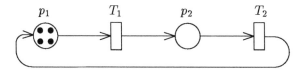

Figure 42 Timed PN model of a timesharing system

The timed PN model of the readers & writers system is shown in Fig. 43. The model comprises three timed and four immediate transitions. Timed transitions are used to represent the reading and writing actions as well as the local activities performed by the processes between two subsequent accesses to the database. Immediate transitions are used to implement the decision of which action a process wants to perform on the data base and to implement the coordination among reading and writing activities. The complete specification of the three timed transitions is the following:

- T_1 models the process activity not related to the data base access. The memory policy for T_1 is age memory (observe that the enabling memory policy can also be chosen, since the transition is not in conflict with other transitions). The timing

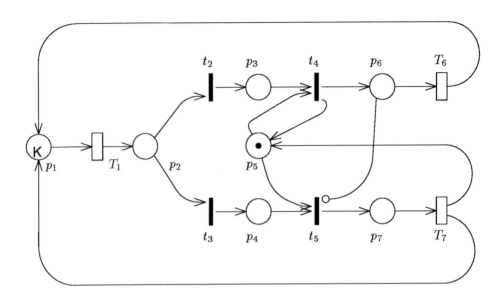

Figure 43   Timed PN model of the readers & writers system

semantics of the transition is infinite-server.

- T_6 models the data base read activity. The memory policy for T_6 is age memory (also in this case the enabling memory policy yields the same behaviour). The timing semantics of the transition is infinite-server.

- T_7 models the data base write activity. The memory policy for T_7 is age memory (once more, the enabling memory policy is equivalent). The timing semantics of the transition is single-server (however, the initial marking of the model – 1 token in place p_5 – prevents the enabling degree of transition T_7 from exceeding 1, thus making inessential the difference between single-server and multiple-server specifications).

The pair of conflicting immediate transitions t_2 and t_3 allows the selection between a read and a write request. The two immediate transitions t_4 and t_5 allow the start of either a read or a write access.

3.7   Performance Measures

The main reason for the introduction of temporal specifications into PN models is the interest for the computation of performance indexes. Consider for example the multiprocessor system modelled by the PN system in Fig. 31. In this case, it may be of interest to answer the following questions:

- For how long is a processor idle waiting for the shared memory ?
- Which is the rate of access of a processor to the shared memory ?

The answers to these questions can be obtained essentially in two different ways: the first one requires to exercise the net simulating its behaviour, whereas the second one, possible only under some specific conditions, requires an analysis based on the reachability graph of the untimed PN system and on the temporal specifications.

Consider first the simulation approach: from a significative execution sequence of the net it is possible to identify all the states (markings) satisfying a given condition and to add (and possibly average) the times spent in each of the markings of interest. This is obviously possible because the model execution generates states in which the PN system sojourns for some time. With reference to Fig. 31, the answer to the first question can be obtained considering all the markings in which a token is present in $p_{requesting\_1}$ (or $p_{requesting\_2}$ for the other processor). The answer to the second question can be obtained in a similar way by considering all the markings in which a token is present in $p_{accessing\_1}$ or $p_{accessing\_2}$.

The second approach in not always possible. As we already pointed out, the introduction of temporal specifications into a PN model or system must be done so as not to modify the basic behaviour, and specifically the non-determinism of the choices occurring in the net execution. Only in this case the reachability set of the untimed PN system contains all execution sequences possible also in the timed PN system.

If the temporal specification is given in a deterministic way, the behaviour of the model is deterministically specified, and the choices due to conflicting transitions may be always solved in the same way. This would make many of the execution sequences in the untimed PN system impossible.

Instead, if the temporal specifications are defined in a stochastic manner, by associating independent continuous random variables with transitions to specify their firing delays, the non-determinism is preserved (in the sense that all the execution sequences possible in the untimed PN system are also possible in the timed version of the PN system) under the condition that the support of the distribution of the random variables is $[0, \infty)$. In this case the temporal specification at the net level can be superimposed over a reachability graph that can be generated using the untimed version of the PN system to obtain the characterization of the behaviour of the timed PN system.

4

PETRI NETS WITH PRIORITY

We noted in the previous chapter that the presence of both timed and immediate transitions in the same timed PN model naturally leads to the concept of priority. On the one hand, the availability of different priority levels in PN models increases their descriptive power, thus giving more flexibility and freedom to the modeller. On the other hand, the introduction of priorities in PN models requires an extension of the standard analysis techniques. In this chapter we first extend the PN model formalism to include several priority levels for transitions and define the dynamics of this new formalism; then we highlight the influence that priorities have on the notion of conflict and related concepts; finally we discuss which of the analysis techniques that are applicable to PN models without priorities still apply to this extended model, and which must be revised in order to account for the peculiarities induced by priority rules.

Although the models considered in this chapter are untimed, the introduction of some concept is motivated in terms of its use in the GSPN framework.

4.1 Definition and Dynamics

The formal definition of a PN model with priority is similar to the usual definition of a PN model given in Definition 2.1.1; the only difference is the introduction of a *priority function* that assigns to each transition a natural number corresponding to its priority level.

Definition 4.1.1 *A PN model with priority is a 9-tuple*

$$\mathcal{M}_\pi = \{P, T, I, O, H, \Pi, PAR, PRED, MP\} \tag{4.1}$$

where

- $\mathcal{M} = \{P, T, I, O, H, PAR, PRED, MP\}$ *defines a PN model and*
- $\Pi : T \to \mathbb{N}$ *is the priority function that maps transitions onto natural numbers representing their priority level.*

For notational convenience we use π_j instead of $\Pi(t_j)$, whenever this does not generate ambiguities. The priority definition that we assume in the book is global: the enabled transitions with a given priority k always fire before any other enabled transition with priority[1] $j < k$.

This kind of priority definition can be used for two different modelling purposes: (1) it allows the partition of the transition set into classes representing actions at different logical levels, e.g. actions that take time versus actions corresponding to logical choices that occur instantaneously; (2) it gives the possibility of specifying a deterministic conflict resolution criterion.

Enabling and firing —   The firing rule in PN models with priority requires the following new definitions:

- a transition t_j is said to *have concession* in marking M if the numbers of tokens in its input and inhibitor places verify the usual enabling conditions for PN models without priority
- a transition t_j is said to *be enabled* in marking M if it has concession in the same marking, and if no transition $t_k \in T$ of priority $\pi_k > \pi_j$ exists that has concession in M. As a consequence, two transitions may be simultaneously enabled in a given marking only if they have the same priority level
- a transition t_j can *fire* only if it is enabled. The effect of transition firing is identical to the case of PN models without priority

Observe that in this new framework all the transitions enabled in a given marking M have the same priority level, say j. In the GSPN formalism, priority level zero is assigned to all timed transitions, and priority levels greater than zero are associated with immediate transitions: this leads to a classification of markings based on the priority level j of the transitions enabled in it. The tangible markings defined in the previous chapter correspond to states characterized by a priority level $j = 0$, plus all the *dead* states (i.e., all states M such that $E(M) = \emptyset$); vanishing markings instead are characterized by a priority level $j > 0$: we may partition the set of vanishing markings into subsets of j-priority level vanishing markings.

Note that the presence of priority only restricts the set of enabled transitions (and therefore the possibilities of firing) with respect to the same PN model without priority. This implies that some properties are not influenced by the addition of a priority structure, while others are changed in a well-determined way, as we shall see in a while.

---

[1] Without loss of generality, we also assume that all lower priority levels are not empty, i.e.:

$$\forall t_j \in T, \quad \pi_j > 0 \implies \exists t_k \in T : \pi_k = \pi_j - 1$$

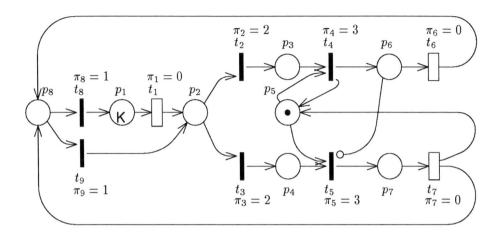

Figure 44   A modified readers & writers model

An example — Let us consider the modified version of the readers & writers example depicted in Fig. 44. The difference with respect to the former model concerns the events following the end of an access: in the new PN model a process can either execute in its local memory for a while before requesting a new access (sequence of transitions t_8, t_1, followed by the choice between t_2 and t_3) or immediately proceed to the next access (transition t_9 followed by the choice between t_2 and t_3).

A possible assignment of transition priorities that is consistent with the interpretation of this PN model as a representation of the readers & writers system is the following: $\pi_1 = \pi_6 = \pi_7 = 0$, and $\pi_2, \pi_3, \pi_4, \pi_5, \pi_8, \pi_9 > 0$. This priority specification is consistent with the timing specification given in Chapter 3: transitions t_1, t_6, and t_7, that represent timed activities, are assigned the lowest priority level (i.e., priority 0) reserved to timed transitions. Transitions t_2 and t_3, that represent the choice between the two access modes, transitions t_4 and t_5, that represent the start of either access mode, and transitions t_8 and t_9, that represent the choice between executing in the local memory for a while and immediately proceeding to the next access, are assigned a priority greater than zero (i.e., they are defined to be immediate), meaning that the corresponding actions are assumed to take place in zero time. Now we could choose either to assign priority level one to all immediate transitions, or to assign a given priority level to t_2 and t_3, a different priority level to t_4 and t_5, and yet another one to t_8 and t_9. The former modelling choice implies no specification of ordering among the conflict resolutions associated with these three transition pairs in case they are enabled together in a given marking. The latter modelling choice instead precisely specifies such an ordering. Notice that since t_2 and t_3 have the same input set, it would be meaningless not to assign them the same priority level: indeed if $\pi_2 > \pi_3$, t_3 could not be live in any marking, and viceversa. The same observation applies to t_8 and t_9. On the contrary, assigning different priority levels to t_4 and t_5, we can model a system where readers (writers) have priority over writers (readers).

Let us consider two examples of priority assignment, and discuss the corresponding interpretations:

- $\pi_2 = \pi_3 = 2$, $\pi_4 = \pi_5 = 3$, $\pi_8 = \pi_9 = 1$; this priority assignment implies that whenever a process chooses to make an access in a given mode, that access should immediately start, provided the corresponding transition is enabled, before any other process can make its choice. In other words, whenever an immediately executable access mode is chosen, the access choice and start events constitute an *atomic* action.

- $\pi_2 = \pi_3 = 2$, $\pi_4 = \pi_5 = 1$, $\pi_8 = \pi_9 = 3$; this priority assignment implies that when several processes are going to choose their access mode, then all of them must make their choice before any access can start.

Both these modelling alternatives are reasonable: the modellist may choose one or the other, according to the actual system behaviour. For example, let us choose the first alternative and play the token game on the resulting model. To play the token game, we need to specify completely the initial marking M_0 by assigning a suitable value to the parameter K; in this example we assume $K = 3$. Let us play the token game starting from marking M_1, reachable from M_0, defined below.

$$M_1 = p_1 + p_4 + p_7$$

Marking M_1 is tangible; indeed, two timed transitions are enabled in this marking: t_1 and t_7. Let us fire transition t_7; we reach the vanishing marking

$$M_2 = p_1 + p_4 + p_5 + p_8$$

from which t_5 can fire. Observe that in this marking transitions t_1, t_8 and t_9 have concession, but they are not enabled. Let us fire transition t_5; we reach the vanishing marking

$$M_3 = p_1 + p_7 + p_8$$

in which t_8 and t_9 are enabled. If now t_9 is fired we reach the vanishing marking

$$M_4 = p_1 + p_2 + p_7$$

in which transitions t_2 and t_3 are enabled. Firing transition t_2 a new tangible marking is finally reached:

$$M_5 = p_1 + p_3 + p_7$$

in which t_1 and t_7 are enabled. Notice that the firing sequence $\sigma = t_5, t_9, t_2$, such that $M_2[\sigma\rangle M_5$ takes zero time: i.e., an external observer who is only capable of perceiving states where the system spends some time, would see the previously described state evolution as an atomic transition leading from M_1 to M_5 (i.e., markings M_2 of priority level 3, M_3 of priority level 1, and M_4 of priority level 2 would vanish).

We could extend this concept of *observability* to higher levels of priority, so that a *level j observer* can perceive the firing of transitions up to priority level j, while firing sequences of higher priority transitions are seen as indivisible actions, and markings of priority level greater than j become, from his point of view, "vanishing".

Choosing the second priority assignment for t_2, t_3, t_4, t_5, t_8, and t_9, the firing sequence leading from M_2 to M_5 would be

$$M_2[t_9\rangle M_3'[t_2\rangle M_4'[t_5\rangle M_5$$

where marking M_2 enables t_8 and t_9 (hence it has priority level 3), marking M_3' enables t_2 and t_3 (hence it has priority level 2), marking M_4' enables t_4 and t_5 (hence it has priority level 1).

Notice that the main difference between the two firing sequences just described is in the firing of transition t_5: it is deterministic in the first firing sequence while it implies a conflict resolution in the second one.

4.2 Conflicts, Confusion and Priority

In this section we study how the notions of conflict and confusion are modified when a priority structure is associated with transitions. The j-observability concept just introduced in the previous section, helps in understanding the new notions. Conflict and related concepts are important in the framework of GSPNs where conflict resolution is performed probabilistically rather than using nondeterminism. In GSPN models, a suitable probability distribution is associated with sets of conflicting transitions for this purpose.

For example, suppose that in the readers & writers system, 30% of the incoming requests are reads, while 70% are writes. Then, every time there is a conflict between t_2 and t_3, the probability that the former is fired should be 0.3 while the probability that the latter is fired should be 0.7. Since t_2 and t_3 are always enabled together, this requirement can be included in the model by associating a *weight* equal to 0.3 with t_2 and a weight equal to 0.7 with t_3.

Let us now consider the conflict due to the presence of both readers and writers competing for the data base (corresponding to a conflict between t_4 and t_5). Readers and writers might have the same probability of being granted access to the data base, or this probability might depend on the number of users of each type waiting to access.

In the latter case, some more complex type of annotation should be added into the model description to take into account all the different possible conflict situations. It is thus very important to be able to clearly identify by inspection of the net structure the sets of potentially conflicting transitions. The SC relation defined in Chapter 2 may seem appropriate to identify sets of potentially conflicting transitions; however, we shall see that this is not always a correct choice.

Conflict — The notion of conflict is drastically influenced by the introduction of a priority structure in PN models. The definition of effective conflict has to be modified with respect to the new notion of *concession*. Instead, the definition of enabling degree given in Chapter 2 remains unchanged for PN models with priority. Observe that this implies that both transitions that have concession and enabled transitions have enabling degree greater than zero. Conflict resolution causes the enabling degree of some transition to be reduced, and this may happen both for transitions with concession and for enabled transitions. Hence the definition of the effective conflict relation is modified as follows.

Definition 4.2.1 *Transition t_i is in* effective conflict *relation with transition t_j in marking M, (t_i $EC(M)$ t_j) iff t_j has concession in M, t_i is enabled in M, and the enabling degree of t_j decreases after the firing of t_i.*

Observe that a necessary condition for the EC relation to hold is that $\pi_i \geq \pi_j$, otherwise t_i would not be enabled in M.

The definition of different priority levels for transitions introduces a further complication, since it destroys the locality of conflicts typical of PN models without priority.

Let us consider the net in Fig. 45. Transitions t_1 and t_2 are both enabled in the marking represented in the figure (since they both have concession, and no higher priority transition has concession), and apparently they are not in conflict, since they do not share input or inhibition places. According to the definition of concurrent transitions given in Chapter 2, one might conclude that t_1 and t_2 are concurrent. However, the firing of t_1 enables t_3, which has higher priority than t_2, so that:

1. transition t_2 becomes disabled while keeping its concession
2. transition t_3 is certainly the next transition to fire
3. the firing of t_3 removes the token from place p_2, thus taking concession away from transition t_2

This sequence of events is not interruptible after the firing of t_1, due to the priority structure, and eventually results in the disabling of t_2 through the firing of a higher priority transition (the example can be extended to a sequence of higher priority transitions). We call this situation *indirect effective conflict* between t_1 and t_2.

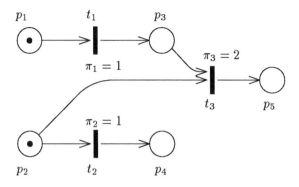

Figure 45   An example of indirect conflict

Definition 4.2.2 *For any priority PN model $\mathcal{M}_\pi$, $\forall t_i, t_j \in T$ such that $t_i \neq t_j$, $\forall M : P \rightarrow \mathbb{N}$, transition t_i is in indirect effective conflict with t_j in marking M (denoted $t_i \ IEC(M) \ t_j$) iff*

- *t_j has concession in M*
- *$t_i \in E(M)$*
- *$\exists \sigma = t_{(1)}, \ldots, t_{(k)}$ such that*

    1. $M[t_i\rangle M_{(1)}[t_{(1)}\rangle \ldots M_{(k)}[t_{(k)}\rangle M'$, and
    2. $\forall 1 \leq h \leq k, \pi_{(h)} > \pi_j$, and
    3. $t_{(k)} EC(M_{(k)}) t_j$.

Notice that this situation cannot occur if priority is removed: if all transitions are at the same priority level, the sequence "t_1 followed by t_3" is interruptible, and a "normal" effective conflict exists only between t_2 and t_3. Indirect effective conflict is the proper generalization of the concept of non-prioritized conflict: in the above example a priority level 1 observer would not see the firing of t_3, hence from his point of view, t_1 and t_2 actually are in EC relation in marking M. In the modified readers & writers example of Fig. 44, indirect conflict could happen only if either t_4 or t_5 had a different priority level with respect to t_2 and t_3. For example, if readers had priority over writers, a correct priority definition could be: $\pi_2 = \pi_3 = \pi_5 = \pi_8 = \pi_9 = 1, \pi_4 = 2$. With this priority definition, an indirect conflict between t_2 and t_5 would be present in marking $p_1 + p_2 + p_4 + p_5$.

Confusion and priority — In Chapter 2, the concept of confusion was discussed in the framework of PN models without priority. In this section we shall see how the introduction of a priority structure can avoid confusion.

Confusion is an important notion because it highlights the fact that, in terms of event ordering, the system behaviour is not completely defined: this underspecification could be due either to a precise modelling choice (the chosen abstraction level does not include any information on the ordering of events, hence the model analysis must investigate the effect of pursuing any possible order) or to a modelling error. The introduction of a priority structure may force a deterministic ordering of conflict resolutions that removes confusion.

For example, let us compare the two examples depicted in Figs. 21 and 45: by associating a higher priority level with transition t_3 we have eliminated the confusion situation due to the firing sequences $\sigma = t_2, t_1$ and $\sigma' = t_1, t_2$ that are both fireable in marking $M = p_1 + p_2$, and that involve different conflict resolutions. Any conflict between t_2 and t_3 is always solved in favour of t_3; as a consequence the sequence $\sigma' = t_1, t_2$ is not fireable in M so that confusion is avoided.

Let us illustrate these concepts on the modified version of the readers & writers example in Fig. 44. If all the immediate transitions in the PN model had priority 1, there would be the possibility for confusion to arise: consider marking $M = (K-2)p_1 + p_3 + p_7$, and assume t_7 fires. In the newly reached marking $M' = (K-2)p_1 + p_3 + p_5 + p_8$, three transitions are enabled, namely t_8, t_9 and t_4. Consider the two firing sequences $\sigma_1 = t_9, t_3, t_4$ and $\sigma_2 = t_4, t_9, t_3$. The first sequence requires three choices to be performed: the one between t_9 and t_8, the one between t_3 and t_2 and finally the one between t_4 and t_5. The second sequence instead requires only two conflicts to be solved: the one between t_9 and t_8 and the one between t_3 and t_2. Confusion can be avoided for example by assigning to t_4 or t_5 a priority level different from that of t_2, t_3, t_8 and t_9.

Observe that even if by inspection of the PN structure we could deduce that a similar confused situation could arise also in the original readers & writers example, actually it can never happen because of the initial marking specification and of the higher priority level of immediate over timed transitions. Indeed, transitions t_2 and t_3 can never be enabled together with t_4 or t_5 in the original example. We shall see later in this chapter that structural necessary conditions for confusion in PN models with priority can be defined. Intuitively, these conditions require the presence of a non free-choice conflict comprising at least two transitions t_i and t_j at the same priority level and a third transition t_k causally connected to either t_i or t_j and such that $\pi_k = \pi_i = \pi_j$.

Concerning indirect conflict, observe that it can never arise if $\pi_4 = \pi_5$. If instead $\pi_4 > \pi_5$ and either (a) $\pi_8 = \pi_9 = \pi_5$ or (b) $\pi_2 = \pi_3 = \pi_5$, then an indirect conflict between t_5 and t_9 or between t_5 and t_2 can be observed. A structural necessary condition for indirect conflict is the presence of a non free-choice conflict comprising at least two transitions t_i and t_j such that $\pi_i > \pi_j$.

4.3   Properties of Priority PN Models

In this section, we discuss the impact of priority on the properties of PN models. In particular, we are interested in observing the relation between the properties of a priority PN model and the properties of the underlying PN model without priority. The practical reason for studying this relation is that some of the properties can be efficiently checked using algorithms that apply only to models without priority. Properties can be divided into two broad classes: properties that must hold for all states in the state space (in the literature these are called *safety* or *invariant* properties) and properties that must hold for some state (called *eventuality* or *progress* properties). Examples of invariant properties are absence of deadlock ($\forall M \in RS(M_0), E(M) \neq \emptyset$), boundedness, and mutual exclusion. Examples of eventuality properties are reachability (a given marking will be eventually reached) and liveness (a transition will eventually become enabled).

Let $\mathcal{M}_\pi$ be a PN model with priority and let $\mathcal{M}$ be the underlying PN model without priority. Since the introduction of priority can only reduce the state space, all the safety properties that can be shown to be true for $\mathcal{M}$, surely hold also for $\mathcal{M}_\pi$. Instead eventuality properties are in general not preserved by the introduction of a priority structure.

It is interesting to observe that P and T-invariants describe properties that continue to hold after the addition of a priority structure. The reason is that they are computed only taking into account the state change caused by transition firing, without any assumption on the possibility for a transition of ever becoming enabled.

Let us consider the properties of PN models of general interest and discuss their extension to priority PN models.

Reachability — The reachability property for PN models with priority is defined in terms of enabling and firing, as was already the case for PN models without priority. If we check reachability by generating the complete reachability set, there is no problem in computing the RS for the PN system with priority since precise enabling and firing rules have been defined for the extended formalism. Moreover, the introduction of priority may considerably reduce the state space size, hence the time and space required to generate the RG of the priority model are usually less than the space and time required to generate the RG of the corresponding model without priority.

Since enabling is more restricted than in the corresponding PN model without priority, in general reachability is not preserved by the addition of a priority structure. However, a marking M' is reachable from a marking M in a PN model with priority only if it is reachable in the corresponding PN model without priority. For example, in the priority PN model representing the readers & writers system, the marking

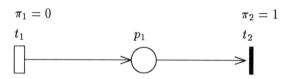

Figure 46   An example of boundedness due to priority

$M' = p_5 + K p_6$ remains reachable after the introduction of priority, while the marking $M'' = K p_2 + p_5$ that was reachable in the PN model without priority, is not reachable after the introduction of priority, if $K > 1$.

Boundedness — Boundedness is preserved by the introduction of a priority structure in the sense that a bounded PN model remains bounded after the introduction of a priority specification. This implies that the use of P-semiflows to study the boundedness of a PN model can be applied to the model without priority $\mathcal{M}$ associated with a priority PN model $\mathcal{M}_\pi$ and if the former model is shown to be structurally bounded, the conclusion can be extended to the latter model. In the examples that will be presented in later chapters of this book we shall use P-invariants to check boundedness of GSPN models exploiting this observation.

Observe that an unbounded PN model may become bounded after the specification of an appropriate priority structure. Consider for example the PN model depicted in Fig. 46. The structure is typical of an unbounded PN model, in which the marking of place p_1 can grow indefinitely due to the repeated firing of transition t_1. If we add the priority specification $\pi_1 = 0$ and $\pi_2 = 1$, however, the PN model with priority becomes 1-bounded (provided that $M_0(p_1) \leq 1$), since transition t_1 is no more enabled (although it still has concession) after putting one token in p_1, until the firing of t_2 removes it. As a consequence, if we cannot show that the model without priority $\mathcal{M}$ associated with a priority PN model $\mathcal{M}_\pi$ is bounded, we have to devise more powerful proof techniques that take into account priority to show the boundedness of model $\mathcal{M}_\pi$. Observe that this kind of problem arises also in PN models with inhibitor/test arcs: indeed the PN model depicted in Fig. 47 is 1-bounded even if the P-semiflows computation doesn't allow this property to be discovered.

Liveness and liveness degree — This property is intimately related to the enabling and firing rules, hence it is greatly influenced by a change in the priority specification: a live PN model may become not live after the introduction of an inappropriate priority structure and, viceversa, a PN model that is not live, may

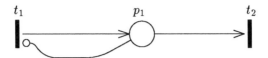

Figure 47   An example of boundedness due to inhibitor arcs

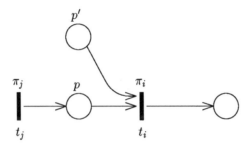

Figure 48   Influence of the priority on the maximum enabling degree of transitions

become live after the addition of an appropriate priority structure. Moreover, even if the net with priority is live, the priority structure could change the maximum enabling degree of transitions. For example, the PN model in Fig. 46 shows a PN model with priority in which t_2 is 1-live, while in the corresponding PN model without priority the same transition would be ∞-live. The reason is that the liveness degree of a transition is related to the possibility of accumulating tokens in its input places. Let us consider the subnet in Fig. 48: input place p of transition t_i receives tokens only from a transition t_j; let's assume that $\pi_j < \pi_i$. Tokens can accumulate in place p, only if the marking of some other input place p' prevents the enabling of t_i immediately after the firing of t_j, and at the same time no other transition sharing an input place p with t_i can take the tokens out from it.

This example shows that liveness, being an eventuality property, does not extend smoothly from a PN model to a priority PN model with the same structure. However, as long as we accept that we have to build the complete RG, we don't have problems in checking any kind of property of priority PN systems. Observe that even for PN models structural liveness is not proved simply by applying an automatic algorithm (except for some simple subclasses of PN models), rather it is proved by the modeller on a case by case basis, using the net structure and some information from P and T-invariants. Hence the addition of priority only adds one more constraint to be taken into account by the modeller when devising the proof.

Reversibility and home states — These are eventuality properties, hence the addition of a priority structure may change drastically the behaviour of a PN model. Like for the other properties in this class, the construction of the RG allows them to be checked on a particular PN system. Also in this case proofs performed on the model can take advantage of the information coming from the P and T-invariants computation.

4.4   Structural Analysis Techniques

4.4.1   Linear algebraic techniques

Structural results based on the incidence matrix apply to PN models with priority in the same way as for PN models without priority. Transition priorities are not taken into account in the incidence matrix, like inhibitor and test arcs. This may result in the loss of some invariance relations, but never in the computation of wrong relations. For example, in the PN model in Fig. 46, the relation $M(p_1) \leq \max(1, M_0(p_1))$ cannot be derived from the incidence matrix since it is enforced by priority.

P- and T-semiflows — P- and T-semiflows define marking-independent invariance relations for which it makes no sense trying to take priority into account. Hence, P- and T-semiflows can be defined, computed and exploited in exactly the same way as for PN models without priority.

The addition of a priority structure may introduce new parametric invariant relations that do not hold true in the corresponding PN model without priority. Fig. 46 provides an example of the existence of such cases. Indeed, in the example, the marking of place p_1 is less than or equal to one, due to the fact that its output transition t_2 has higher priority than its input transition t_1, that $O(t_2) = I(t_1) = 1$, and that $M_0(p_1) = 0$.

Another example is provided by the priority PN model of Fig. 49. It is covered by a unique P-semiflow comprising all the places. Hence the model has one P-invariant: $M(p_1) + M(p_2) + M(p_3) = K$.

However, if the priority structure is taken into account it is clear that also the following P-invariant holds for this model:

$$M(p_3) \leq M_0(p_3) = 0$$

which implies that

$$M(p_1) + M(p_2) = K$$

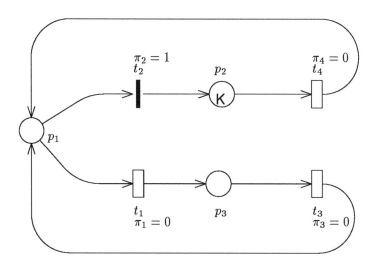

Figure 49   An example of modified P-invariant due to priority

The problem with such invariant relations is that no general algorithm is known to compute a minimal set of independent invariants due to priority, unlike for P- and T-semiflows. Hence, these properties must be proved on a case-by-case basis, using the intuition and the ingenuity of the modeller.

4.4.2   Graph based analysis

Structural conflict — For PN models without priority, we defined the notion of *structural conflict* relation (SC) to identify potentially conflicting pairs of transitions by inspection of the net structure. Intuitively, two transitions t_i and t_j are in structural conflict if they share at least one input place or if the output set of t_i is not disjoint from the inhibition set of t_j. The definition does not change for Petri nets with priority.

In this case we can also define the *indirect structural conflict* (ISC) relation that gives a necessary condition for two transitions to be in indirect effective conflict relation in some marking. Intuitively, we have first to find a pair of transitions t_k and t_j such that $\pi_k > \pi_j$ and $t_k SC t_j$; then we have to follow the net arcs backwards starting from transition t_k until we find a new transition t_i such that $\pi_i \leq \pi_j$. All the transitions on the path (including t_i) with priority greater than or equal to π_j, are in indirect structural conflict relation with t_j. Indeed, any transition on the path can trigger a firing sequence of transitions with priority higher than π_j, that may eventually enable transition t_k whose firing decreases the enabling degree of transition t_j. Notice that the transitions on the path are in causal connection relation. A formal recursive definition for the ISC relation follows:

Definition 4.4.1 *Given a priority PN model, two transitions t_i and t_j are in indirect structural conflict relation (denoted t_i ISC t_j) iff*

- $\pi_i \geq \pi_j$;
- $\exists t_k : (\pi_k > \pi_j) \wedge (t_i SCC t_k) \wedge ((t_k SCt_j) \vee (t_k ISCt_j))$

where SCC is the structural causal connection relation (see Definition 2.5.8).

Let us consider the model in Fig. 45; since transition t_3 is in SC relation with transition t_2, $\pi_3 > \pi_2$ and $t_1 SCCt_3$, it is possible to conclude that $t_1 ISCt_2$.

Given the definition of structural conflict, it is possible to introduce the notion of *conflict set* and *extended conflict set*. The motivation for the introduction of these concepts will become apparent in the following chapters.

We define the *symmetric structural conflict* as follows:

Definition 4.4.2 *Transition t_i is in symmetric structural conflict with t_j (denoted t_i SSC t_j) iff*

- $\pi_i = \pi_j$ *and*
- $t_i SCt_j \vee t_j SCt_i \vee t_i ISCt_j \vee t_j ISCt_i$.

The conflict set associated with a given transition t_i is the set of transitions that might be in conflict with t_i in some marking.

Definition 4.4.3 *The conflict set associated with a given transition t_i is defined as*

$$CS(t_i) = \{t_j : (t_i SSCt_j)\}$$

The transitive closure of the SSC relation is an equivalence relation that allows the partition of the set T into equivalence classes called *extended conflict sets*.

Definition 4.4.4 $ECS(t_i) = \{t_j : t_i \ SSC^* \ t_j \wedge \sim (t_i \ SME \ t_j)\}.$

Here the SME relation represents the mutual exclusion in enabling due to structural properties. The notation $t_i \ SME \ t_j$ (*structural mutual exclusion*) is used as a synonym of $t_i \ HME \ t_j \quad \vee \quad t_i \ MME \ t_j \quad \vee \quad t_i \ \Pi ME \ t_j$ where HME indicates the structural mutual exclusion due to inhibitor arcs, MME indicates the structural mutual exclusion due to invariants (see Chapter 2), and ΠME is defined as follows:

Definition 4.4.5 *Structural mutual exclusion due to priority (denoted ΠME) is:* $t_l \ \Pi ME \ t_m \quad iff \quad \exists t_k :$

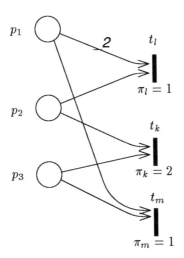

Figure 50   An example of ΠME relation

- $\pi_k > \pi_l \wedge \pi_k > \pi_m$ *and*

- $\forall p_j \in P,$

  - $I(t_k, p_j) \leq \max(I(t_l, p_j), I(t_m, p_j))$ *and*

  - $(H(t_k, p_j) = 0 \vee H(t_k, p_j) \geq \min(H(t_l, p_j), H(t_m, p_j)) > 0)$

Informally, two transitions (at the same priority level) are ΠME if, in order for them to have concession at the same time, a third higher priority transition must also have concession; an example is shown in Fig. 50 where transitions t_l and t_m can have concession together in a given marking M only if $M(p_1) \geq 2$, $M(p_2) \geq 1$ and $M(p_3) \geq 1$; however in this situation also t_k has concession, and since $\pi_k > \pi_l = \pi_m$, then t_l and t_m are not enabled together in this marking.

   Any one of the three structural mutual exclusion conditions can be checked without computing the actual transition sequences, and is sufficient for the mutually exclusive enabling of two transitions.

4.5   Reachability Analysis Techniques

The analysis of the reachability graph in the case of PN models with priority is similar to that for PN models without priority. The only difference is in the enabling rule that

		p_1	p_2	p_3	p_4	p_5	p_6	p_7
M_0	$=$	$2p_1 +$				p_5		
M_1^{**}	$=$	$p_1 +$	$p_2 +$			p_5		
M_2^{*}	$=$	$p_1 +$		$p_3 +$		p_5		
M_3^{*}	$=$	$p_1 +$			$p_4 +$	p_5		
M_4	$=$	$p_1 +$				$p_5 +$	p_6	
M_5	$=$	$p_1 +$						p_7
M_6^{**}	$=$		$p_2 +$			$p_5 +$	p_6	
M_7^{*}	$=$			$p_3 +$		$p_5 +$	p_6	
M_8	$=$				$p_4 +$	$p_5 +$	p_6	
M_9	$=$					$p_5 +$	$2p_6$	
M_{10}^{**}	$=$		$p_2 +$					p_7
M_{11}	$=$			$p_3 +$				p_7
M_{12}	$=$				$p_4 +$			p_7

Figure 51 Reachability set of the readers & writers PN system with priority

in the case of a priority structure may produce a smaller reachability graph (in terms of both numbers of arcs and nodes).

Reachability graph of PN models with priority — Fig. 51 and Fig. 52 depict the reachability set and reachability graph of the readers & writers PN system with two processes, and with the following priority definition: $\pi_1 = \pi_6 = \pi_7 = 0$, $\pi_2 = \pi_3 = 2$, $\pi_4 = \pi_5 = 1$. The reader may wish to compare this RG with that of the PN system without priority shown in Fig. 14. The total number of markings in the RS is reduced from 19 to 13. Moreover, markings can be partitioned into classes, according to the priority level of enabled transitions. In our example, markings can be partitioned in three classes, corresponding to the enabling of transitions at priority levels 0, 1, and 2. Seven markings enable priority 0 transitions, three markings enable priority 1 transitions (namely M_2, M_3, and M_7), and three enable priority 2 transitions (namely M_1, M_6, and M_{10}). In Fig. 51 and Fig. 52, markings at priority level 1 have a $*$ superscript, while markings at priority level 2 have a $**$ superscript.

Reduced reachability graphs — Often, when performing the analysis of a priority PN model, we are interested only in a part of the model behaviour, such as the enabling and firing of transitions with priority level less than or equal to a given threshold. This is in particular the case when the priority PN model describes the underlying logic of a timed PN model, in which higher priority transitions are

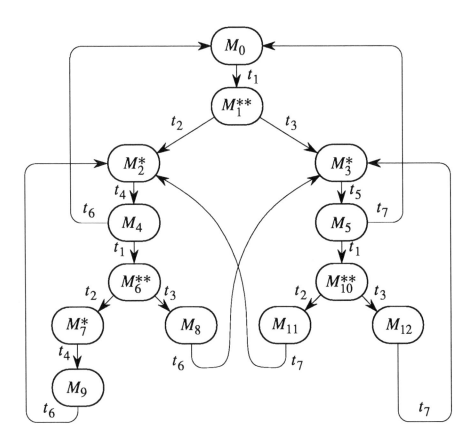

Figure 52   Reachability graph of the readers & writers PN system with priority

immediate and fire in zero time, while the enabling of lowest priority transitions lasts
for non-negligible amounts of time. In such cases, it is convenient to introduce the
construction of a *reduced reachability graph up to priority level L* (denoted *L*–RRG),
in which all markings enabling transitions of priority greater than *L* "vanish". The
indirect conflict between transitions at priority level *L* can be directly recognized by
the analysis of the *L*–RRG as if it was a regular conflict on that graph. In the GSPN
framework, the 0–RRG is usually called *Tangible Reachability Graph* (TRG), because
its nodes are the tangible markings.

Figs. 53 and 54 depict the 1–RRG and the 0–RRG, respectively, associated with the
readers & writers PN model with priority. Notice the labelling of the arcs representing
sequences of higher priority transition firings that substitute higher priority sequences
of markings. These sequences should contain an indication of the higher priority

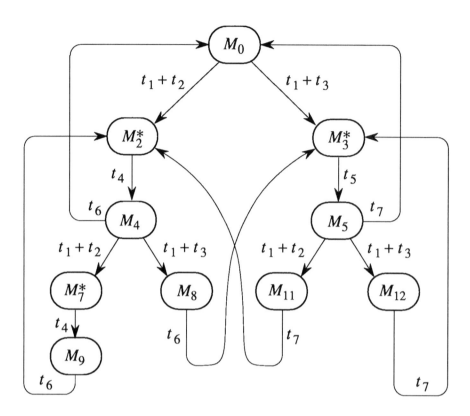

Figure 53   1–reduced reachability graph of the readers & writers PN system with priority

transition firings, together with the extended conflict sets in which these transitions were enabled in the vanished markings. This is the minimal information required to give an interpretation of the original model behaviour in terms of conflict resolutions. For example, the arc from marking M_0 to marking M_5 in Fig. 54 should contain the following information: (1) the firing sequence associated with the arc is $t_1 + t_3 + t_5$, (2) the firing of t_1 didn't involve any conflict resolution, the firing of t_3 involved a conflict resolution between transitions t_2 and t_3, and the firing of t_5 didn't involve any conflict resolution.

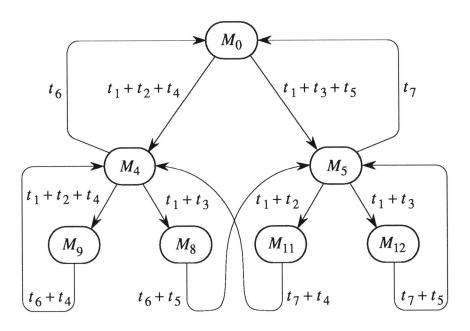

Figure 54 0–reduced reachability graph of the readers & writers PN system with priority

5

GSPN BASICS

In this chapter we provide an intuitive explanation of the characteristics and dynamics of the PN models obtained by associating a random, exponentially distributed firing delay with timed transitions. In the first section we consider the case of nets with timed transitions only, thus obtaining an informal introduction to the models that are known by the name Stochastic PNs (SPNs). A discussion on the impact of the introduction of immediate transitions in SPN models is contained in the other sections of the chapter. Some restrictions are initially assumed, for the sake of simplicity, leading to a first approach to generalized SPN (GSPN), which is limited to the case of free-choice conflicts, marking-independent firing rates and weights, and one level of priority for immediate transitions. The general case of multiple priorities, non-free-choice conflicts, and marking-dependency is then informally described, and subsequently the formal definition of GSPNs is provided. Simple examples of SPN and GSPN models are used throughout the chapter, to illustrate in some details the concepts introduced and the differences among the various definitions.

Some subtleties relating to the basic GSPN behaviour are finally addressed in the last part of this chapter.

5.1   Exponential Distributions for Transition Delays

In Chapter 3 we observed that a simple sufficient condition to guarantee that the qualitative behaviour of PN models with timed transitions is identical to that of the underlying untimed PN model, that is, to guarantee that the possible transition sequences are the same in the two models, is that the delays associated with transitions be random variables whose distributions have infinite support.

If this is the case, a probabilistic metrics transforms the nondeterminism of the untimed PN model into the probabilism of the timed PN model, so that the theory of discrete-state stochastic processes in continuous time can be applied for the evaluation of the performance of the real system described with the timed PN model.

As we note in the appendix on stochastic processes, discrete-state stochastic processes in continuous time may be very difficult to characterize from a probabilistic viewpoint and virtually impossible to analyse. Their characterization and analysis become instead reasonably simple in some special cases that are often used just because of their mathematical tractability.

The simplicity in the characterization and analysis of discrete-state stochastic processes in continuous time can be obtained by eliminating (or at least drastically reducing) the amount of *memory* in the dynamics of the process. This is the reason for the frequent adoption of the negative exponential probability density function (pdf) for the specification of random delays. Indeed, the negative exponential is the only continuous pdf that enjoys the memoryless property, i.e., the only continuous pdf for which the residual delay after an arbitary interval has the same pdf as the original delay (for more details see Appendix A).

In the case of PN models with timed transitions adopting the race policy, a random delay with negative exponential pdf can be associated with each transition. This guarantees that the qualitative behaviour of the resulting timed PN model is the same as the qualitative behaviour of the PN model with no temporal specification. The timed PN models that are obtained with such an approach are known by the name Stochastic PNs (SPNs). This modelling paradigm was independently proposed by G.Florin and S.Natkin [FN85] and by M.Molloy [Mol81]. Similar ideas appeared also in the works of F.Symons [Sym78].

An SPN model is thus a PN model augmented with a set of rates (one for each transition in the model). The rates are sufficient for the characterization of the pdf of the transition delays (remember that the only parameter of the negative exponential pdf is its rate, obtained as the inverse of the mean).

The use of negative exponential pdfs for the specification of the temporal characteristics in a PN model has some interesting effects that deserve comment. Let us consider the dynamic evolution of an SPN model. As in Chapter 3, for the description we can assume that each timed transition possesses a timer. The timer is set to a value that is sampled from the negative exponential pdf associated with the transition, when the transition becomes enabled for the first time after firing (thus we are assuming an *age memory* policy). During all time intervals in which the transition is enabled, the timer is decremented. For the time being, let us assume that the speed at which the timer is decremented is constant in all markings. Transitions fire when their timer reading goes down to zero.

With this interpretation, each timed transition can be used to model the execution of an activity in a distributed environment; all activities execute in parallel (unless otherwise specified by the PN structure) until they complete. At completion, activities induce a local change of the system state that is specified with the interconnection of the transition to input and output places. Note that no special mechanism is necessary

for the resolution of timed conflicts: the temporal information provides a metric that
allows the conflict resolution (the probability that two timers expire at the same
instant is zero — a fine point on which we shall return).

It must be observed that the memoryless characteristics of the negative exponential
pdf render immaterial the distinction among the three policies [AMBB$^+$89] described
in Chapter 3, i.e.:

- race policy with resampling
- race policy with enabling memory
- race policy with age memory

Indeed, whether the timer is reset or not, the pdf of the remaining time to fire is
always distributed according to a negative exponential pdf, with the same mean, due
to the memoryless property of such a pdf. Going back to the example of a timed PN
system with age memory policy presented in Fig. 38, consider the timed transition
T_{end}, whose timing describes the duration of the execution of a local process that
may be interrupted by external requests. The exponential assumption implies that
the whole duration of the execution of a local process is a random variable with
negative exponential pdf with a given mean, and that also the remaining execution
time after an interruption is a random variable with negative exponential pdf with the
same mean (again, for more details see Appendix A). This aspect is quite relevant for
the transformation of an SPN model into its underlying stochastic process, and for its
analysis.

As an example of an SPN model, consider the timed version of the PN model in
Fig. 8, describing a simple parallel computation. For the readers' convenience, the
model, in its timed version, is repeated in Fig. 55. Observe that the only difference
between the model in Fig. 8 and that in Fig. 55 is in the graphical look of transitions,
that are depicted as bars in the former, and as boxes in the latter. This is due to the
formalism adopted for the representation of timed transitions throughout the book,
as we already mentioned in Chapter 3.

To associate a meaningful temporal specification with the model, transition
$T_{newdata}$, which describes the activity of reading new data, is associated with a random
delay, with a negative exponential pdf, whose mean matches the average time for the
new data read operation. If the observed average time for the new data read is 10
time units, the negative exponential pdf has rate 0.1. Note that the observation of
the real system might reveal that the data read activity is far from having a negative
exponentially distributed duration. However, with the SPN modelling paradigm we
have no flexibility on the type of pdf for the description of the activity duration, and
we can thus only match the average observed duration. The rate of a timed transition
is the only parameter necessary for the specification of the firing delay pdf.

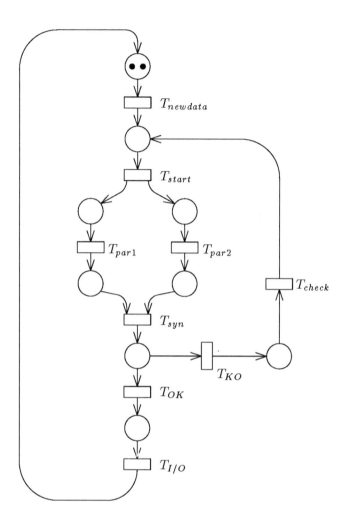

Figure 55 SPN description of a simple parallel system

In a similar way:

- transition T_{start}, which describes the activation of the two parallel processes, is associated with a random delay, with negative exponential pdf whose mean matches the average time for the activation operation,

- transition T_{par1}, which describes the first parallel process, is associated with a random delay, with negative exponential pdf whose mean matches the average time for the execution of the first process,

- transition T_{par2}, which describes the second parallel process, is associated with a random delay, with negative exponential pdf whose mean matches the average time for the process execution,

- transition T_{syn}, which describes the process synchronization, is associated with a random delay, with negative exponential pdf whose mean matches the average time for the synchronization to take place,

- transition T_{check}, which describes the control of the results, is associated with a random delay, with negative exponential pdf whose mean matches the average time for the control operation,

- transition $T_{I/O}$, which describes the output of the results, is associated with a random delay, with negative exponential pdf whose mean matches the average time for the output operation.

The situation is slightly different for the two transitions T_{OK}, and T_{KO}, that form a free-choice conflict set. Indeed, in this case the association of the rate of the negative exponential pdf to the two transitions must account for two aspects: the duration of the consistency check operation, and the probability of obtaining either a positive or a negative result. If the average duration of the consistency check is 2 time units, and the probability of a success is 0.9, then the resulting rate associated with T_{OK} is $0.9/2 = 0.45$, while the rate associated with T_{KO} is $0.1/2 = 0.05$. Note that the sum of the two rates equals the inverse of the average consistency check time.

SPN models have quite nice features: their qualitative behaviour is identical to that of their underlying PN model with no temporal specifications, so that the reachability and structural analysis results obtained from the PN model are valid also for the SPN model. Moreover, as we shall see in the next chapter, SPN models are isomorphic to continuous-time Markov chains: a class of stochastic processes for which a well-developed theory exists.

5.2 Mixing Exponentially Distributed and Null Delays

Several reasons suggest the introduction of the possibility of using immediate transitions into PN models together with timed transitions. As we observed in Chapter 3, the firing of a transition may describe either the completion of a time-consuming activity, or the verification of a logical condition. It is thus natural to use timed transitions in the former case, and immediate transitions in the latter. Moreover, as we noted in the previous example, when all transitions are timed the temporal specification of the model must in some cases consider at one time both the timing and the probability inherent in a choice. It seems natural to separate the two aspects in the modelling paradigm, to simplify the model specification. Furthermore, by allowing the use of immediate transitions, some important benefits can be obtained in the model solution. They will be described in detail in the next chapter; we only mention here the fact that the use of immediate transitions may significantly reduce the cardinality of the reachability set, and may eliminate the problems due to the presence in the model of timed transitions with rates that differ by orders of magnitude. The latter situation results in so-called "stiff" stochastic processes, that are quite difficult to handle from a numerical viewpoint. On the other hand, the introduction of immediate transitions in an SPN does not raise any significant complexity in the analysis, as we shall see in the next chapter.

SPN models in which immediate transitions coexist with timed transitions with race policy and random firing delays with negative exponential pdf are known by the name *generalized SPNs* (GSPNs).

In the graphical representation of GSPNs, immediate transitions are drawn as bars or segments and are denoted by a name that is normally of the form t_x, where x is either a number or a mnemonic string; timed transitions are drawn as (white or black) rectangular boxes, and are denoted by a name that is normally of the form T_x.

Immediate transitions are fired with priority over timed transitions. Thus, if timing is disregarded, the resulting PN model comprises transitions at different priority levels. The adoption of the race policy may seem to implicitly provide the priority of immediate over timed transitions; this is indeed the case in most situations, but the explicit use of priority simplifies the development of the theory. We shall return to this subtle point later in this chapter.

Recall that markings in the reachability set can be classified as *tangible* or *vanishing*. A tangible marking is a marking in which (only) timed transitions are enabled. A vanishing marking is a marking in which (only) immediate transitions are enabled (the "only" is in parentheses since the different priority levels make it impossible for timed and immediate transitions to be enabled in the same marking, according to the definition of the enabling condition for PN models with priority given in Chapter 4). A marking in which no transition is enabled is tangible. The time spent in any vanishing marking is deterministically equal to zero, while the time spent in tangible markings is positive with probability one. Similarly, a place is said to be vanishing if it can contain tokens only in vanishing markings.

To describe the GSPN dynamics, we separately observe the timed and the immediate behaviour, hence referring to tangible and vanishing markings, respectively. Let us start with the timed dynamics (hence with tangible markings); this is identical to the dynamics in SPNs, that was described before. We can assume that each timed transition possesses a timer. The timer is set to a value that is sampled from the negative exponential pdf associated with the transition, when the transition becomes enabled for the first time after firing. During all time intervals in which the transition is enabled, the timer is decremented. Transitions fire when their timer reading goes down to zero.

With this interpretation, each timed transition can be used to model the execution of some activity in a distributed environment; all enabled activities execute in parallel (unless otherwise specified by the PN structure) until they complete. At completion, activities induce a change of the system state, only as regards their local environment. No special mechanism is necessary for the resolution of timed conflicts: the temporal information provides a metric that allows the conflict resolution.

In the case of vanishing markings, the GSPN dynamics consumes no time: everything takes place instantaneously. This means that if only one immediate transition is enabled, it fires, and the following marking is produced. If several immediate transitions are enabled, a metric is necessary to identify which transition will produce the marking modification. Actually, the selection of the transition to be fired is relevant only in those cases in which a conflict must be resolved: if the enabled transitions are concurrent, they can be fired in any order. For this reason, GSPNs associate *weights* with immediate transitions belonging to the same conflict set.

For the time being, let us consider only free-choice conflict sets; the case of non-free-choice conflict sets will be considered later on, but we can anticipate at this point that it can be tackled in a similar manner by exploiting the definition of ECS introduced in Chapter 4. The transition weights are used to compute the firing probabilities of the simultaneously enabled transitions comprised within the conflict set. The restriction to free-choice conflict sets guarantees that transitions belonging to different conflict sets cannot disable each other, so that the selection among transitions belonging to different conflict sets is not necessary.

We can thus observe a difference between the specification of the temporal information for timed transitions and the specification of weights for immediate transitions. The temporal information associated with a timed transition depends only on the characteristics of the activity modelled by the transition. Thus, the temporal specification of a timed transition requires no information on the other (possibly conflicting) timed transitions, or on their temporal characteristics. On the contrary, for immediate transitions, the specification of weights must be performed considering at one time all transitions belonging to the same conflict set. Indeed, weights are normalized to produce probabilities by considering all enabled transitions within a conflict set, so that the specification of a weight, independent of those of the other transitions in the same conflict set, is not possible.

As a first simple example of a GSPN model, we use again the parallel system model that was described in the Introduction in its untimed version (see Fig. 8), and earlier in this chapter in its SPN version (see Fig. 55). Now we describe the GSPN version of the model, illustrated in Fig. 56.

Transitions $T_{newdata}$, T_{par1}, T_{par2}, $T_{I/O}$, and T_{check} are timed also in this version of the model, and are associated with the same rates as in the SPN model of Fig. 55.

Instead, transitions t_{start}, t_{syn}, t_{OK}, and t_{KO} are immediate in the GSPN model.

The timed transition $T_{newdata}$ describes the activity by which a set of new input data is read, and it is assumed to be timed with rate $\lambda = 0.1$. As soon as the new data are available, two processes are started in parallel with the fork operation described by the immediate transition t_{start}, whose weight is set to 1. The execution of the two processes consumes exponentially distributed amounts of time with rates μ_1 and μ_2, so that the two timed transitions T_{par1} and T_{par2} are associated with rates μ_1 and μ_2, respectively. When both processes complete, a synchronization takes place through the join operation described by the immediate transition t_{syn}, whose weight is again equal to 1. The two immediate transitions t_{OK} and t_{KO} form a free-choice conflict set. If the probability of inconsistent results is 0.1, a weight 1 is assigned to transition t_{KO}, and a weight 9 is assigned to transition t_{OK}. If the results are not consistent (t_{KO} fires), the whole parallel execution is repeated, after a further control modelled by the timed transition T_{check}, with rate γ. Otherwise, the output of the results is modelled by transition $T_{I/O}$, which is timed with parameter δ.

It must be observed that the values of the weights associated with t_{start}, and t_{syn} are irrelevant, because these two transitions are never enabled in conflict with other immediate transitions. On the contrary, the choice of the weights associated with t_{OK} and t_{KO} is important for the model, since they define the probability of inconsistent results after the parallel execution.

In the next chapter, we shall observe the differences resulting from the analysis of SPN and GSPN models. We can anticipate here that the GSPN model produces a smaller reachability set, and is thus easier to analyse than the SPN model, while producing very similar results.

5.3   Some Extensions

Some additional features can be included in a GSPN model, with an advantage in the power of the modelling paradigm and little increase in the analysis complexity. These extensions are the possibility of using non-free-choice conflicts of immediate transitions, the availability of multiple priority levels for immediate transitions, and the marking-dependency of transition annotations (rates for timed transitions and weights for immediate transitions).

The availability of multiple priority levels for immediate transitions, and the marking-dependency of transition annotations has quite a beneficial impact on the modelling power, and hardly any impact on the complexity of the model specification and analysis. In particular, the availability of multiple priority levels for immediate

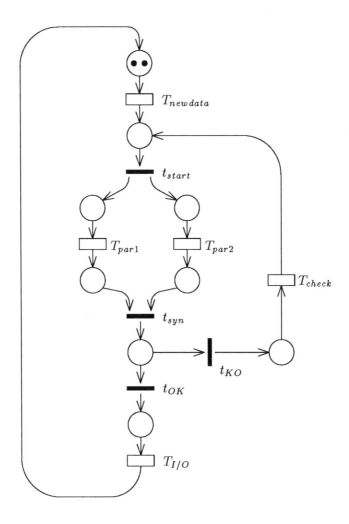

Figure 56   GSPN description of a simple parallel system

transitions permits the simple specification of complex sequential selection algorithms, while the marking-dependency of transition annotations allows the development of compact models in which the behaviours of a number of different entities are synthetically described.

Employing non-free-choice conflicts of immediate transitions, the user has the possibility of describing a much wider range of dynamic behaviours in vanishing markings, but he must be able to correctly associate the immediate transitions with the metrics that define the probabilistic conflict resolution. This requires the knowledge of the sets of simultaneously enabled non-concurrent immediate transitions in any

vanishing marking. This knowledge may not be easy to obtain without the generation
of the reachability set, which is however very costly in most cases. The definition of
extended conflict sets (*ECS*s) was introduced in Chapter 4 to provide the user with
the information on the sets of transitions that *may* be in effective conflict (either direct
or indirect) in a marking, thus helping in the definition of weights.

One extension that is not possible within the GSPN framework is the introduction of
more general forms of pdf for the firing delays associated with transitions. Nevertheless,
also in this respect, the availability of immediate and exponential transitions in one
modelling paradigm can be exploited for the construction of somewhat more general
pdfs in the description of the duration of the real system activities. How this can be
done will be shown in Chapter 7.

5.4   The Definition of a GSPN Model

GSPNs were originally defined in [AMBC84]. The definition was later improved to
better exploit the structural properties of the modelling paradigm [AMBCC87]. The
definition we present here is based on the version contained in this second proposal.

Formally, a GSPN model is an 8-tuple

$$\mathcal{M}_{\text{GSPN}} = (P, T, \Pi, I, O, H, W, PAR, PRED, MP) \tag{5.1}$$

where $\mathcal{M}_\pi = (P, T, \Pi, I, O, H, PAR, PRED, MP)$ is a PN model with
priorities and inhibitor arcs as defined in Chapter 4, that is called the *underlying PN
model*, and $W : T \to I\!R$ is a function defined on the set of transitions.

Timed transitions are associated with priority zero, whereas all other priority levels
are reserved for immediate transitions.

The underlying PN model constitutes the structural component of a GSPN model,
and it must be confusion-free at priority levels greater than zero (i.e., in subnets of
immediate transitions).

The function W allows the definition of the stochastic component of a GSPN model.
In particular, it maps transitions into real positive functions of the GSPN marking.
Thus, for any transition t it is necessary to specify a function $W(t, M)$. In the case of
marking independency, the simpler notation w_k is normally used to indicate $W(t_k)$, for
any transition $t_k \in T$. The quantity $W(t_k, M)$ (or w_k) is called the "rate" of transition
t_k in marking M if t_k is timed, and the "weight" of transition t_k in marking M if t_k
is immediate.

Since in any marking all firing delays of timed transitions have a negative exponential
pdf, and all the delays are independent random variables, the sojourn time in a tangible
marking is a random variable with a negative exponential pdf whose rate is the sum
of the rates of all enabled timed transitions in that marking. This result stems from

the fact that the minimum of a set of independent random variables with negative exponential pdf also has a negative exponential pdf whose rate is the sum of the rates of the individual pdfs.

In the case of vanishing markings, the weights of the immediate transitions enabled in an *ECS* can be used to determine which immediate transition will actually fire, if the vanishing marking enables more than one conflicting immediate transition.

When transitions belonging to several different *ECS*s are simultaneously enabled in a vanishing marking, as we already explained, the choice among these transitions is irrelevant. The irrelevance implies that no choice is needed among the different *ECS*s, and that the transitions can fire concurrently. It is thus possible to say that either transitions fire simultaneously, or a fixed ordering among *ECS*s exists, or the *ECS*s comprising enabled transitions are selected with equal probability, or an *ECS* is chosen with a probability proportional to the sum of the weights of the enabled immediate transitions it contains.

It must be emphasized that the irrelevance in the order of transition firings is an important consequence of the restriction that subnets of immediate transitions must be confusion-free. The restriction to confusion-free immediate subnets also has a beneficial impact on the model definition, since the association of weights with immediate transitions requires only the information about *ECS*s, not about reachable markings. For each *ECS* the analyst thus defines a *local* association of weights from which probabilities are then derived.

5.5 An Example of a GSPN Model

In this section we illustrate an example of the application of the GSPN methodology to the modelling of systems.

Several steps must be followed in the study of a system with the GSPN approach:

1. the model must be constructed, possibly using a structured technique, either top-down or bottom-up, depending on the system to be modelled;
2. the model must then be validated using the results of the structural analysis, possibly formally proving some behavioural properties of the model;
3. the performance indices of interest must be defined in terms of GSPN markings and of transition firings;
4. the reachability set and the reachability graph must then be generated, to obtain the continuous-time Markov chain associated with the GSPN system (see the next chapter);
5. the Markov chain must be solved;
6. the performance indices must be computed from the Markov chain solution.

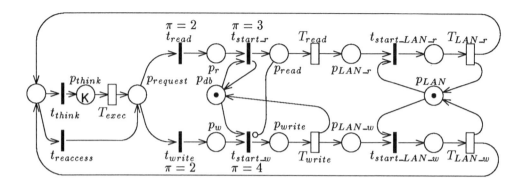

Figure 57   The example GSPN model: a modification of the readers & writers model

All steps must be performed with a suitable software tool that provides the GSPN modelling environment, allowing the graphical creation and modification of a model, the definition of performance indices, the structural analysis, and the stochastic analysis of the model.

In this chapter we only provide an example of a GSPN model, but in the second part of the book, after the analysis of GSPN models will be discussed (this is the topic of the next chapter), the various steps of the modelling process are illustrated.

The example that we illustrate next is obtained with a modification of the standard readers & writers model. Actually, the GSPN model that we use, which is depicted in Fig. 57, results from a further complication of the model presented in Fig. 44 as an example of a PN model with priority. The new feature introduced in the model is a local area network (LAN) transfer phase that follows each read or write access to the shared memory.

The GSPN model comprises 13 places and 13 transitions, five timed and eight immediate. To simplify the model description, we use mnemonic names for all transitions and places. The initial parametric marking assigns K tokens to place p_{think} to model the fact that K processes are initially assumed to be executing in their private memories; one token to place p_{db} to indicate that the database is initially idle; and one token to place p_{LAN} to indicate that the LAN is initially idle as well. All other places contain no tokens in the initial parametric marking.

Transition T_{exec} models the execution phase of processes in their private memories; it is timed with parameter λ, and has infinite-server semantics. The average execution time in private memory is assumed to be $1/\lambda$, and since all executions proceed in parallel the infinite-server semantics is used.

The firing of T_{exec} models the end of the execution phase and the generation of a database access request that is modelled by a token in place $p_{request}$.

The free-choice conflict set comprising the two immediate transitions t_{read} and t_{write} at priority level 2 models the fact that the request for the database access can be either a read or a write request, so that a token is generated in either place p_r, or p_w, respectively. Assuming that 80% of the requests are read requests, and only 20% are write requests, the weights of t_{read} and t_{write} are set to 8 and 2, respectively.

The priorities of t_{start_r} and t_{start_w} are set to 3 and 4, respectively, so that the write requests have priority over the read requests, and the two transitions are in different conflict sets. The weights associated with the two transitions are thus irrelevant (they are set to 1 by default).

Place p_{write} can contain at most one token, and transition T_{write} is timed with a rate μ_w which is the inverse of the average write time; the transition semantics is single-server. The firing of T_{write} models the end of a database access for a write and generates a token in place p_{LAN_w}.

Place p_{read} can contain several tokens, and transition T_{read} is timed with a rate μ_r which is the inverse of the average read time; the transition semantics is infinite-server since all read accesses proceed in parallel. The firing of T_{read} models the end of a database access for a read and generates a token in place p_{LAN_r}.

Transitions $t_{start\_LAN\_r}$ and $t_{start\_LAN\_w}$ have equal priority set to 1, and thus form a non-free-choice conflict set of immediate transitions. Their weights are both set to 1, to indicate that the allocation of the LAN to processes that have just completed a read or write database access is equally likely. [1]

Transitions T_{LAN_r} and T_{LAN_w} model the data transfer activities on the LAN after the two types of database access. They are timed with rates ρ_r and ρ_w, respectively, and their semantics is single-server, since no more than one LAN transfer activity can be in progress at a time.

Transitions t_{think} and $t_{reaccess}$ have equal priority set to 1, and form a free-choice conflict set of immediate transitions. Their weights are set to 9 and 1, respectively, to indicate that 10% of the time processes immediately reissue a database access request after completing the previous access, while 90% of the time processes go back to execute in their private memory.

The characteristics of the five timed transitions are summarized in Table 15, and those of the eight immediate transitions in Table 16.

Note that in the GSPN model we have four different priority levels of immediate

---

[1] With this choice, when processes that have just completed a read and write database access are waiting, the LAN is allocated with probability 0.5 to one of the processes that have just completed a read database access, and with probability 0.5 to one of the processes that have just completed a write database access. If, instead the weights of transitions $t_{start\_LAN\_r}$ and $t_{start\_LAN\_w}$ are made equal to the numbers of tokens in places p_{LAN_r} and p_{LAN_w}, respectively, the LAN is allocated to any waiting process with equal probability.

Table 1   Characteristics of the timed transitions in the example GSPN model

transition	rate	semantics
T_{exec}	λ	infinite-server
T_{write}	μ_w	single-server
T_{read}	μ_r	infinite-server
T_{LAN_r}	ρ_r	single-server
T_{LAN_w}	ρ_w	single-server

Table 2   Characteristics of the immediate transitions in the example GSPN model

transition	weight	priority	ECS
t_{read}	8	2	1
t_{write}	2	2	1
t_{start_r}	1	3	2
t_{start_w}	1	4	3
$t_{start\_LAN\_r}$	1	1	4
$t_{start\_LAN\_w}$	1	1	4
t_{think}	9	1	5
$t_{reaccess}$	1	1	5

transitions, which are necessary to guarantee that the underlying PN model with priority is not confused. Timed transitions have semantics both of single-server and of infinite-server type. Immediate transitions form conflict sets that are either free-choice or non-free-choice. Note also that only the relative values of weights associated with immediate transitions are important: if all weights are multiplied or divided by an arbitrary constant, the model behaviour does not change.

5.6   Some Fine Points

Let us return to the points we raised in the previous sections, but left unanswered. These are:

1. the need for an explicit priority of immediate over timed transitions;

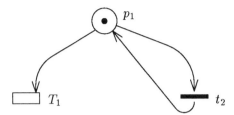

Figure 58   A conflict set comprising a timed and an immediate transition

2. the irrelevance of the distinction between resampling, enabling memory, and age
   memory;
3. the impossibility for two timers to expire at the same time.

   All three points relate to the properties of the negative exponential pdf. This
distribution characterizes a continuous random variable, hence it is a continuous
function defined in the interval $[0, \infty)$, that integrates to one. The lack of
discontinuities in the function makes the probability of any specific value x being
sampled equal to zero (however, obviously, the probability that a value is sampled
between two distinct values $x_1 \geq 0$ and $x_2 > x_1$ is positive). The particular shape of
the negative exponential pdf is such that the *memoryless property* [Kle75] holds, as
explained in Appendix A. This means that, if the exponentially distributed random
variable models a lifetime, at any time instant the residual life has the same negative
exponential pdf as the entire lifetime.

   Let us look now at the three previous points in order.

1. Consider a free-choice conflict set comprising an immediate and a timed transition,
   and assume for a moment that priority does not exist. The race policy makes
   the immediate transition always win, except for the case in which a zero delay is
   sampled from the negative exponential pdf. Although the probability of selecting
   the value zero is null, some problem may arise when the conflict set is enabled
   infinitely often in a finite time interval. For example, in the case of Fig. 58, the
   timed and the immediate transitions are always enabled, because the firing of the
   immediate transition t_2 does not alter the PN marking. The situation is changed
   only when the timed transition T_1 fires. This happens with probability one in
   time zero, possibly after an infinite number of firings of the immediate transition.
   To avoid these (sometimes strange) limiting behaviours, the priority of immediate
   over timed transitions was introduced in the GSPN definition. This makes the timed
   transition T_1 in Fig. 58 never enabled.

2. The mentioned *memoryless property* of the negative exponential pdf, at any time instant makes the residual time until a timer associated with a transition expires statistically equivalent to the originally sampled timer reading. Thus, whether a new timer value is set at every change of marking, or at every instant a transition becomes enabled after disabling, or after firing, makes no difference from the point of view of the probabilistic metrics of the GSPN.

3. Since the probability that a sample extracted from a negative exponential pdf takes a specific value x equals zero, the probability of two timers expiring at the same time is null. Indeed, given the value sampled by the first timer, the probability that the second one samples the same value is zero.

6

ANALYSIS OF GSPN MODELS

In this chapter we show how GSPN systems can be converted into Markov chains and how their analysis can be performed to compute interesting performance indices. The construction of the Markov chain associated with a Stochastic Petri Net (SPN) system is described first, to set the ground for the subsequent derivation of the probabilistic model associated with a GSPN. Only GSPNs with finite state space are considered in this chapter, as they yield Markov chains that are solvable with standard numerical techniques. In particular, we are not discussing more advanced solution methods based on matrix-geometric theory [FN89, Neu81] that allow the analysis of unbounded GSPNs when their reachability graphs are characterized by regular repetitive structures. Some more advanced material is discussed in the second part of the chapter where we illustrate reduction techniques that can be employed to obtain smaller reachability graphs. Finally, the chapter ends with a section devoted to GSPN simulation that can be used to estimate performance indices of models with very general structures and whose state space is either unbounded or simply too large to be treated with numerical methods.

6.1   The Stochastic Process Associated with a SPN

In Chapter 5 we discussed the motivations behind the work of several authors that led to the proposal of Stochastic Petri Nets (SPNs) [FN85, Mol81, Sym78]. Due to the memoryless property of the exponential distribution of firing delays, it is relatively easy to show [FN85, Mol81] that SPN systems are isomorphic to continuous time Markov chains (CTMCs). In particular, a k-bounded SPN system can be shown to be isomorphic to a finite CTMC. The CTMC associated with a given SPN system is obtained by applying the following simple rules:

1. The CTMC state space $S = \{s_i\}$ corresponds to the reachability set $RS(M_0)$ of the PN associated with the SPN ($M_i \leftrightarrow s_i$).
2. The transition rate from state s_i (corresponding to marking M_i) to state s_j (M_j) is obtained as the sum of the firing rates of the transitions that are enabled in M_i

and whose firings generate marking M_j.

To keep the discussion simple, transitions in SPNs are initially assumed to be associated with a single-server semantics and with a marking-independent speed. This restriction will be relaxed later on in this chapter, when the modelling implications of the general case will be discussed. The type of race policy that we assume for the model is irrelevant for the construction of the stochastic process associated with the SPN, as we observed at the end of Chapter 5. A race policy with resampling is thus used to simplify the explanation of the expressions derived in the rest of the chapter.

Based on the simple rules listed before, it is possible to devise algorithms for the automatic construction of the infinitesimal generator (also called the state transition rate matrix) of the isomorphic CTMC, starting from the SPN description. Denoting this matrix by $\mathbf{Q}$, with w_k the firing rate of T_k, and with $E_j(M_i) = \{T_h \in E(M_i) : M_i[T_h\rangle M_j\}$ the set of transitions whose firings bring the net from marking M_i to marking M_j, the components of the infinitesimal generator are:

$$
q_{ij} = \begin{cases} \sum_{k:T_k \in E_j(M_i)} w_k & i \neq j \\[2mm] -q_i & i = j \end{cases} \tag{6.1}
$$

where

$$
q_i = \sum_{k:T_k \in E(M_i)} w_k \tag{6.2}
$$

In this book we consider only SPNs originating ergodic CTMCs. A k-bounded SPN system is said to be ergodic if it generates an ergodic CTMC; it is possible to show that a SPN system is ergodic if M_0, the initial marking, is a home state (see Section 2.4). A presentation of the most important results of the theory of ergodic CTMCs is contained in Appendix A; this must be considered as a reference for all the discussion contained in this chapter.

Let the row vector $\boldsymbol{\eta}$ represent the steady-state probability distribution on markings of the SPN. If the SPN is ergodic, it is possible to compute the steady-state probability distribution vector solving the usual linear system expressed in matrix form as:

$$
\begin{cases} \boldsymbol{\eta}\, \mathbf{Q} = \mathbf{0} \\[2mm] \boldsymbol{\eta}\, \mathbf{1}^{\mathrm{T}} = 1 \end{cases} \tag{6.3}
$$

where $\mathbf{0}$ is a row vector of the same size as $\boldsymbol{\eta}$ and with all its components equal to zero and $\mathbf{1}^{\mathrm{T}}$ is a column vector (again of the same size as $\boldsymbol{\eta}$) with all its components equal to one, used to enforce the normalization condition typical of all probability distributions.

To keep the notation simple, in the rest of this chapter we will use η_i instead of $\eta(M_i)$ to denote the steady state probability of marking M_i. The *sojourn time* is the time spent by the PN system in a given marking M. As we already observed in Chapter 5, the fact that a CTMC can be associated with the SPN system ensures that the sojourn time in the ith marking is exponentially distributed with rate q_i. The pdf of the sojourn time in a marking corresponds to the pdf of the minimum among the firing times of the transitions enabled in the same marking; it thus follows that the probability that a given transition $T_k \in E(M_i)$ fires (first) in marking M_i has the expression:

$$P\{T_k|M_i\} = \frac{w_k}{q_i} \tag{6.4}$$

Using the same argument, we can observe that the average sojourn time in marking M_i is given by the following expression:

$$E[SJ_i] = \frac{1}{q_i} \tag{6.5}$$

6.1.1   SPN performance indices

The steady-state distribution η is the basis for a quantitative evaluation of the behaviour of the SPN that is expressed in terms of performance indices. These results can be computed using a unifying approach in which proper index functions (also called *reward functions*) are defined over the markings of the SPN and an average reward is derived using the steady-state probability distribution of the SPN. Assuming that $r(M)$ represents one of such reward functions, the average reward can be computed using the following weighted sum:

$$R = \sum_{i:M_i \in RS(M_0)} r(M_i)\, \eta_i \tag{6.6}$$

Different interpretations of the reward function can be used to compute different performance indices. In particular, the following quantities can be computed using this approach.

(1) The *probability of a particular condition* of the SPN. Assuming that *condition* $\Upsilon(M)$ is *true* only in certain markings of the PN, we can define the following reward function:

$$r(M) = \begin{cases} 1 & \Upsilon(M) = true \\ 0 & otherwise \end{cases} \tag{6.7}$$

The desired probability $P\{\Upsilon\}$ is then computed using (6.6). The same result can also be expressed as:

$$P\{\Upsilon\} = \sum_{i:M_i \in A} \eta_i \tag{6.8}$$

where $A = \{M_i \in RS(M_0) : \Upsilon(M_i) = true\}$.

(2) The *expected value of the number of tokens in a given place*. In this case the reward function $r(M)$ is simply the value of the marking of that place (say place j):

$$r(M) \; = \; n \;\; \text{iff} \;\; M(p_j) \; = \; n \tag{6.9}$$

Again this is equivalent to identifying the subset $A(j,n)$ of $RS(M_0)$ for which the number of tokens in place p_j is n $(A(j,n) \; = \; \{M_i \in RS(M_0) : M_i(p_j) \; = \; n\})$; the expected value of the number of tokens in p_j is given by:

$$E[M(p_j)] \; = \; \sum_{n>0} n \; P\{A(j,n)\} \tag{6.10}$$

where the sum is obviously limited to values of $n \leq k$, if the place is k-bounded.

(3) The *mean number of firings per unit of time of a given transition*. Assume that we want to compute the firing frequency of transition T_j (the *throughput* of T_j); observing that a transition may fire only when it is enabled, we have that the reward function assumes the value w_j in every marking that enables T_j:

$$r(M) \; = \; \begin{cases} w_j & T_j \in E(M) \\ \\ 0 & otherwise \end{cases} \tag{6.11}$$

The same quantity can also be computed using the more traditional approach of identifying the subset A_j of $RS(M_0)$ in which a given transition T_j is enabled $(A_j \; = \; \{M_i \in RS(M_0) : T_j \in E(M_i)\})$. The mean number of firings of T_j per unit of time is then given by:

$$f_j \; = \; \sum_{i:M_i \in A_j} w_j \, \eta_i \tag{6.12}$$

These results show that indeed, Petri nets can be used not only as a formalism for describing the behaviour of distributed/parallel systems and for assessing their qualitative properties, but also as a tool for computing performance indices that allow the efficiency of these systems to be evaluated.

To illustrate the details of this last analysis step, a simple example is presented in the following subsection, with the explicit derivation of the CTMC infinitesimal generator, of the steady-state probability distribution of the different markings, and of some performance indices.

6.1.2 An example SPN system

Consider the SPN version of the example of a shared memory system introduced in Chapter 1 (Fig. 5), representing two processors accessing a common shared memory. The net comprises seven places and six timed transitions with single-server semantics;

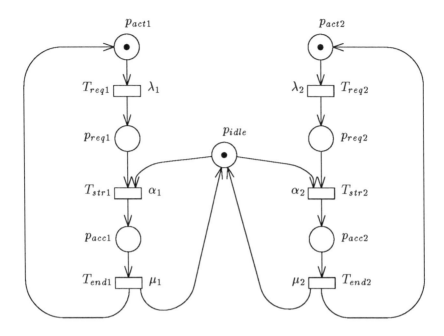

Figure 59   The SPN description of shared memory system

for convenience the SPN is depicted in Fig. 59 and the additional specifications are contained in Tables 3 and 4.

Starting from the initial marking shown in Fig. 59, in which the two processors are both in a locally active state $(p_{act1} + p_{act2} + p_{idle})$, a possible evolution of the SPN marking that focuses on the processing cycle of processor 1, may be the following. Processor 1 works locally for an exponentially distributed random amount of time with average $1/\lambda_1$, and then requests an access to the common memory. Transition T_{req1} fires, and the token contained in p_{act1} is removed while a token is added in p_{req1}. Since the common memory is available (place p_{idle} is marked), the acquisition of the memory starts immediately and takes an average of $1/\alpha_1$ units of time to complete; this is represented by the firing of transition T_{str1} whose associated delay has a negative-exponential distribution with rate α_1; when transition T_{str1} fires, one token is removed from places p_{req1} and p_{idle}, and another token is deposited into place p_{acc1}, where it stays for the entire time required by the first processor to access the common memory. Such a time lasts on the average $1/\mu_1$ units of time, and ends when transition T_{end1} fires returning the net to its initial state. Obviously, a similar processing cycle is possible for processor 2 and many interleavings between the activities of the two processors may be described by the evolution of the net.

Table 3   Specification of the transitions of the SPN of Fig. 59

transition	rate	semantics
T_{req1}	λ_1	single-server
T_{req2}	λ_2	single-server
T_{str1}	α_1	single-server
T_{str2}	α_2	single-server
T_{end1}	μ_1	single-server
T_{end2}	μ_2	single-server

Table 4   Initial marking of the SPN of Fig. 59

place	initial marking
p_{act1}	1
p_{act2}	1
p_{idle}	1

A conflict exists in the behaviour of this system when both processors want to simultaneously access the common memory, i.e., when transitions T_{str1} and T_{str2} are both enabled. According to equation (6.1), in this situation, transition T_{str1} fires with probability:

$$P\{T_{str1}\} \;=\; \frac{\alpha_1}{\alpha_1 + \alpha_2} \qquad\qquad (6.13)$$

whereas transition T_{str2} fires with probability:

$$P\{T_{str2}\} \;=\; \frac{\alpha_2}{\alpha_1 + \alpha_2} \qquad\qquad (6.14)$$

Notice that when the two transitions T_{str1} and T_{str2} are both enabled in a given marking M, the speed at which the PN model exits from that marking is the sum of the individual speeds of the two transitions and the conflict is actually resolved only when the first transition fires.

The reachability set of the SPN system of Fig. 59 is depicted in Table 5. The reachability graph is shown in Fig. 60, while the corresponding CTMC state transition rate diagram is presented in Fig. 61. Finally, the infinitesimal generator is reported in Fig. 62.

Assuming $\lambda_1 = 1$, $\lambda_2 = 2$, $\alpha_1 = \alpha_2 = 100$, $\mu_1 = 10$, and $\mu_2 = 5$, we can write the

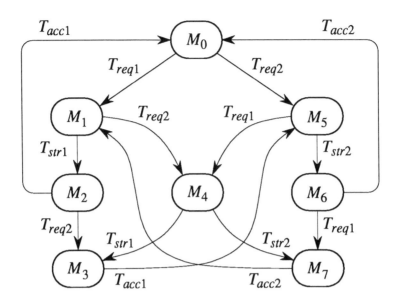

Figure 60   The reachability graph of the SPN system in Fig. 59

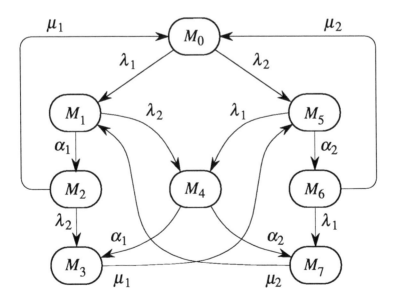

Figure 61   The state transition rate diagram of the Markov chain associated with the
SPN in Fig. 59

Table 5   Reachability set of the SPN in Fig. 59

$M_0 = p_{act1} +$			$p_{idle} +$	p_{act2}	
$M_1 =$	$p_{req1} +$		$p_{idle} +$	p_{act2}	
$M_2 =$		$p_{acc1} +$		p_{act2}	
$M_3 =$		$p_{acc1} +$			p_{req2}
$M_4 =$	$p_{req1} +$		$p_{idle} +$		p_{req2}
$M_5 = p_{act1} +$			$p_{idle} +$		p_{req2}
$M_6 = p_{act1} +$					p_{acc2}
$M_7 =$	$p_{req1} +$				p_{acc2}

$$
Q \; = \;
\begin{bmatrix}
-\lambda_1 - \lambda_2 & \lambda_1 & 0 & 0 & 0 & \lambda_2 & 0 & 0 \\
0 & -\alpha_1 - \lambda_2 & \alpha_1 & 0 & \lambda_2 & 0 & 0 & 0 \\
\mu_1 & 0 & -\lambda_2 - \mu_1 & \lambda_2 & 0 & 0 & 0 & 0 \\
0 & 0 & 0 & -\mu_1 & 0 & \mu_1 & 0 & 0 \\
0 & 0 & 0 & \alpha_1 & -\alpha_1 - \alpha_2 & 0 & 0 & \alpha_2 \\
0 & 0 & 0 & 0 & \lambda_1 & -\alpha_2 - \lambda_1 & \alpha_2 & 0 \\
\mu_2 & 0 & 0 & 0 & 0 & 0 & -\lambda_1 - \mu_2 & \lambda_1 \\
0 & \mu_2 & 0 & 0 & 0 & 0 & 0 & -\mu_2
\end{bmatrix}
$$

Figure 62   The Infinitesimal Generator of the Markov Chain in Fig. 61

system of linear equations whose solution yields the steady-state distribution over the CTMC states:

$$
(\eta_0,\ \eta_1,\ \eta_2,\ \eta_3,\ \eta_4,\ \eta_5,\ \eta_6,\ \eta_7)
\begin{bmatrix}
-3 & 1 & 0 & 0 & 0 & 2 & 0 & 0 \\
0 & -102 & 100 & 0 & 2 & 0 & 0 & 0 \\
10 & 0 & -12 & 2 & 0 & 0 & 0 & 0 \\
0 & 0 & 0 & -10 & 0 & 10 & 0 & 0 \\
0 & 0 & 0 & 100 & -200 & 0 & 0 & 100 \\
0 & 0 & 0 & 0 & 1 & -101 & 100 & 0 \\
5 & 0 & 0 & 0 & 0 & 0 & -6 & 1 \\
0 & 5 & 0 & 0 & 0 & 0 & 0 & -5
\end{bmatrix}
= 0
$$

and

$$
\sum_{i=0}^{7} \eta_i \; = \; 1
$$

By solving this linear system we obtain:

$$\eta_0 = 0.61471, \quad \eta_1 = 0.00842, \quad \eta_2 = 0.07014, \quad \eta_3 = 0.01556$$

$$\eta_4 = 0.00015, \quad \eta_5 = 0.01371, \quad \eta_6 = 0.22854, \quad \eta_7 = 0.04876$$

As an example, we can now compute the average number of tokens in place p_{idle} from which we can easily compute the utilization of the shared memory. Since one token is present in place p_{idle} in markings M_0, M_1, M_4, and M_5, we have:

$$E[M(p_{idle})] = \eta_0 + \eta_1 + \eta_4 + \eta_5 = 0.6370$$

and the utilization of the shared memory is:

$$U[shared\_memory] = 1.0 - E[M(p_{idle})] = 0.3630$$

The throughput of transition T_{req1}, that represents the actual rate of access to the shared memory from the first processor, can be obtained using equation (6.12) and observing that T_{req1} is enabled only in M_0, M_5, and M_6. The following expression allows the desired quantity to be obtained:

$$f_{req1} = (\eta_0 + \eta_5 + \eta_6) \lambda_1 = 0.8570$$

6.2 The Stochastic Process Associated with a GSPN

In Chapter 5 we described the qualitative effect that immediate transitions have on the behaviour of a GSPN system. GSPNs adopt the same firing policy of SPNs; when several transitions are enabled in the same marking, the probabilistic choice of the transition to fire next depends on parameters that are associated with these same transitions and that are not functions of time. The general expression for the probability that a given (timed or immediate) transition t_k, enabled in marking M_i, fires is:

$$P\{t_k|M_i\} = \frac{w_k}{q_i} \tag{6.15}$$

where q_i is the quantity defined by equation (6.2). Equation (6.15) represents the probability that transition t_k fires first, and is identical to equation (6.4) for SPNs, with a difference in the meaning of the parameters w_k. When the marking is vanishing, the parameters w_k are the weights of the immediate transitions enabled in that marking and define the selection policy used to make the choice. When the marking is tangible, the parameters w_k of the timed transitions enabled in that marking are the rates of their associated negative exponential distributions. The average sojourn time in vanishing markings is zero, while the average sojourn time in tangible markings is given by equation (6.5).

Observing the evolution of the GSPN system, we can notice that the distribution of the sojourn time in an arbitrary marking can be expressed as a composition of negative exponential and deterministically zero distributions: we can thus recognize that the marking process $\{M(t), t \geq 0\}$ is a semi-Markov stochastic process whose analysis is discussed in Appendix A.

When several immediate transitions are enabled in the same vanishing marking, deciding which transition to fire first makes sense only in the case of conflicts. If these immediate transitions do not "interfere", the choice of firing only one transition at a time becomes an operational rule of the model that hardly relates with the actual characteristics of the real system. In this case the selection is inessential from the point of view of the overall behaviour of the net. The concept of ECS introduced in Chapter 4 represents a basic element for identifying these situations and for making sure that both the specification of the model and its operational rules are consistent with the actual behaviour of the system we want to analyse.

Assuming, as we have already pointed out in the previous chapter, that the GSPN is not confused (see Section 2.3.4 for a definition), the computation of the ECSs of the net corresponds to partitioning the set of immediate transitions into equivalence classes such that transitions of the same partition may be in conflict among each other in possible markings of the net, while transitions of different ECSs behave in a truly concurrent manner.

When transitions belonging to the same ECS are the only ones enabled in a given marking, one of them (say transition t_k) is selected to fire with probability:

$$P\{t_k|M_i\} = \frac{w_k}{\omega_k(M_i)} \qquad (6.16)$$

where $\omega_k(M_i)$ is the weight of $ECS(t_k)$ in marking M_i and is defined as follows:

$$\omega_k(M_i) = \sum_{j : t_j \in [ECS(t_k) \wedge E(M_i)]} w_j \qquad (6.17)$$

Within the ECS we may have transitions that are in direct as well as in indirect conflict. This means that the distributions of the firing selection probabilities computed for different markings may assign different probabilities of firing to the same transition in different markings. Equation (6.16) however ensures that if we have two transitions (say transitions t_i and t_j), both enabled in two different markings (say markings M_r and M_s), the ratios between the firing probabilities of these two transitions in these two markings remain constant and in particular equal to the ratio between the corresponding weights assigned at the moment of the specification of the model.

In particular, referring to the example of Fig. 63 and of Table 6, we can observe that in marking $M_r = (p_1 + p_2 + p_3)$ these probabilities are:

$$P\{t_a|M_r\} = \frac{w_a}{(w_a + w_b + w_d)}$$

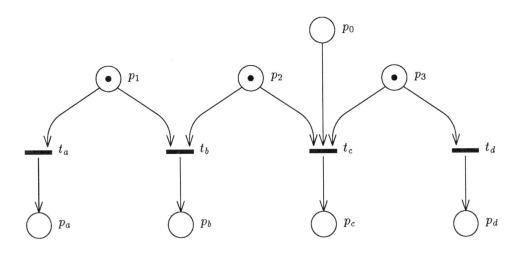

Figure 63   An example of ECS

Table 6   Specification of the transitions of the SPN of Fig. 63

transition	weight	priority	ECS
t_a	w_a	1	1
t_b	w_b	1	1
t_c	w_c	1	1
t_d	w_d	1	1

$$P\{t_b|M_r\} = \frac{w_b}{(w_a + w_b + w_d)}$$

$$P\{t_c|M_r\} = 0$$

and

$$P\{t_d|M_r\} = \frac{w_d}{(w_a + w_b + w_d)}$$

while in marking $M_s = (p_0 + p_1 + p_2 + p_3)$ we have:

$$P\{t_a|M_s\} = \frac{w_a}{(w_a + w_b + w_c + w_d)}$$

$$P\{t_b|M_s\} = \frac{w_b}{(w_a + w_b + w_c + w_d)}$$

$$P\{t_c|M_r\} = \frac{w_c}{(w_a + w_b + w_c + w_d)}$$

and

$$P\{t_d|M_s\} = \frac{w_d}{(w_a + w_b + w_c + w_d)}$$

The corresponding probabilities within the two markings are different, but their relative values, when the transitions are enabled, remain constant and completely characterized by the initial specification of the model. For instance,

$$\frac{P\{t_a|M_r\}}{P\{t_d|M_r\}} = \frac{P\{t_a|M_s\}}{P\{t_d|M_s\}} = \frac{w_a}{w_d}$$

During the evolution of a GSPN, it may happen that several ECSs are simultaneously enabled in a vanishing marking. According to the usual firing mechanism of Petri nets, we should select the transition to fire by first non-deterministically choosing one of the ECSs and then a transition within such ECS. The assumption that the GSPN is not confused guarantees that the way in which the choice of the ECS is performed is irrelevant with respect to the associated stochastic process. One possibility is that of computing the weight of the ECS by adding the parameters of all the enabled transitions that belong to that ECS and of using this weight to select the ECS with a method suggested by (6.15). A simple derivation shows that the use of this method implies that the selection of the immediate transition to be fired in a vanishing marking can be performed with the general formula (6.15) that was originally derived for timed transitions (and thus for tangible markings) only [AMBCC87, CAMBC93]. Moreover, it is possible to show that if we consider the probabilities associated with the many different sequences of immediate transitions whose firings lead from a given vanishing marking to a target tangible one, they turn out to be all equal [AMBCC87].

This last property strongly depends on the absence of confusion in the GSPN; the fact that the presence of confused subnets of immediate transitions within a GSPN is an undesirable feature of the model can also be explained considering the following example.

Suppose that a subnet is identified as confused using the structural confusion condition of Section 2.3.4. Suppose also that the subnet has the structure depicted in Fig. 21 of Chapter 2 and repeated here in Fig. 64(a) for convenience. Given the initial marking $M_0 = (p_0 + p_2)$ and the parameters listed in Table 7, markings $M_1 = p_3$ and $M_2 = (p_1 + p_4)$ are reached with total probabilities

$$P\{M_0, M_1\} = \frac{w_0}{(w_0 + \alpha)} \frac{\beta}{(\alpha + \beta)}$$

$$P\{M_0, M_2\} = \frac{\alpha}{(w_0 + \alpha)} + \frac{w_0}{(w_0 + \alpha)} \frac{\alpha}{(\alpha + \beta)}$$

From these expressions we can see that, although the picture suggests transitions t_0 and t_2 as concurrent, and transitions t_1 and t_2 as members of a conflict set, the

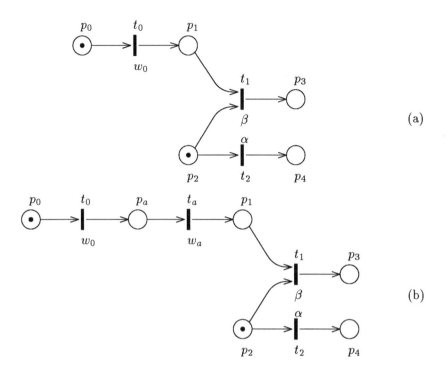

Figure 64 Comparison of two simple confused GSPN systems

Table 7 Specification of the transitions of the SPN of Fig. 64

transition	weight	priority	ECS
t_0	w_0	1	-
t_1	β	1	-
t_2	α	1	-
t_a	w_a	1	-

first choice of firing either t_0 or t_2 is actually crucial for the possibility of reaching the desired markings. In this case the value assigned by the analyst to w_0 becomes fundamental for the quantitative evaluation of the model.

Much more intriguing however is the behaviour of the subnet in Fig. 64(b) that differs from that of Fig. 64(a) for the simple addition of place p_a and transition t_a between transition t_0 and place p_1. Given the initial marking $M_0 = (p_0 + p_2)$ and the parameters listed in Table 7, markings $M_1 = p_3$ and $M_2 = (p_1 + p_4)$ are reached in the case of the subnet of Fig. 64(b) with total probabilities

$$P\{M_0, M_1\} = \frac{w_0}{(w_0 + \alpha)} \frac{w_a}{(w_a + \alpha)} \frac{\beta}{(\alpha + \beta)}$$

and

$$P\{M_0, M_2\} = \frac{\alpha}{(w_0 + \alpha)} + \frac{w_0}{(w_0 + \alpha)} \frac{\alpha}{(w_a + \alpha)} + \frac{w_0}{(w_0 + \alpha)} \frac{w_a}{(w_a + \alpha)} \frac{\alpha}{(\alpha + \beta)}$$

From a modelling point of view, there are good reasons to consider the two subnets of Figs. 64(a) and 64(b) equivalent since the sequence of immediate actions represented by t_0 and t_a of Fig. 64(b) should be reducible to transition t_0 of Fig. 64(a) without affecting the behaviour of the model. Instead, the difference among the total probabilities that we have just computed shows that, in the case of confused models, the trivial action of splitting an atomic (and instantaneous) action in two has drastic effects not only on the graphical description of the model, but also (and more important) on the values of the results obtained from its quantitative evaluation.

6.2.1 Marking dependency

The firing times and the weights that we considered so far were assumed to be independent of the marking of the GSPN system. In principle, however, it is possible to work with transition parameters that are marking-dependent. When one or more timed transitions are enabled in a given marking, we can compute the distribution of the sojourn time in that marking, as well as the probability of the transition that fires first, using negative exponential distributions whose firing rates may depend on that specific marking. Similarly, the selection of the immediate transition that fires in a vanishing marking enabling several immediate transitions can be computed using weighting factors that may be marking-dependent. In all these cases, equations (6.5), (6.15), (6.16), and (6.17) can be generalized assuming that all the parameters are functions of the marking for which they are computed.

In practice, the generality allowed by this extension (which was indeed assumed by the original GSPN proposal [AMBC84]) is in contrast with the claim of GSPNs as a high-level language for the description of complex systems. In fact, while the construction of a GSPN model requires a local view of the behaviour of the real system, the specification of (general) marking-dependent parameters requires the analyst to be aware of the possible (global) states of the system. Moreover, a dependency of the weights of conflicting immediate transitions on the marking of places that are not part of the input set of any of the transitions comprised in their ECS could lead to a new form of "confusion" that is not captured by the definitions contained in Chapter 2 and discussed in the previous section.

For this reason, a restriction of the type of marking-dependency allowed in GSPN models was informally proposed in [CAMBC93]. A definition of marking dependency that satisfies these restrictions can be obtained by allowing the specification of marking dependent parameters as the product of a nominal rate (or weight in the case of immediate transitions) and of a dependency function defined in terms of the marking of the places that are connected to a transition through its input and inhibition functions.

Denote with $M_{/t}$ the restriction of a generic marking M to the input and inhibition sets of transition t:

$$M_{/t} = \bigcup_{p \in (\bullet t \cup \circ t)} M(p) \qquad (6.18)$$

Let $f(M_{/t})$ be the marking dependency function that assumes positive values every time transition t is enabled in M; using this notation, the marking dependent parameters may be defined in the following manner:

$$\begin{cases} \mu_i(M) = f(M_{/T_i})\, w_i & \text{in the case of marking dependent firing rates} \\ \\ \omega_j(M) = f(M_{/t_j})\, w_j & \text{in the case of marking dependent weights} \end{cases} \qquad (6.19)$$

Multiple-servers and infinite-servers can be represented as special cases of timed transitions with marking dependent firing rates that are consistent with this restriction. In particular, a timed transition T_i with a negative-exponential delay distribution with parameter w_i and with an infinite-server policy, has a marking dependency function of the following form:

$$f(M_{/T_i}) = ED(T_i, M) \qquad (6.20)$$

where $ED(T_i, M)$ is the enabling degree of transition T_i in marking M (see Section 2.3.4). Similarly, a timed transition T_i with multiple-server policy of degree K has a marking dependency function defined in the following way:

$$f(M_{/T_i}) = min\,(ED(T_i, M),\, K) \qquad (6.21)$$

Other interesting situations can be represented using the same technique, Fig. 65 depicts two such cases. In Fig. 65(a), we have a situation of two competing infinite servers: transition T_1 fires with rate $w_1 M(p_1)$ if place p_0 is marked; similarly for transition T_2. Obviously both transitions are interrupted when the first of the two fires removing the token from place p_0.

Using $\delta(x)$ to represent the following step function:

$$\delta(x) = \begin{cases} 0 & x = 0 \\ \\ 1 & x > 0 \end{cases} \qquad (6.22)$$

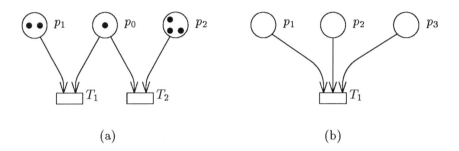

Figure 65   Examples of complex marking dependency situations

we can define the marking dependency function as follows:

$$
\begin{cases}
f(M_{/T_1}) = \delta(ED(T_1, M))M(p_1) \\
f(M_{/T_2}) = \delta(ED(T_2, M))M(p_2)
\end{cases}
\tag{6.23}
$$

Fig. 65(b) represents instead a server whose speed depends on a linear combination of the markings of all its input places. In this case the marking dependency function may assume the form:

$$
f(M_{/T_1}) = \delta(ED(T_1, M)) \sum_{i:p_i \in \,\bullet T_1} \alpha_i M(p_i) \qquad \alpha_i \geq 0, \qquad \sum_{i:p_i \in \,\bullet T_1} \alpha_i = 1 \quad (6.24)
$$

6.2.2   An example GSPN system

Consider the example of a parallel system introduced in Chapter 1 (Fig. 8) and discussed at some length in Chapter 5 (Fig. 55). The GSPN system comprises nine places and nine transitions (five of which are timed) and is repeated in Fig. 66 for convenience. The characteristics of the transitions of this model are summarized in Table 8.

Three ECSs can be identified within this system. Two of them can be considered "degenerate" ECSs as they comprise only one transition each (transitions t_{start} and t_{syn}, respectively). The third ECS corresponds instead to a free choice conflict among the two immediate transitions t_{OK} and t_{KO} that have weights α and β, respectively.

Starting from the initial marking shown in Fig. 66, a possible evolution of the GSPN state may be the following. After an exponentially distributed random time with average $1/(2\lambda)$, transition T_{ndata} fires, and one of the two tokens contained in p_1 is removed, while a token is added in p_2. Then, in zero time t_{start} fires, placing one token in p_3 and one token in p_4. The two timed transitions T_{par1} and T_{par2} are now enabled and their probabilities of firing depend on their speeds. Using equation (6.15),

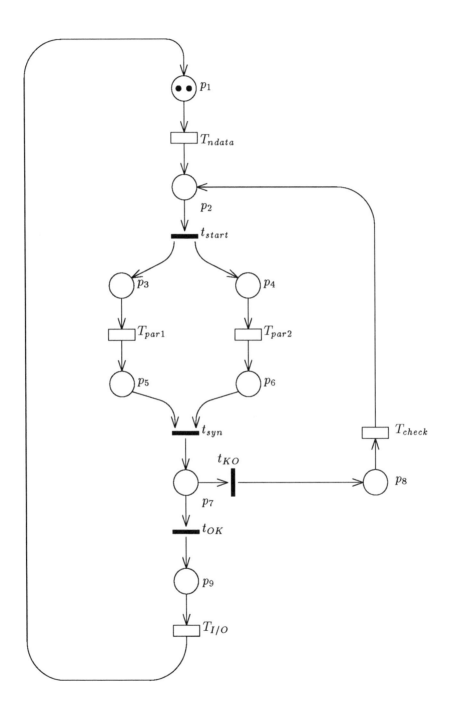

Figure 66   The GSPN description of a parallel system

Table 8 Specification of the transitions of the SPN of Fig. 66

transition	rate	semantics
T_{ndata}	λ	infinite-server
T_{par1}	μ_1	single-server
T_{par2}	μ_2	single-server
$T_{I/O}$	ν	single-server
T_{check}	θ	single-server

transition	weight	priority	ECS
t_{start}	1	1	1
t_{syn}	1	1	2
t_{OK}	α	1	3
t_{KO}	β	1	3

transitions T_{par1} and T_{par2} fire with probabilities:

$$P\{T_{par1}\} = \frac{\mu_1}{\mu_1 + \mu_2 + \lambda} \qquad P\{T_{par2}\} = \frac{\mu_2}{\mu_1 + \mu_2 + \lambda} \qquad (6.25)$$

If T_{par1} fires first, one token moves from p_3 to p_5; subsequently, T_{par2} can fire, moving one token from p_4 to p_6, and enabling immediate transition t_{syn}. This transition fires immediately, removing the two tokens from p_5 and p_6 and depositing one token in p_7. The free-choice conflict is now enabled, and one of the two immediate transitions is selected to fire with probabilities:

$$P\{t_{OK}\} = \frac{\alpha}{\alpha + \beta} \qquad P\{t_{KO}\} = \frac{\beta}{\alpha + \beta} \qquad (6.26)$$

Assume that t_{OK} fires, so that a token is removed from p_7 and a token is put in p_9. Now transition $T_{I/O}$ is enabled; if it fires before T_{ndata}, the GSPN system returns to its initial marking, and its evolution continues.

Of course, many other evolution patterns are possible. Table 9 shows the reachability set of the GSPN system of Fig. 66. It comprises 38 markings, whereas the reachability set of the associated PN system (without priority) comprises 44 states. It must be pointed out that in general the reachability set of a GSPN system is a subset of the reachability set of the associated PN system, because the priority rules introduced by immediate transitions may not allow some states to be reached. The reachability set of an SPN system is, instead, the same as for the associated PN system. Moreover, as was pointed out in Chapter 5, the reachability set of the GSPN system can be divided in two disjoint subsets, one of which comprises tangible markings, i.e., markings that enable timed transitions only, while the other one comprises markings that enable immediate transitions (vanishing markings); in our case the set of tangible markings comprises 20 elements while the number of vanishing markings is 18.

Once the GSPN system is defined, some structural properties may be computed to perform a validation of the model. First, P- and T- semiflows can be computed to check whether the net is structurally bounded and whether it may have home-states.

In the case of the GSPN system of this example, two P- semiflows are identified ($PS_1 = p_1 + p_2 + p_3 + p_6 + p_7 + p_8 + p_9$ and $PS_2 = p_1 + p_2 + p_4 + p_5 + p_7 + p_8 + p_9$) that completely cover the PN system that is thus structurally bounded. Similarly, two T- semiflows are obtained ($TS_1 = T_{ndata} + t_{start} + T_{par1} + T_{par2} + t_{syn} + t_{OK} + T_{I/O}$ and $TS_2 = t_{start} + T_{par1} + T_{par2} + t_{syn} + t_{KO} + T_{check}$) that again cover the whole net, making the presence of home-states possible. Other structural results that may be computed are the ECSs of this model that, as we already said before, are $\{t_{start}\}$, $\{t_{syn}\}$, and $\{t_{OK}, t_{KO}\}$.

These results ensure that the net is suitable for a numerical evaluation yielding the steady-state probabilities of all its markings.

6.3   Numerical Solution of GSPN Systems

The stochastic process associated with k-bounded GSPN systems with M_0 as their initial marking can be classified as a finite state space, stationary (homogeneous), irreducible, and continuous-time semi-Markov process.

In Appendix A we show that semi-Markov processes can be analysed identifying an embedded (discrete-time) Markov chain that describes the transitions from state to state of the process. In the case of GSPNs, the embedded Markov chain (EMC) can be recognized disregarding the concept of time and focusing the attention on the set of states of the semi-Markov process. The specifications of a GSPN system are sufficient for the computation of the transition probabilities of such a chain.

Let RS, TRS, and VRS indicate the state space (the reachability set), the set of tangible states (or markings) and the set of vanishing markings of the stochastic process, respectively. The following relations hold among these sets:

$$RS = TRS \bigcup VRS, \quad TRS \bigcap VRS = \emptyset.$$

The entries of the transition probability matrix U of the EMC can be obtained from the specification of the model using the following expression:

$$u_{ij} = \frac{\sum_{k:T_k \in E_j(M_i)} w_k}{q_i} \tag{6.27}$$

Assuming for the sake of simplicity, that all enabled transitions produce a different change of marking upon their firing, the sum contained in (6.27) reduces to a single element. In this way, except for the diagonal elements of matrix U, all the other transition probabilities of the EMC can be computed using equation (6.15) independently of whether the transition to be considered is timed or immediate, according to the discussion contained at the end of Section 6.2.

Table 9   Reachability set of the GSPN of Fig. 66

Marking	
$M_0 = 2p_1$	
$M_1 = p_1 + p_2$	*
$M_2 = p_1 + p_3 + p_4$	
$M_3 = p_2 + p_3 + p_4$	*
$M_4 = 2p_3 + 2p_4$	
$M_5 = p_1 + p_4 + p_5$	
$M_6 = p_1 + p_3 + p_6$	
$M_7 = p_3 + 2p_4 + p_5$	
$M_8 = 2p_3 + p_4 + p_6$	
$M_9 = p_2 + p_4 + p_5$	*
$M_{10} = p_1 + p_5 + p_6$	*
$M_{11} = p_1 + p_7$	*
$M_{12} = p_1 + p_9$	
$M_{13} = p_1 + p_8$	
$M_{14} = p_2 + p_3 + p_6$	*
$M_{15} = 2p_4 + 2p_5$	
$M_{16} = p_3 + p_4 + p_5 + p_6$	*
$M_{17} = p_3 + p_4 + p_7$	*
$M_{18} = p_3 + p_4 + p_9$	
$M_{19} = p_3 + p_4 + p_8$	
$M_{20} = 2p_3 + 2p_6$	
$M_{21} = p_2 + p_9$	*
$M_{22} = p_2 + p_8$	*
$M_{23} = p_4 + 2p_5 + p_6$	*
$M_{24} = p_4 + p_5 + p_7$	*
$M_{25} = p_4 + p_5 + p_9$	
$M_{26} = p_4 + p_5 + p_8$	
$M_{27} = p_3 + p_6 + p_9$	
$M_{28} = p_3 + p_6 + p_8$	
$M_{29} = p_3 + p_5 + 2p_6$	*
$M_{30} = p_3 + p_6 + p_7$	*
$M_{31} = p_5 + p_6 + p_9$	*
$M_{32} = p_7 + p_9$	*
$M_{33} = 2p_9$	
$M_{34} = p_8 + p_9$	
$M_{35} = p_5 + p_6 + p_8$	*
$M_{36} = p_7 + p_8$	*
$M_{37} = 2p_8$	

By ordering the markings so that the vanishing ones correspond to the first entries of the matrix and the tangible ones to the last, the transition probability matrix U can be decomposed in the following manner:

$$U = A + B = \begin{bmatrix} C & D \\ 0 & 0 \end{bmatrix} + \begin{bmatrix} 0 & 0 \\ E & F \end{bmatrix} \qquad (6.28)$$

The elements of matrix A correspond to changes of markings induced by the firing of immediate transitions; in particular, those of submatrix C are the probabilities of moving from vanishing to vanishing markings, while those of D correspond to transitions from vanishing to tangible markings. Similarly, the elements of matrix B correspond to changes of marking caused by the firing of timed transitions: E accounts for the probabilities of moving from tangible to vanishing markings, while F comprises the probabilities of remaining within tangible markings.

The solution of the system of linear equations

$$\begin{cases} \psi = \psi\,U \\ \psi\,\mathbf{1}^{\mathrm{T}} = 1 \end{cases} \qquad (6.29)$$

in which ψ is a row vector representing the steady-state probability distribution of the EMC, can be interpreted in terms of numbers of (state-) transitions performed by the EMC. Indeed, $1/\psi_i$ is the mean recurrence time for state s_i (marking M_i) measured in number of transition firings (see Appendix A). The steady-state probability distribution of the stochastic process associated with the GSPN system is then obtained by weighting each entry ψ_i with the average sojourn time of its corresponding marking $E[SJ_i]$ and by normalizing the whole distribution (see Appendix A).

The solution method outlined so far, is computationally acceptable whenever the size of the set of vanishing markings is small (compared with the size of the set of tangible markings). However, this method requires the computation of the steady-state probability of each vanishing marking that does not increase the information content of the final solution since the time spent in these markings is known to be null. Moreover, vanishing markings not only require useless computations, but, by enlarging the size of the transition probability matrix U, tend to make the computation of the solution more expensive and in some cases even impossible to obtain.

In order to restrict the solution to quantities directly related with the computation of the steady-state probabilities of tangible markings, we must reduce the model by computing the total transition probabilities among tangible markings only, thus identifying a Reduced EMC (REMC).

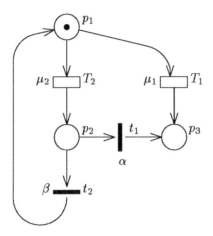

Figure 67   A GSPN system with multiple paths between tangible markings

Table 10   Specification of the transitions of the SPN of Fig. 67

transition	rate	semantics		transition	weight	priority	ECS
T_1	μ_1	single-server		t_1	α	1	1
T_2	μ_2	single-server		t_2	β	1	1

To illustrate the method of reducing the EMC by removing the vanishing markings, consider first the example of Fig. 67. This system contains two free-choice conflicts corresponding to transitions T_1 , T_2, and t_1, t_2, respectively. The transition characteristics are specified in Table 10. From the initial marking $M_i = p_1$, the system can move to marking $M_j = p_3$ following two different paths. The first corresponds to the firing of transition T_1, that happens with probability $\frac{\mu_1}{(\mu_1+\mu_2)}$, and that leads to the desired (target) marking M_j in one step only. The second corresponds to selecting transition T_2 to fire first, followed by transition t_1. The first of these two events happens with probability $\frac{\mu_2}{(\mu_1+\mu_2)}$, and the second with probability $\frac{\alpha}{(\alpha+\beta)}$. The total probability of this second path from M_i to M_j amounts to $\frac{\mu_2}{(\mu_1+\mu_2)}\frac{\alpha}{(\alpha+\beta)}$. Notice that firing transition T_2 followed by transition t_2 would lead to a different marking (in this case the initial one). Firing transition T_2 leads the system into an intermediate (vanishing) marking M_r. The total probability of moving from marking M_i to marking

M_j is thus in this case:

$$u'_{ij} = \frac{\mu_1}{(\mu_1 + \mu_2)} + \frac{\mu_2}{(\mu_1 + \mu_2)} \frac{\alpha}{(\alpha + \beta)} \qquad (6.30)$$

In general, upon the exit from a tangible marking, the system may "walk" through several vanishing markings before ending in a tangible one. To make the example more interesting, and to illustrate more complex cases, let us modify the net of Fig. 67 as depicted in Fig. 68 and specified in Table 11. In this new case the system can move from marking $M_1 = p_1$ to marking $M_2 = p_2$ following four different paths. The first corresponds again to firing transition T_1 and thus to a direct move from the initial marking to the target one. This happens with probability $\frac{\mu_1}{(\mu_1 + \mu_2 + \mu_3)}$. The second path corresponds to firing transition T_2 followed by t_1 (total probability $\frac{\mu_2}{(\mu_1 + \mu_2 + \mu_3)} \frac{\alpha}{(\alpha + \beta)}$); the third path corresponds to firing transition T_3 followed by transition t_4 (total probability $\frac{\mu_3}{(\mu_1 + \mu_2 + \mu_3)} \frac{\gamma}{(\gamma + \delta)}$). Finally, the last path corresponds to firing transition T_3 followed by transition t_3 and then by transition t_1 which happens with probability $\frac{\mu_3}{(\mu_1 + \mu_2 + \mu_3)} \frac{\delta}{(\gamma + \delta)} \frac{\alpha}{(\alpha + \beta)}$.

In this case the total probability of moving from marking M_i to marking M_j becomes:

$$u'_{ij} = \frac{\mu_1}{(\mu_1 + \mu_2 + \mu_3)} + \frac{\mu_2}{(\mu_1 + \mu_2 + \mu_3)} \frac{\alpha}{(\alpha + \beta)} +$$

$$\frac{\mu_3}{(\mu_1 + \mu_2 + \mu_3)} \frac{\gamma}{(\gamma + \delta)} + \frac{\mu_3}{(\mu_1 + \mu_2 + \mu_3)} \frac{\delta}{(\gamma + \delta)} \frac{\alpha}{(\alpha + \beta)} \qquad (6.31)$$

In general, recalling the structure of the U matrix, a direct move from marking M_i to marking M_j corresponds to a non-zero entry in block F ($f_{ij} \neq 0$), while a path from M_i to M_j via two intermediate vanishing markings corresponds to the existence of

1. a non-zero entry in block E corresponding to a move from tangible marking M_i to a generic intermediate vanishing marking M_r;
2. a non-zero entry in block C from this generic vanishing marking M_r to another arbitrary vanishing marking M_s;
3. a corresponding non-zero entry in block D from vanishing marking M_s to tangible marking M_j.

These informal considerations are precisely captured by the following formula:

$$u'_{ij} = f_{ij} + \sum_{r:M_r \in VRS} e_{ir} P\{r \rightarrow s\} d_{sj} \qquad (6.32)$$

where $P\{r \rightarrow s\} d_{sj}$ is the probability that the net moves from vanishing marking M_r to tangible marking M_j in an arbitrary number of steps, following a path through vanishing markings only.

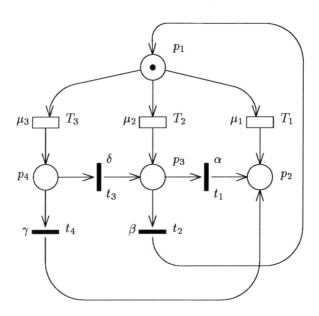

Figure 68   A GSPN system with several multiple paths between tangible markings

Table 11   Specification of the transitions of the SPN of Fig. 68

transition	rate	semantics
T_1	μ_1	single-server
T_2	μ_2	single-server
T_3	μ_3	single-server

transition	weight	priority	ECS
t_1	α	1	1
t_2	β	1	1
t_3	δ	1	1
t_4	γ	1	1

In order to provide a general and efficient method for the computation of the state transition probability matrix U' of the REMC, we can observe that (6.32) can be rewritten in matrix notation in the following form:

$$U' = F + E\,G\,D \qquad (6.33)$$

where each entry g_{rs} of matrix G represents the probability of moving from vanishing marking M_r to vanishing marking M_s in any number of steps, but without hitting any intermediate tangible marking. Observing that each entry c_{rs}^n of matrix C^n represents the probability of moving from vanishing marking M_r to vanishing marking M_s in exactly n steps without hitting any intermediate tangible marking, we can conclude that

$$G = \sum_{n=0}^{\infty} C^n$$

In the computation of C^n, two possibilities may arise. The first corresponds to the situation in which there are no loops among vanishing markings. This means that for any vanishing marking $M_r \in VRS$ there is a value n_{0r} such that any sequence of transition firings of length $n \geq n_{0r}$ starting from such marking must reach a tangible marking $M_j \in TRS$. In this case

$$\exists n_0 \; : \quad \forall \; n \geq n_0 \quad C^n = 0$$

and

$$G = \sum_{k=0}^{\infty} C^k = \sum_{k=0}^{n_0} C^k$$

The second corresponds to the situation in which there are possibilities of loops among vanishing markings, so that there is a possibility for the GSPN to remain "trapped" within a set of vanishing markings. In this case the irreducibility property of the semi-Markov process associated with the GSPN system ensures that the following results hold [Var62]:

$$\lim_{n \to \infty} C^n = 0$$

so that

$$G = \sum_{k=0}^{\infty} C^k = [I - C]^{-1}.$$

We can thus write (see [AMBC86, AMBC84] for details):

$$H = \begin{cases} \left(\sum_{k=0}^{n_0} C^k \right) D & \text{\textit{no loops among vanishing states}} \\[2em] [I - C]^{-1} D & \text{\textit{loops among vanishing states}} \end{cases}$$

from which we can conclude that an explicit expression for the desired total transition probability among any two tangible markings is:

$$u'_{ij} = f_{ij} + \sum_{r:M_r \in VRS} e_{ir} \, h_{rj} \quad \forall \; i, j \in TRS$$

The transition probability matrix of the REMC can thus be expressed as

$$U' = F + E H \tag{6.34}$$

The solution of the problem

$$\begin{cases} \psi' = \psi' U' \\[1em] \psi' \, 1^{\mathrm{T}} = 1 \end{cases} \tag{6.35}$$

in which ψ' is a row vector representing the steady-state probability distribution of the REMC, allows the direct computation of the mean number of visits performed by the net to tangible markings only between two subsequent visits to a reference marking. By selecting one of the markings of the REMC as a reference marking for the chain (say marking M_i), the mean number of visits to an arbitrary marking M_j, between two subsequent visits to marking M_i, is obtained as:

$$v_{ij} = \frac{\psi'_j}{\psi'_i} \tag{6.36}$$

The stationary probability distribution associated with the set of tangible markings is thus readily obtained by means of their average sojourn times (see (6.5)) using the following formula:

$$\eta'_j = \frac{v_{ij}\, E[SJ_j]}{CY(M_i)} \tag{6.37}$$

where $CY(M_i)$ represents the mean cycle time of the GSPN with respect to state M_i, i.e., the average amount of time that the GSPN takes to return to marking M_i. $CY(M_i)$ has the following expression:

$$CY(M_i) = \sum_{k:M_k \in TRS} v_{ik}\, E[SJ_k] \tag{6.38}$$

The construction of the REMC defined over the set of tangible markings TRS implies that a transformation exists of the semi-Markov process associated with every GSPN system into a CTMC. The steady-state probability distribution over the tangible markings can thus be also obtained by a direct solution of this CTMC. Appendix A contains the details of the relationships between CTMCs and their corresponding EMCs defined at transition instants. In our case, the infinitesimal generator Q' of the CTMC associated with a GSPN can be constructed from the transition probability rate matrix U' of the REMC by dividing each of its rows by the mean sojourn time of the corresponding tangible marking. To conform with the standard definition of the infinitesimal generators, the diagonal elements of Q' are set equal to the negative sum of the off-diagonal components:

$$q'_{ij} = \begin{cases} \frac{1}{E[SJ_i]}\, u'_{ij} & i \neq j \\[2ex] -\sum_{j \neq i} q'_{ij} & i = j \end{cases} \tag{6.39}$$

An alternative way of computing the steady-state probability distribution over the tangible markings is thus that of solving the following system of linear equations:

$$\begin{cases} \eta'\, Q' = 0 \\[2ex] \eta'\, \mathbf{1}^{T} = 1 \end{cases} \tag{6.40}$$

This result shows that GSPNs, like SPNs, can be analysed by solving proper associated CTMCs. This obviously implies that the computation of performance indices defined over GSPN models can be performed using the reward method discussed in Section 6.1 without any additional difficulty.

The advantage of solving the system by first identifying the REMC is twofold. First, the time and space complexity of the solution is reduced in most cases, since the iterative methods used to solve the system of linear equations tend to converge more slowly when applied with sparse matrices and an improvement is obtained by eliminating the vanishing states thus obtaining a denser matrix [Cia89, Bla89]. Second, by decreasing the impact of the size of the set of vanishing states on the complexity of the solution method, we are allowed a greater freedom in the explicit specification of the logical conditions of the original GSPN, making it easier to understand.

6.3.1 Evaluation of the steady-state probability distribution for the example GSPN system

The GSPN system of Fig. 66 can now be analysed to compute the steady-state probability distribution of the states of the parallel processing system that it represents.

As was mentioned in Section 6.2.2, the 38 markings of this net can be grouped within two subsets comprising 20 tangible and 18 vanishing markings, respectively. Vanishing markings are tagged with a star in Table 9.

Using the notation introduced in Section 6.3, we have $|RS| = 38$, $|TRS| = 20$, and $|VRS| = 18$. The transition probability matrix U of the EMC associated with the GSPN can be subdivided into four blocks whose entries are computed from the parameters of the model (the W function of the GSPN system specification). The four submatrices C, D, E, and F of equation (6.28) have dimensions (18×18), (18×20), (20×18), and (20×20), respectively. Because of the relatively simple structure of the model, all these four blocks are quite sparse (few of the entries are different from zero). Table 12 reports the non-zero values of all these matrices, with the understanding that $x_{i,j}(r, s)$ represents the non-zero component of the X matrix located in row i and column j, and corresponding to the transition probability from state r to state s.

Table 12   Non-zero entries of the transition probability matrix of the EMC

Component	Probability	Component	Probability
$c_{4,5}(10,11)$	1.0	$d_{1,2}(1,2)$	1.0
$c_{7,8}(16,17)$	1.0	$d_{2,3}(3,4)$	1.0
$c_{11,12}(23,24)$	1.0	$d_{3,6}(9,7)$	1.0
$c_{13,14}(29,30)$	1.0	$d_{5,8}(11,12)$	α
$c_{15,16}(31,32)$	1.0	$d_{5,9}(11,13)$	β
$c_{17,18}(35,36)$	1.0	$d_{6,7}(14,8)$	1.0
		$d_{8,11}(17,18)$	α
		$d_{8,12}(17,19)$	β
		$d_{9,11}(21,18)$	1.0
		$d_{10,12}(22,19)$	1.0
		$d_{12,14}(24,25)$	α
		$d_{12,15}(24,26)$	β
		$d_{14,16}(30,27)$	α
$e_{1,1}(0,1)$	1.0	$d_{14,17}(30,28)$	β
$e_{2,2}(2,3)$	$\lambda / (\lambda + \mu_1 + \mu_2)$	$d_{16,18}(32,33)$	α
$e_{4,3}(5,9)$	$\lambda / (\lambda + \mu_2)$	$d_{16,19}(32,34)$	β
$e_{4,4}(5,10)$	$\mu_2 / (\lambda + \mu_2)$	$d_{18,19}(36,34)$	α
$e_{5,4}(6,10)$	$\mu_1 / (\lambda + \mu_1)$	$d_{18,20}(36,37)$	β
$e_{5,6}(6,14)$	$\lambda / (\lambda + \mu_1)$		
$e_{6,7}(7,16)$	$\mu_2 / (\mu_1 + \mu_2)$	$f_{2,4}(2,5)$	$\mu_1 / (\lambda + \mu_1 + \mu_2)$
$e_{7,7}(8,16)$	$\mu_1 / (\mu_1 + \mu_2)$	$f_{2,5}(2,6)$	$\mu_2 / (\lambda + \mu_1 + \mu_2)$
$e_{8,9}(12,21)$	$\lambda / (\lambda + \nu)$	$f_{3,6}(4,7)$	$\mu_1 / (\mu_1 + \mu_2)$
$e_{9,1}(13,1)$	$\theta / (\lambda + \theta)$	$f_{3,7}(4,8)$	$\mu_2 / (\mu_2 + \mu_2)$
$e_{9,10}(13,22)$	$\lambda / (\lambda + \theta)$	$f_{6,10}(7,15)$	$\mu_1 / (\mu_1 + \mu_2)$
$e_{10,11}(15,23)$	1.0	$f_{7,13}(8,20)$	$\mu_2 / (\mu_1 + \mu_2)$
$e_{12,2}(19,3)$	$\theta / (\mu_1 + \mu_2 + \theta)$	$f_{8,1}(12,0)$	$\nu / (\lambda + \nu)$
$e_{13,13}(20,29)$	1.0	$f_{11,2}(18,2)$	$\nu / (\mu_1 + \mu_2 + \nu)$
$e_{14,15}(25,31)$	$\mu_2 / (\mu_2 + \nu)$	$f_{11,14}(18,25)$	$\mu_1 / (\mu_1 + \mu_2 + \nu)$
$e_{15,3}(26,9)$	$\theta / (\mu_2 + \theta)$	$f_{11,16}(18,27)$	$\mu_2 / (\mu_1 + \mu_2 + \nu)$
$e_{15,17}(26,35)$	$\mu_2 / (\mu_2 + \theta)$	$f_{12,15}(19,26)$	$\mu_1 / (\mu_1 + \mu_2 + \theta)$
$e_{16,15}(27,31)$	$\mu_1 / (\mu_1 + \nu)$	$f_{12,17}(19,28)$	$\mu_2 / (\mu_1 + \mu_2 + \theta)$
$e_{17,6}(28,14)$	$\theta / (\mu_1 + \theta)$	$f_{14,4}(25,5)$	$\nu / (\mu_2 + \nu)$
$e_{17,17}(28,35)$	$\mu_1 / (\mu_1 + \theta)$	$f_{16,5}(27,6)$	$\nu / (\mu_1 + \nu)$
$e_{19,9}(34,21)$	$\theta / (\theta + \nu)$	$f_{18,8}(33,12)$	1.0
$e_{19,10}(37,22)$	1.0	$f_{19,9}(34,13)$	$\nu / (\theta + \nu)$

Table 13   Non-zero entries of the transition probability matrix of the REMC

Component	Probability	Component	Probability
$u'_{1,2}(0,2)$	1.0	$u'_{11,2}(18,2)$	$\frac{\nu}{(\mu_1+\mu_2+\nu)}$
$u'_{2,3}(2,4)$	$\frac{\lambda}{(\lambda+\mu_1+\mu_2)}$	$u'_{11,14}(18,25)$	$\frac{\mu_1}{(\mu_1+\mu_2+\nu)}$
$u'_{2,4}(2,5)$	$\frac{\mu_1}{(\lambda+\mu_1+\mu_2)}$	$u'_{11,16}(18,27)$	$\frac{\mu_2}{(\mu_1+\mu_2+\nu)}$
$u'_{2,5}(2,6)$	$\frac{\mu_2}{(\lambda+\mu_1+\mu_2)}$	$u'_{12,3}(19,4)$	$\frac{\theta}{(\mu_1+\mu_2+\theta)}$
$u'_{3,6}(4,7)$	$\frac{\mu_1}{(\mu_1+\mu_2)}$	$u'_{12,15}(19,26)$	$\frac{\mu_1}{(\mu_1+\mu_2+\theta)}$
$u'_{3,7}(4,8)$	$\frac{\mu_2}{(\mu_2+\mu_2)}$	$u'_{12,17}(19,28)$	$\frac{\mu_2}{(\mu_1+\mu_2+\theta)}$
$u'_{4,6}(5,7)$	$\frac{\lambda}{(\lambda+\mu_2)}$	$u'_{13,16}(20,27)$	α
$u'_{4,8}(5,12)$	$\frac{\alpha\mu_2}{(\lambda+\mu_2)}$	$u'_{13,17}(20,28)$	β
$u'_{4,9}(5,13)$	$\frac{\beta\mu_2}{(\lambda+\mu_2)}$	$u'_{14,4}(25,5)$	$\frac{\nu}{(\mu_2+\nu)}$
$u'_{5,7}(6,8)$	$\frac{\lambda}{(\lambda+\mu_1)}$	$u'_{14,18}(25,33)$	$\frac{\alpha\mu_2}{(\mu_2+\nu)}$
$u'_{5,8}(6,12)$	$\frac{\alpha\mu_1}{(\lambda+\mu_1)}$	$u'_{14,19}(25,34)$	$\frac{\beta\mu_2}{(\mu_2+\nu)}$
$u'_{5,9}(6,13)$	$\frac{\beta\mu_1}{(\lambda+\mu_1)}$	$u'_{15,6}(26,7)$	$\frac{\theta}{(\mu_2+\theta)}$
$u'_{6,10}(7,15)$	$\frac{\mu_1}{(\mu_1+\mu_2)}$	$u'_{15,19}(26,34)$	$\frac{\alpha\mu_2}{(\mu_2+\theta)}$
$u'_{6,11}(7,18)$	$\frac{\alpha\mu_2}{(\mu_1+\mu_2)}$	$u'_{15,20}(26,37)$	$\frac{\beta\mu_2}{(\mu_2+\theta)}$
$u'_{6,12}(7,19)$	$\frac{\beta\mu_2}{(\mu_1+\mu_2)}$	$u'_{16,5}(27,6)$	$\frac{\nu}{(\mu_1+\nu)}$
$u'_{7,11}(8,18)$	$\frac{\alpha\mu_1}{(\mu_1+\mu_2)}$	$u'_{16,18}(27,33)$	$\frac{\alpha\mu_1}{(\mu_1+\nu)}$
$u'_{7,12}(8,19)$	$\frac{\beta\mu_1}{(\mu_1+\mu_2)}$	$u'_{16,19}(27,34)$	$\frac{\beta\mu_1}{(\mu_1+\nu)}$
$u'_{7,13}(8,20)$	$\frac{\mu_2}{(\mu_1+\mu_2)}$	$u'_{17,7}(28,8)$	$\frac{\theta}{(\mu_1+\theta)}$
$u'_{8,1}(12,0)$	$\frac{\nu}{(\lambda+\nu)}$	$u'_{17,19}(28,34)$	$\frac{\alpha\mu_1}{(\mu_1+\theta)}$
$u'_{8,11}(12,18)$	$\frac{\lambda}{(\lambda+\nu)}$	$u'_{17,20}(28,37)$	$\frac{\beta\mu_1}{(\mu_1+\theta)}$
$u'_{9,2}(13,2)$	$\frac{\theta}{(\lambda+\theta)}$	$u'_{18,8}(33,12)$	1.0
$u'_{9,12}(13,19)$	$\frac{\lambda}{(\lambda+\theta)}$	$u'_{19,9}(34,13)$	$\frac{\nu}{(\theta+\nu)}$
$u'_{10,14}(15,25)$	α	$u'_{19,11}(34,18)$	$\frac{\theta}{(\theta+\nu)}$
$u'_{10,15}(15,26)$	β	$u'_{20,12}(37,19)$	1.0

Using the method outlined by (6.3) we obtain the transition probability matrix of the REMC reported in Table 13. Solving the system of linear equations (6.35), we obtain the steady state probabilities for all the states of the REMC.

Supposing that the transition weights assume the following values:

$$\lambda = 0.2, \quad \mu_1 = 2.0, \quad \mu_2 = 1.0, \quad \theta = 0.1, \quad \nu = 5.0, \quad \alpha = 0.99, \quad \text{and } \beta = 0.01$$

we obtain, for example:

$$\psi'_0 = 0.10911, \quad \psi'_2 = 0.11965, \quad \text{and } \psi'_{37} = 0.00002$$

Assuming marking 1 as a reference, we compute the visits to any other state using (6.36). Focusing our attention on markings M_0, M_2, and M_{37}, we obtain:

$$v_{0,0} = 1.0, \quad v_{2,0} = 1.09666, \quad \text{and} \quad v_{37,0} = 0.00020.$$

Knowing the mean sojourn time for the markings of the GSPN:

$$E[SJ_0] = 2.5, \quad E[SJ_2] = 0.3125, \quad \text{and} \quad E[SJ_{37}] = 10.0$$

we can compute the mean cycle time with respect to reference marking M_0:

$$CY(M_0) = 4.31108$$

and consequently the steady-state probability of each marking. For the three markings arbitrarily chosen before we have:

$$\eta_0 = 0.57990, \quad \eta_2 = 0.07949, \quad \text{and} \quad \eta_{37} = 0.00047$$

6.3.2   Performance analysis of the example GSPN

The performance of the parallel processing system of Fig. 66 can be conveniently studied by evaluating the probability of having at least one process waiting for synchronization. For this purpose, we can use the following reward function:

$$r(M) = \begin{cases} 1 & (M(p_5) \geq 1) \vee (M(p_6) \geq 1) \\ 0 & otherwise \end{cases} \tag{6.41}$$

With this definition the desired probability is computed to have the value $R = 0.23814$.

Similarly, the processing power of this system (i.e., the average number of processors doing useful work accessing local data only) can be obtained using the following reward function:

$$r(M) = M(p_1) \tag{6.42}$$

which provides $R = 1.50555$.

6.4   Reducing GSPNs to SPNs

As we saw in the previous sections, immediate transitions, that have quite a beneficial impact on the modelling power of GSPNs, on the other hand make the overall analysis of GSPNs more complex than that of SPNs. Indeed, while for the latter the reachability graph is isomorphic to the state transition rate diagram of the CTMC

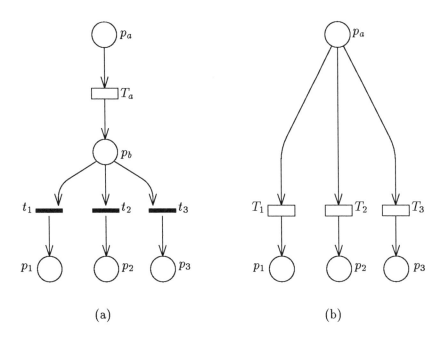

(a)   (b)

Figure 69   Removing immediate transitions: the free-choice case

underlying the SPN, such isomorphism does not exist for GSPNs, but is obtained
only after the elimination of vanishing markings. An analysis procedure different from
that described in the previous sections consists in the elimination of all immediate
transitions from a given GSPN before starting the generation of its reachability set,
so as to produce an SPN whose underlying continuous-time Markov chain is identical
to that corresponding to the GSPN.

This section provides a concise and informal overview of the rules for the reduction
of a GSPN model to an equivalent SPN by eliminating all immediate transitions. A
complete and formal description of these reduction rules and of the sub-class of GSPNs
for which it is possible to compute an equivalent SPN, can be found in [CDF91, Don90].

The basic idea behind the elimination of immediate transitions is quite simple and
can be easily explained in its simplest form by means of an example. The model
depicted in Fig. 69(a) is a free-choice GSPN subnet whose SPN counterpart is shown
in Fig. 69(b). The two systems are equivalent as far as tangible states are concerned.

To understand how we can transform the GSPN into its corresponding SPN, consider
what happens in the GSPN when T_a fires: the three immediate transitions t_1, t_2, and
t_3 become enabled, due to the arrival of one token in place p_b; they are the only
transitions that are enabled in the subnet, and the choice about which one to fire

is made according to their associated weights. The basic behaviour of the subnet in Fig. 69(a) is therefore that of "moving" tokens from place p_a to one of the three places p_1, p_2, and p_3. The net in Fig. 69(b) is clearly equivalent to that of Fig. 69(a) from the point of view of the flow of tokens (token flow equivalence was defined in [Ber87]).

When time is involved, token flow equivalence is not enough to ensure the possibility of freely interchanging the two types of models. In particular, the equivalence notion we are interested in must preserve the underlying stochastic behaviour of the net. We must therefore take into account not only the possible final states of the subnet, but also the rates at which the model transits from state to state.

The operations of the GSPN subnet induce a movement of a token from p_a to p_k, $k = 1, 2, 3$, with rate

$$\frac{w_a w_k}{\sum_{j=1}^{3} w_j} \tag{6.43}$$

where w_a is the rate of the exponential distribution associated with timed transition T_a, and w_k is the weight of immediate transition t_k, so that

$$\frac{w_k}{\sum_{j=1}^{3} w_j} \tag{6.44}$$

is the probability that t_k is the transition that actually fires when t_1, t_2, and t_3 are all enabled.

The timed transition T_k in the SPN model represents the firing of timed transition T_a followed by immediate transition t_k. If we define its firing rate as in (6.43), then the rate at which the SPN subnet in Fig. 69(b) induces a movement of a token from p_a to p_k, given that transition T_a is enabled, is exactly the same as for the GSPN subnet, and therefore the rates of the underlying Markov processes are the same. Note that place p_b was deleted in the reduction process: this is not surprising because p_b is a vanishing place, i.e., a place that is never marked in a tangible marking.

The elimination procedure is somewhat more complex if the set of immediate transitions enabled by the firing of a timed transition does not form a free-choice conflict. Indeed, in this case the probability of firing an immediate transition may depend also on the other simultaneously enabled immediate transitions. We are thus forced to consider all possible cases. As an example, consider the subnet in Fig. 70(a).

The firing of timed transition T_a may enable either only t_1, or only t_2, or both t_1 and t_2, or neither of them, depending on the marking of p_3 and p_4. In any case, at most one of the two immediate transitions can fire (only one token is in p_2 after the firing of T_a). The probability that, for example, t_1 is the transition that actually fires is different in the two cases where t_1 is enabled alone, or together with t_2: we have therefore to distinguish the two cases. A similar consideration holds for t_2, so that we have two more cases, plus the additional case in which the firing of the timed transition

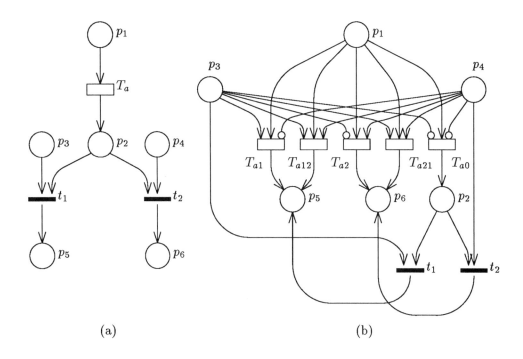

(a)   (b)

Figure 70   Removing immediate transitions: the non-free-choice case

cannot be followed by that of any immediate transition. We hence have five possible situations:

1. T_a is followed by t_1 when only t_1 is enabled (transition T_{a1} with rate w_a);
2. T_a is followed by t_1 when both t_1 and t_2 are enabled (transition T_{a12} with rate $w_a w_1/(w_1 + w_2)$);
3. T_a is followed by t_2 when only t_2 is enabled (transition T_{a2} with rate w_a);
4. T_a is followed by t_2 when both t_2 and t_1 are enabled (transition T_{a21} with rate $w_a w_2/(w_1 + w_2)$);
5. T_a is not followed by any immediate transition (transition T_{a0} with rate w_a).

In the GSPN subnet resulting from the reduction of t_1 and t_2 over T_a, shown in Fig. 70(b), five timed transitions take the place of T_a. No vanishing place existed in the original GSPN, so that no place could be deleted. The size of the state space has been reduced, as all vanishing markings of the original GSPN are not reachable any longer (for example, the marking $\{p_2, p_3, p_4\}$ is not generated by the reduced net of Fig. 70(b)). Observe that the subnet depicted in Fig. 70(a) includes only one of the timed transitions that may deposit tokens in the input places of the ECS composed by

t_1 and t_2, but in general there can be more than one. This is the reason why the two immediate transitions t_1 and t_2 are still present in the reduced subnet of Fig. 70(b), since they shall also be reduced over all timed transitions that add tokens to p_3 and/or p_4.

Let us now apply the two rules to the reduction of the example GSPN in Fig. 66 to an equivalent SPN. First of all, the immediate transition t_{start} can be removed. We can view t_{start} as a free-choice conflict comprising just one transition, and thus incorporate it into the two timed transitions T_{ndata} and T_{check}. As a result, the output set of the two timed transitions T_{ndata} and T_{check} becomes $\{p_3, p_4\}$, as shown in Fig. 71. No modification of the transition rates is necessary, since the weight of t_{start} is equal to 1.

As a second step, we can remove the immediate transition t_{syn}, that can be viewed as a non-free-choice conflict comprising just one transition. It is thus necessary to consider the possible situations at the firing of either of the two timed transitions T_{par1} and T_{par2}. When T_{par1} fires, t_{syn} fires if p_6 contains a token; otherwise, the token produced by the firing of T_{par1} waits for the synchronization in p_5. The elimination of t_{syn} thus requires the introduction of two timed transitions T_a and T_b in place of T_{par1}, and T_c and T_d for T_{par2}. The resulting GSPN is shown in Fig. 72. Also in this case, no modification of the transition rates is necessary, since the weight of t_{syn} is equal to 1.

Finally, the free-choice conflict formed by transitions T_{OK} and T_{KO} can be eliminated by splitting the two timed transitions T_a and T_d in two timed transitions each. From transition T_a we generate $T_{a'}$ and $T_{a''}$ to account for the two cases in which either T_{OK} or T_{KO} fires. The rate of the timed transition $T_{a'}$ is obtained as the product of the rate of the timed transition T_a by the weight of the immediate transition T_{OK}, and similarly in the other cases. The resulting SPN model is shown in Fig. 73.

It should be observed that the SPN model in Fig. 73 is much more complex than the original model in Fig. 66, and much less adherent to our natural description of the system operations. This is usually the case, and provides a demonstration of the greater expressivness of GSPNs over SPNs. However, the transformation from GSPNs to SPNs can be easily automated, and made invisible to the user, as a useful intermediate step instrumental for the generation of the continuous-time Markov chain underlying the GSPN system.

6.5   Simulation of GSPN Systems

One of the problems that hamper the analysis of GSPN systems is the exponential growth of the size of their state space that makes it often impossible to construct (and

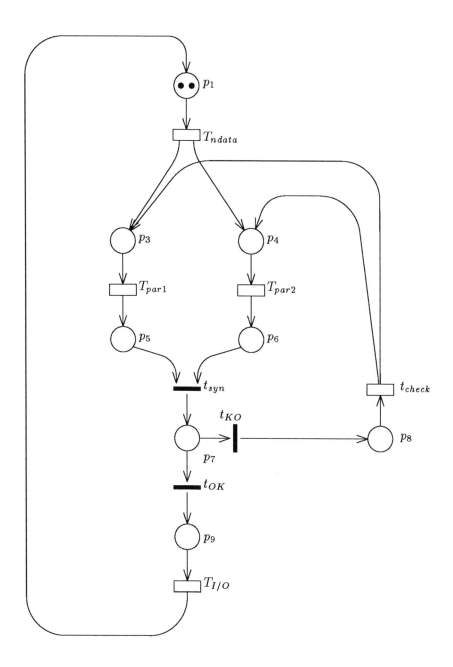

Figure 71 First reduction step for the GSPN of Fig. 66

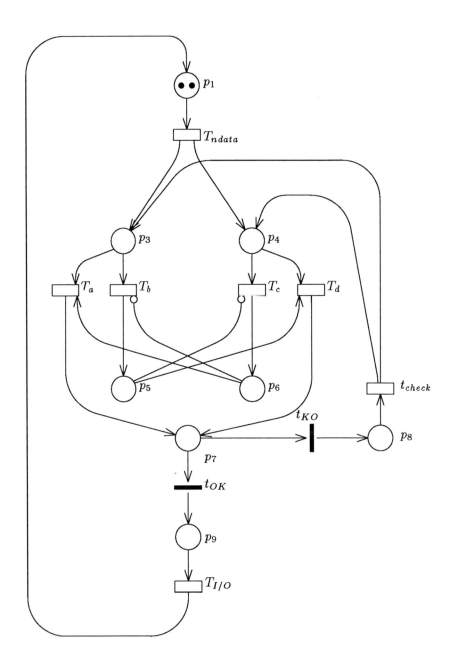

Figure 72 Second reduction step for the GSPN of Fig. 66

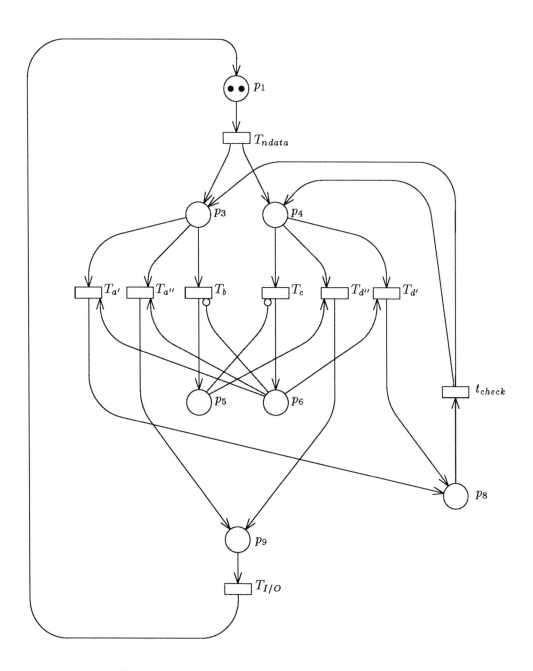

Figure 73 Third reduction step for the GSPN of Fig. 66

store) their reachability sets. In these cases it becomes also impossible to construct the associated stochastic processes, so that it often happens that the only way of assessing the properties of the corresponding systems is via simulation.

The simulation of a GSPN system for performance evaluation purposes corresponds to generating a sample path through the state space of the system, and to collecting measurements on particular aspects of GSPN system behaviour.

GSPN systems are suitable for discrete-event simulation in which the events that characterize the changes of states and the times spent in states are the only relevant aspects of model behaviour. Events correspond to transition firings and the time spent in states derives from the temporal distance between transition firings. The simulation of a GSPN system corresponds to identifying a *current event* that is certain to happen given the *current marking*, as well as the other events that may happen in the future given the information provided by the same marking (*scheduled events*). Firing the transition that corresponds to the current event produces a change of marking in which new transitions may become enabled, and other transitions (that were previously enabled) may become disabled.

The identification of the transitions that are enabled in a given marking as well as the transitions that are affected by the change of marking due to a transition firing is one of the main problem in the efficient simulation of large GSPN systems. When the set of transitions of the GSPN is large, testing at each change of marking all the elements of the set to see which transitions are enabled may be extremely time consuming. A considerable advantage can be gained by exploiting interesting relationships among transitions that can be obtained from a structural analysis of the model.

Consider the set $E(M)$ of transitions that are enabled in a given marking M. This set is usually substantially smaller than the set of transitions of the GSPN. Supposing that transition t $(t \in E(M))$ has been selected to fire, let $\Delta_t^+(M)$ and $\Delta_t^-(M)$ represent the set of transitions whose enabling is caused by the firing of t and the set of transitions that become disabled after the firing of t, respectively. The set of transitions enabled in the new marking M' $(E(M'))$ is related with the old one by the following relation:

$$E(M') = E(M) + \Delta_t^+(M) - \Delta_t^-(M) \qquad (6.45)$$

Since the number of transitions affected by the firing of t is usually small, this "incremental" construction of the new set of enabled transitions has the potential of greatly reducing the time needed for its computation with respect to the trivial method of testing all the transitions of the model for their enabling in the new marking.

In order to support this simulation strategy, the relationships of causal connection, structural conflict, and mutual exclusion (see Sections 2.3 and 2.5.2) can be computed for all the transitions of the GSPN during an initial phase of the simulation and stored into proper data structures to speed up the updating of the event list after the firing of each transition [Chi91b]. Indeed, after the firing of an arbitrary transition t, only the transitions that are causally connected with t must be tested for inclusion in the set of newly enabled transitions. Letting $\Omega(t)$ represent the set of transitions that are causally connected with t, we can observe that the following inclusion relation holds:

$$\Delta_t^+(M) \subseteq \Omega(t) = \{t_i : t \; SCC \; t_i\} \tag{6.46}$$

Similarly, after the firing of transition t only the transitions that are in structural conflict with t itself and that are not mutually exclusive must be tested to be removed from the new set of enabled transitions. Letting $\Theta(t)$ represent the set of transitions that satisfy this condition, we can observe that:

$$\Delta_t^-(M) \subseteq \Theta(t) = \{t_i : (t \; SC \; t_i) \wedge (t \; \neg ME \; t_i)\} \tag{6.47}$$

The small amount of extra storage that is needed to keep track of these sets and that is filled up at the beginning of the simulation allows a considerable speed-up of the operations needed for managing each transition firing and for updating the event list of the simulator.

The memoryless property of the negative exponential distributions of firing delays greatly simplifies the operations related with the management of the event list. Each time a new timed transition is included in the set of the enabled transitions, an instance τ of its associated random delay is generated, a projected firing time is computed by adding τ to the current clock of the simulator, and the associated firing event is inserted in the event list in firing time order. Transitions that were enabled before the firing and that have not been affected by the firing, keep their projected firing times unchanged and their corresponding firing events remain scheduled in the event list. Transitions that were enabled before the firing of transition t and that are now disabled have their associated firing events removed from the event list and their remaining firing delays are discarded.

The updating of the event list at the time of a transition firing can be slightly more complex when the GSPN comprises timed transitions with marking-dependent firing rates. In this case a reordering of the event list may be needed even with respect to transitions whose enabling conditions have not been affected by the firing of transition t except for their enabling degree.

When several immediate transitions are enabled in a given marking the choice of the transition to fire first is made by computing the probability distribution over the enabled transitions using the expresssion in (6.16) and selecting the transition via the generation of a random number.

Extending the simulation methodology discussed so far to the case of GSPN systems with general firing time distributions is quite simple. In this case firing delay instances for newly enabled transitions are generated with well-known techniques that are standard in the simulation field [Kob78] and the only major difference concerns the way of managing the firing delays of transitions that were enabled in the previous marking and that became disabled due to the firing of another transition. Two ways of treating these firing delays need to be implemented, depending on their specific memory policies [HS86]. Transitions that have been specified with an enabling memory policy have their remaining firing delays discarded and new firing delay instances are generated for them when they become enabled again in a new marking. Transitions that have been specified instead with an age memory policy keep record of their remaining firing delays by means of proper auxiliary variables. When they become enabled in a new marking, new firing delay instances are generated only if their associated auxiliary variables have zero values [1]. In all the other cases the value of the auxiliary variable is directly interpreted as the new instance of the firing delay that is used to insert a corresponding firing event in the event list. The auxiliary variable associated with a timed transition with age memory policy is set to zero when the transition fires.

The statistical analysis of the simulation output can be performed in the case of GSPN with the *regenerative method* [Kob78], because of the existence of an underlying CTMC. The only problem may be that of identifying a suitable regeneration point (marking) that is visited sufficiently often during the simulation run. When the restriction of the negative exponential distribution of the firing delays is relaxed, the regenerative structure of the associated stochastic process is maintained only in very special cases [HS86] and it may become more convenient to obtain interval estimates for the performance figures of interest using the *independent replication method* [Kob78].

6.5.1 Simulation of the example GSPN system

The effectiveness of simulation for the analysis of complex systems can be demonstrated with the use of the simple parallel processing example of Fig. 66, by assuming that a large number of customers are considered in the system. Table 14 summarizes the results of an experiment in which simulation estimates for the throughput and for the processing power (i.e., the mean number of tokens in place p_1) of the system are compared with the exact ones computed with numerical methods in the case of small populations. The size of the reachability set of this model grows quickly according to the following formula

$$|TRG(N)| = \binom{N + |P| - 1}{|P| - 1} - \binom{N + |P| - 3}{|P| - 1} \tag{6.48}$$

---

[1] Some attention must be paid in the case of firing delays with discrete distributions, since it may happen that several transitions are scheduled to fire at the same time and an auxiliary variable with zero value does not necesserely mean that the corresponding transition has fired.

Table 14 Comparison of performance figures computed via numerical and simulation
methods for the parallel system of Fig. 66

N	|TRG|	System Throughput		Processing Power		Sim. Time
		Num.	Sim.	Num.	Sim.	
2	20	0.3011	0.2979 $\mp$ 0.0137	1.5055	1.5173 $\mp$ 0.0179	15 sec.
8	825	0.8996	0.8718 $\mp$ 0.0354	4.4877	4.4137 $\mp$ 0.2077	23 sec.
20	19481	0.9900	1.0008 $\mp$ 0.0349	4.9500	4.9494 $\mp$ 0.2448	27 sec.
50	609076	-	1.0402 $\mp$ 0.0474	-	5.2243 $\mp$ 0.2533	24 sec.

where N is the number of customers in the model and $|P|$ is the number of places
of the net. It thus happens that when 50 customers are in the system, the numerical
solution becomes practically impossible and simulation remains the only reasonable
analysis technique.

Due to the size of the reachability set in the case of 50 customers, an independent
replication method was used to obtain interval estimates with a 5% precision and a
confidence level of 99%. The results are reported in Table 14 where the confidence
interval of the simulation estimates is shown to cover the numerical results when the
size of the problem allowed the use of both evaluation methods. Table 14 reports also
an indication of the time needed to obtain the simulation estimates that shows that the
cost of simulation does not increase dramatically when the state space explodes making
the numerical solution impossible for both time and space complexity considerations.

7

GSPN REPRESENTATION OF PHASE-TYPE DISTRIBUTIONS

In this chapter we show how GSPN models can account for activities with generally distributed durations. An expansion of timed transitions by means of subnets that approximate the desired delay distributions is proposed with a simple example. The aim of this chapter is to show the possibility of accounting for general distributions without the need of special solution algorithms, while highlighting the subtleties that must be considered to avoid the construction of incorrect models. The technique allows a correct modelling of the race firing policies and outlines the importance of representing interruptions and preemptions of activities.

The example chosen to illustrate this possibility is a simple central server system in which the CPU can be interrupted by the arrival of higher priority tasks as well as by failures. The implications that these two types of phenomena may have on the work carried on by the CPU are discussed and proper modelling representations are developed to show the problems that may arise when non-exponential firing time distributions are considered.

7.1 The Central Server Model Example

The GSPN modelling formalism described in the first part of this book assumes that timed transitions have negative exponential firing time distributions. This choice was motivated by the desire of ensuring that the qualitative properties exhibited by the models when time considerations are ignored (untimed nets with priorities) remain valid also when time is explicitly considered in the models and by the simplicity of the underlying stochastic process. With these characteristics, GSPN models can be used for both validation and performance evaluation purposes.

Within this framework, the introduction of general firing time distributions must

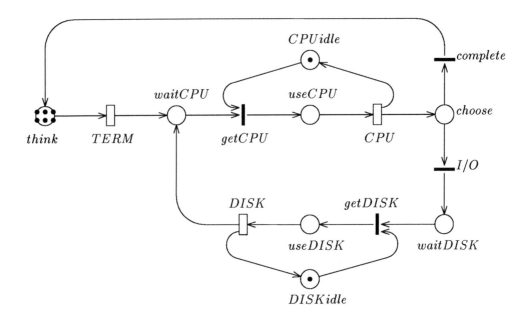

Figure 74   The GSPN system representing a Central Server Model

be performed without hampering the possibilities for a qualitative analysis of GSPN models, but, at the same time, accounting for the effects that different distributions may have on the performance evaluation aspects. This is in general very difficult with a direct representation of general firing time distributions at the level of the stochastic process underlying the GSPN model. The use of Markovian approximations allows instead the inclusion in GSPN models of general firing time distributions in a convenient manner.

The implications that timed transitions with non-exponential distributions have on the behaviour of GSPN models can be easily described by means of a simple example.

Consider the basic version of the classical *Central Server Model* depicted in Fig. 74 in which jobs are submitted by a set of terminals to a central system comprising a CPU and an I/O subsystem.

Assuming that all the timed transitions of the GSPN system behave according to an infinite server semantics (see Section 3.5), we can easily recognize that tokens in place *think* represent thinking customers that submit jobs to the CPU when transition *TERM* fires. A number of tokens may accumulate in place *waitCPU*. The first token entering this place finds the CPU idle and starts using it (a token is deposited in place *useCPU*); subsequent arriving tokens wait for their turn in place *waitCPU*. This

Table 15 Specification of the transitions of the Central Server Model of Fig. 74

transition	rate	semantics
TERM	0.1	infinite-server
CPU	1.0	infinite-server
DISK	0.8	infinite-server

transition	weight	priority	ECS
getCPU	1	1	1
getDISK	1	1	2
complete	1	1	3
I/O	9	1	3

Table 16 Initial marking of the Central Server Model of Fig. 74

place	initial marking
think	6
CPUidle	1
DISKidle	1

place represents the CPU queue that is served in *random order*. A job that completes its service (transition *CPU* fires) proceeds to a selection point where, with a certain probability, it decides to continue requesting service from the I/O subsystem; with a complementary probability, the job leaves the central system and the corresponding customer starts a new thinking period (immediate transition *complete* is chosen to fire). The disk representing the I/O subsystem is used in a single server manner and the *waitDISK* place represents the disk queue. No specific policy is specified for this queue and a random order is assumed to fit the purposes of the analysis as long as the actual discipline excludes preemption.

A structural analysis of this basic model shows that it is bounded and live, and that its initial marking is a home state. Using the algebraic techniques discussed in Chapter 2, three P-semiflow vectors can be identified ($PS_1 = think + waitCPU + useCPU + choose + waitDISK + useDISK$, $PS_2 = CPUidle + useCPU$, and $PS_3 = DISKidle + useDISK$). The first P-semiflow corresponds to the possibilities that customers have of moving throughout the net and it identifies the possible execution cycle of jobs; it generates a P-invariant with token count of 6 that proves the conservation of customers in the system. The second P-semiflow corresponds to the CPU cycle through idle and busy states. The third corresponds to the DISK cycle: the disk may also be either idle or busy. These last two P-semiflows generate two P-invariants with token count of 1. Since all the places of the GSPN are covered by P-semiflows, the net is structurally bounded: its reachability graph is finite and the corresponding Markov chain has a finite state space. Following again the algebraic techniques of Chapter 2, two T-semiflows are computed ($TS_1 = TERM + getCPU + CPU + complete$ and $TS_2 = getCPU + CPU + I/O + getDISK + DISK$) that include all the transitions of the GSPN model. The first T-semiflow corresponds to the sequence of transitions that bring the GSPN back to its initial marking without using the I/O. The second is a sequence of transitions that cannot be fired from the initial marking. However, the sum of the two T-semiflows yields a transition sequence that can be fired from the initial marking and that brings the GSPN back to such a marking. Finally, using the conditions discussed in Chapter 2, it is possible to identify three Extended Conflict Sets. Two of them are "degenerate" as they consist of one transition only (immediate transitions $getCPU$, and $getDISK$, respectively); the third is instead a proper ECS since it corresponds to the free-choice conflict between the immediate transitions *complete* and *I/O* and for which a set of weights must actually be defined.

Starting from this example, additional features of the system can be easily studied with the associated GSPN system considering, for instance, the possibility for the CPU to break down or to be interrupted by higher priority tasks.

7.1.1 CPU interruptions

Focusing our attention on the effect that these two phenomena may have on the customers using the Central Server System, we can represent these two different cases by adding a simple subnet that models the CPU interruption. Figure 75 represents the interruption cycle of a high priority external task. This task operates locally without any CPU need for a certain amount of time (token in place *noINT*) and occasionally requests the CPU when transition *INT* fires. The action of acquiring the CPU (token in place *grabCPU*) is performed by two mutually exclusive events implemented by immediate transitions *stopW* and *stopI* that reflect the fact that when the interruption occurs the CPU can either be working on regular jobs or idle. The state of the CPU prior to the interruption is recorded by alternatively marking places *stoppedW* and *stoppedI* to allow the situation to be re-established at the end of the interruption. The CPU remains busy while working on the high-priority task and then becomes again available when timed transition *CPUbusy* fires followed by the firing of one of the two immediate transitions *returnW* and *returnI*. In this model, the dynamics of the interrupting phenomena are represented in a very abstract manner by simply considering the frequency of the interruptions and the lengths of their effects on regular customers.

The modified Central Server Model in which CPU interruptions may take place at any point in time is obtained by merging places *CPUidle* and *useCPU* in the GSPNs

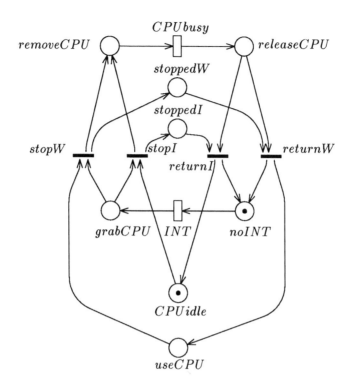

Figure 75   The GSPN representation of a CPU interruption cycle

of Figs. 74 and 75, obtaining the model of Fig. 76.

The structural analysis of this new GSPN system shows that all the places are covered by P-semiflows, so that the net is bounded. These semiflows can also be conveniently used to prove several properties of this GSPN system. The semiflow *useCPU + CPUidle + stoppedW + stoppedI* reveals that transitions *stopW* and *stopI* are mutually exclusive since, although they share a common input place (place *grabCPU*), they cannot be simultaneously enabled due to the fact that the token count of the semiflow is one, and only one of the two places *CPUidle* and *useCPU* can be marked at any given time. A similar argument (and in particular the same P-semiflow) can be used to show that also transitions *returnW* and *returnI* are mutually exclusive. Finally, through the combined use of the semiflows *useCPU + CPUidle + stoppedW + stoppedI, useCPU + CPUidle + removeCPU + releaseCPU* and *noINT + grabCPU + removeCPU + releaseCPU* it can be proved that once transition *INT* fires the token originally put in place *noINT* inevitably returns in this same place. Indeed, if place *grabCPU* is marked with one token, then another token must be in

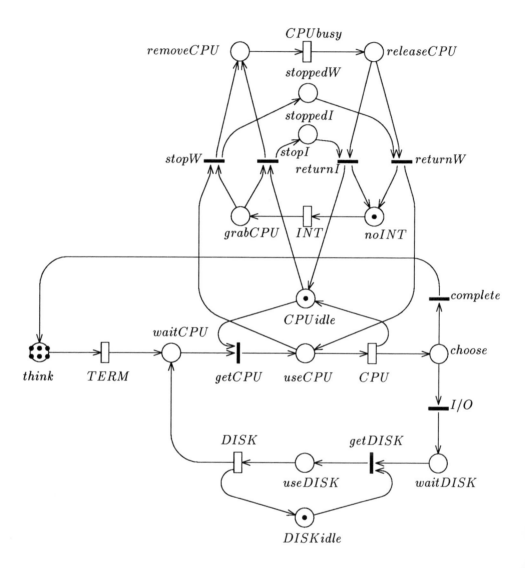

Figure 76   The GSPN system representing a Central Server Model with CPU
interruptions

either *CPUidle* or *useCPU*; when one token is put in place *removeCPU* another
token is eventually deposited in place *releaseCPU*; finally if place *releaseCPU* is
marked then necessarily a token is present in either *stoppedW* or *stoppedI*.

The computation of the ECSs that are needed for the correct specification of the
immediate transition weights identifies the following pairs of immediate transitions:

Table 17 Specification of the transitions of the Central Server Model of Fig. 76

transition	rate	semantics
TERM	0.1	infinite-server
CPU	1.0	infinite-server
DISK	0.8	infinite-server
INT	1.0	infinite-server
CPUbusy	1.0	infinite-server

transition	weight	priority	ECS
getCPU	1	1	1
stopI	1	1	1
getDISK	1	1	2
complete	1	1	3
I/O	9	1	3
stopW	1	1	4
returnW	1	1	5
returnI	1	1	6

Table 18 Initial marking of the Central Server Model of Fig. 76

place	initial marking
think	6
CPUidle	1
DISKidle	1
noINT	1

(*complete*, *I/O*) and (*getCPU*, *stopI*). Transitions *getCPU* and *stopI* are obviously in conflict since they share *CPUidle* as an input place. Also transitions *stopI* and *stopW* share an input place (place *grabCPU*), but they are not part of the same ECS since they are mutually exclusive, as we already observed before, due to the token count of the P-invariant *useCPU* + *CPUidle* + *removeCPU* + *releaseCPU*. This property is identified by the *MME* condition (see Section 2.5.2) and is used to properly define the ECSs of the GSPN system. A further analysis of the way the interruption subnet works allows us to notice that the weights associated with transitions *getCPU* and *stopI* are actually inessential for the evolution of the GSPN. Indeed, assume that both transitions are enabled and thus that a token is present in place *CPUidle*. It is easy to show that this token will be removed from the place and that another token will eventually appear in place *removeCPU* independently of the weights associated with the conflicting transitions *getCPU* and *stopI*. If *stopI* wins the race against *getCPU* a token is immediately deposited in place *removeCPU*; if however the race is won by transition *getCPU*, one token is first deposited in place *useCPU*, but at this point transition *stopW* becomes enabled, which yields again a token in place *removeCPU*, leaving both places *useCPU* and *grabCPU* empty.

A complete structural analysis of the GSPN system of Fig. 76 allows an informal demonstration that the model correctly represents the system we intend to study. The same structural analysis can also be used to observe that when place *stoppedW* is marked, place *stoppedI* is not, and vice-versa. It thus follows that one of these two places can be removed from the net and that its effect can be reproduced by the introduction of an inhibitor arc. The GSPN system of Fig. 77 is equivalent to that of Fig. 76 with the advantage of a simpler graphical representation.

7.1.2 CPU memory policies

When an interrupt occurs while the CPU is in use, different possibilities must be considered with respect to the amount of work already performed for the interrupted job before the interruption occurred. On the one hand it may be reasonable to assume that if the interruption is due to a higher priority task that needs immediate attention, the work already performed for the interrupted job should not be lost; on the other hand, if the interruption corresponds to a CPU failure, it is likely that the work performed before the interruption is lost and that the interrupted job should start anew when the CPU becomes available again after its repair. The subnet added to the original Central Server Model and depicted in Fig. 76 can be interpreted according to both the phenomena that we want to model, while the specification of the way of treating interrupted work must be added as an "attribute" to transition *CPU* specifying whether it behaves according to an age or an enabling memory policy, respectively (see Section 3.4 for a discussion of this topic).

When the firing time distributions are negative exponential, the distinction between the two policies is inessential, due to the memoryless property of the distribution (see Chapter 6) and the model of Fig. 76 can be used to study both phenomena without the need for any additional specification [1]. When instead the firing time distributions are not negative exponential, considerable differences exist between the two cases.

The objective of the methodology discussed in this chapter is to allow treating these cases with GSPN models. In the next section, we will show how predefined subnets can replace the exponential transitions taking automatically into account all the details that need to be considered for the correct implementation of the different types of distributions and of memory policies.

---

[1] This is indeed the case, provided that we don't need to implement a preemptive-repeat-identical execution policy

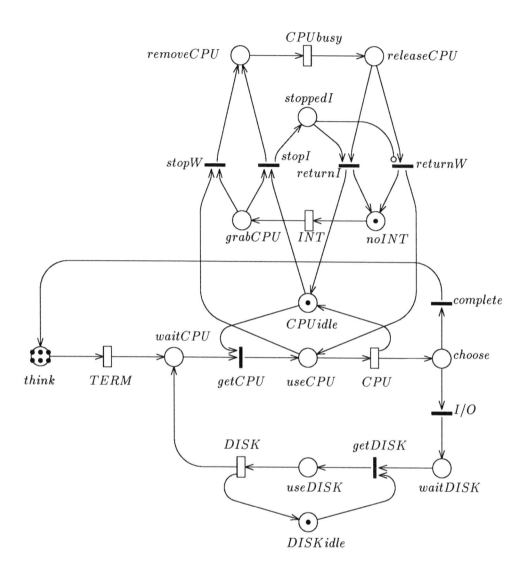

Figure 77   Alternative GSPN representation of a Central Server Model with CPU
interruptions

7.2   Phase-Type Distributions

The possibility of including timed transitions with general firing time distributions in
GSPN models is provided by the phase expansion [Neu81] that allows the behaviour
of a random variable with general distribution to be approximated by means of a
combination of negative exponential random variables with appropriate parameters.

These distributions are called *Phase-Type* (*PH*) distributions. This means that an activity that lasts for a generally distributed random amount of time can be modelled by breaking it down into a set of stages (phases), all lasting for exponentially distributed periods of time. Considering that the state of an activity represented by an exponentially distributed random variable is completely captured by the indication that the activity is under way, because of the memoryless property of this distribution (see Appendix A), in the case of the phase expansion, the same state is characterized by the additional indication of the index of the stage that is currently active. As a consequence, a multidimensional CTMC can be used to describe the evolution of any activity represented with *PH* distributions, and an overall CTMC (albeit more complex) can still be recognized as the probabilistic model underlying SPNs and GSPNs including timed transitions with *PH* distributed firing times.

A complete treatment of how to include *PH* distributions in GSPN models can be found in [Cum85, AMBB+89, CBB89]. In [Cum85] the expansion is performed at the CTMC level with the use of an algorithm that maps the reachability graph of the GSPN into the expanded state space of the CTMC. With this approach, the timed transitions of the GSPN model are annotated with attributes that specify the characteristics of their distributions and of their memory policies. These attributes are used by the expansion algorithm to obtain the desired extended CTMC. In [CBB89] a methodology is proposed to perform the expansion at the net level. With this approach, timed transitions with PH distributions and with specified memory policies are substituted by proper subnets. After the substitution takes place, the resulting model is a standard (but expanded) GSPN that can be analyzed with usual techniques. In this book we consider only this second method and we limit our discussion to simply highlighting the fundamental aspects of the problem by using our example. For this purpose we assume that the CPU service time for the customers of the Central Server System has one of the simplest possible *PH* distributions, namely an Erlang-3. The discussion of this simple example will be sufficient to illustrate a technique that can be applied to embed into GSPN models any *PH* distribution.

7.2.1 Erlang distributions

Erlang distributions correspond to series of exponential stages all with the same mean. A random variable x with Erlang-k distribution can be interpreted as a sum of k independent and identically distributed random variables. Each of these components has a negative exponential distribution with parameter $k\mu$. Under this assumption, the expected value of the Erlang-k variable is $E[x] = 1/\mu$ and its variance is $VAR[x] = 1/(k\mu^2)$. Timed transitions with Erlang firing time distributions can be easily specified with GSPN models in which each stage is represented by an

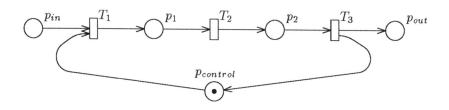

Figure 78   The GSPN representation of an Erlang-3 server

exponentially timed transition. As usual, the single-server policy can be enforced by using a control place to insure that at most one stage is active at any given time. Considering as an example an Erlang distribution with three exponential stages, Fig. 78 depicts one of the possible GSPN representations of such a distribution in which transitions T_1, T_2, and T_3 implement the three exponential stages and have all the same firing rate.

This straightforward representation of an Erlang distribution is, however, not suited for conflicting timed transitions in which the race policy requires the firing action to be instantaneous after a generally distributed amount of time is elapsed. Consider for instance the GSPN system of Fig. 79 in which a token in place p_{in} enables two conflicting transitions. The observation that the "horizontal" subnet provides an Erlang-3 delay could lead to the superficial impression that this is a correct implementation of a conflict between a transition with negative exponential firing time distribution (transition T_4) and a subnet representing an activity with an Erlang-3 distribution. The model of Fig. 79 instead solves the conflict by making transition T_1 race against transition T_4. In this way only the first stage of the Erlang distribution takes part in the race that is won by the whole subnet whenever transition T_1 fires before transition T_4, thus removing the token from place p_{in}.

In order to overcome this problem, an alternative representation of PH distributions was proposed in [CBB89]. According to this proposal, the subnet corresponding to the PH distribution comprises an input place that, upon the enabling of the subnet, is kept marked until the completion of the last stage of the distribution. For the case of the Erlang-3 distribution considered in Fig. 78, the new GSPN representation is depicted in Fig. 80.

When place p_{in} becomes marked and the whole subnet is idle (place $p_{control}$ is marked), two tokens[2] are immediately deposited in place p_1 and the first delay stage starts; at the same time the token in place $p_{control}$ is withdrawn to signal that the

---

[2] The multiplicity of the arcs between t_1 and p_1, and between p_3 and T_3, depends on the degree of the Erlang distribution that is being modelled; Erlang-k distributions require a $k - 1$ multiplicity.

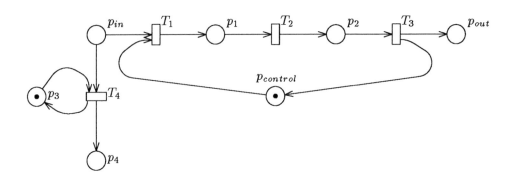

Figure 79   The GSPN model of a conflict between Erlang-3 and exponential servers

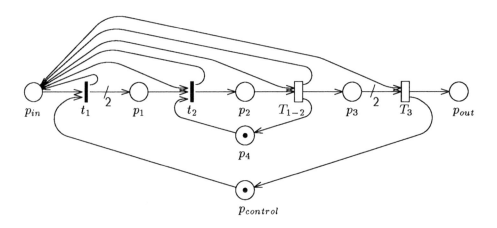

Figure 80   The interruptible GSPN model of an Erlang-3 server

subnet is busy and a token is put back in place p_{in} to mean that the original request (arrival of a token in place p_{in}) is undergoing service, but has not been completed yet. At the same time, the first delay stage starts with the firing of t_2, but no token is removed from place p_{in}. The control place p_4 is introduced to ensure a single-server semantics for timed transition T_{1-2}. Transition T_{1-2} plays the role of transitions T_1 and T_2 in the net of Fig. 78 and is fired twice to implement the first two stages of the Erlang-3 distribution. When two tokens are finally accumulated in place p_3, timed transition T_3 becomes enabled and its firing corresponds to the end of the overall delay that indeed lasted for three exponential stages. Only when transition T_3 fires, the token deposited in p_{in} is removed to mean that the whole subnet completed its

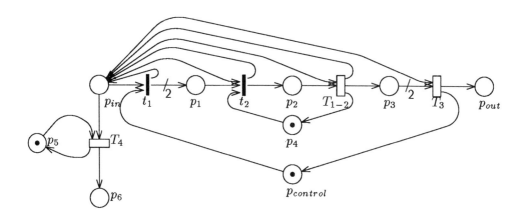

Figure 81   Age memory conflict

evolution. In this case a conflict arising because of a race between (macro-)transitions with Erlang type distributions would be decided only on the basis of which of the transitions actually completed its work (fired) first.

The computation of the P- and T- semiflows for the GSPN systems of Figs. 78 and 80 (with the Input/Output places connected with an immediate transition) allows the equivalence of the two representations to be established in a formal manner. In particular, looking at the T-semiflows of the two nets we can notice that for the subnets to transfer a token from the input place (place p_{in}) to the output place (place p_{out}) the firing of three timed transitions is needed in both cases. Moreover, the use of the semiflows shows that a token deposited in place p_{in} of the subnet of Fig. 80 is eventually withdrawn, leaving the net in its original (idle) state.

As we briefly discussed at the beginning of this section, the type of memory policy needs to be specified in the case of generally distributed firing times because of different possible attitudes with respect to the work performed before an interruption.

The Erlang-3 representation of Fig. 80 corresponds to the specification of an *age memory* policy (see Chapter 3) since the tokens representing the stages that are still to be executed before completion are unaffected by the interruption. When the subnet is enabled again in the future the firing delay will account only for the stages of service not executed yet. This can be easily seen by examining Fig. 81 where the Erlang-3 subnet is in conflict with the exponential transitions T_4. Assuming that place p_{in} is marked, the firing of transition T_4 disables the Erlang-3 subnet that keeps memory of its internal state and that will restart from it when a new token is later deposited in place p_{in}. Indeed, the firing of T_4 removes the token from place p_{in} disabling the

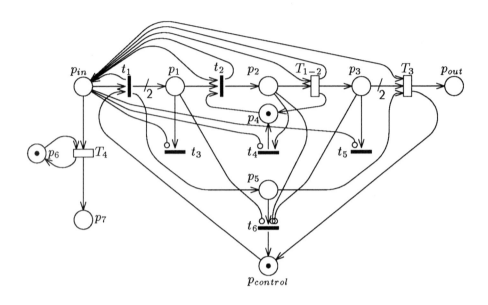

Figure 82   Enabling memory conflict

transition of the Erlang subnet that is currently enabled. The internal state of the subnet is represented by the marking of places p_1, p_2, and p_3 which make sure that the work of the transition starts from where it was interrupted at the exact moment of the arrival of a new token in place p_{in}.

If we want instead to represent an enabling memory policy, the subnet must be reset by any interruption. This means that the subnet must lose track of the stages of service completed before the interruption. To achieve this, we must modify the internal structure of the subnet as depicted in Fig. 82.

In this case, removing a token from p_{in} (because of the firing of T_4) when $p_{control}$ is not marked, causes those places that are non-empty among p_1, p_2, and p_3 to be cleared from tokens, thus returning the subnet to its initial "idle" state. Places p_1, p_2, and p_3 may contain several tokens because of the multiplicity of the output arc of transition t_1. The clearing of these places is accomplished in two steps and with the help of place p_5 that signals the condition "the firing of the subnet is in progress" (place p_5 is marked upon firing of transition t_1 and is returned empty either on completion – firing of T_3 – or at the end of the clearing action we are discussing). As soon as place p_{in} becomes empty, immediate transitions t_3, t_4, and t_5 fire as many times as is needed to remove all the tokens that may be found in these three places. At the end of this first step, places p_4 and p_5 are marked with one token each. The return to the initial state is finally performed by transition t_6 that puts one token in place $p_{control}$, making sure that this action takes place only after places p_1, p_2, and p_3 are empty using inhibitor arcs. The part of the GSPN system that we have just described appears cumbersome, but has the advantage of confining within the subnet itself the entire "mechanism" that is needed to lose memory of the work performed before the interruption. To make sure that these actions take place in the proper sequence, different priority levels may also be assigned to transitions t_3, t_4, t_5, and t_6. In particular, transitions t_3, t_4, and t_5 may be defined of priority level 3 and transition t_6 of priority level 2.

The Erlang-3 representations of Figs. 80 and 82 share the important features of being of the *one-input/one-output* type and of having the specifications of the race memory policies completely "self-contained". This makes possible the definition of a reduction/expansion rule that allows the automatic interchanging of simple timed transitions with more complex subnets that represent their internal expansions and vice versa. Indeed, the two Erlang-3 representations of Figs. 80 and 82 can be easily included in the Central Server Model of Fig. 76 to replace transition CPU, yielding the GSPN systems of Figs. 83 and 84, respectively. In both cases, a structural analysis of the resulting GSPN systems shows that immediate transitions $stopW$, t_1, and t_2 belong to the same ECS. Although not very likely, the possibilities for these three transitions to be in apparent conflict exist and corresponding weights must be assigned during the specification of the model. In practice, any assignment of weights to these transitions works, since transitions t_1 and t_2 are mutually exclusive due to the presence of only one token in place $p_{control}$ and since transitions t_1 and t_2 only test the presence of tokens in place $useCPU$ so that their firings do not disable transition $stopW$ when place $grabCPU$ is marked.

The GSPN systems of Figs. 76, 83, and 84 can now be considered as different representations of the same problem that can be used for different purposes: the original GSPN system of Fig. 76 can be used for a qualitative analysis of the problem as it hides the complexity of the firing time distribution of the timed transition CPU as well as of its associated memory policy, which do not affect the qualitative properties of the model. At the moment of the performance analysis, the three models can then be used to study the effects that the time specifications may have on the efficiency of the system.

7.2.2 Numerical evaluation

The importance of the higher moments of certain firing time distributions and of the firing memory policies is shown experimentally by comparing the results of the evaluation of the GSPN models in Figs. 76, 83, and 84.

Tables 21 and 22 contain the parameters of the model of Fig. 84 that can be used

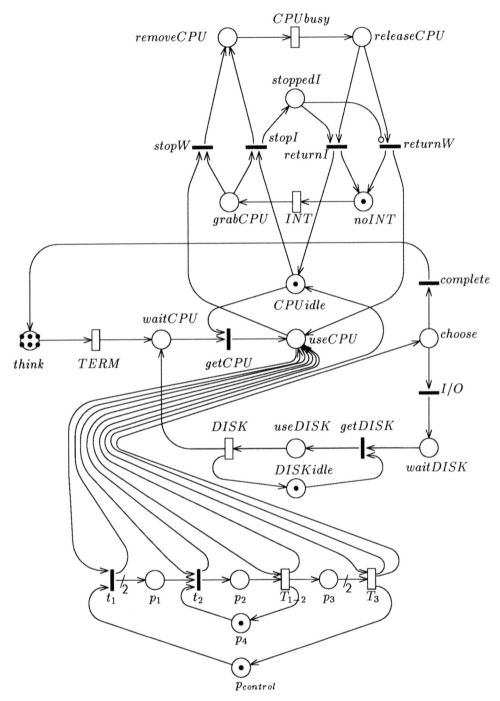

Figure 83   The GSPN representation of a Central Server Model with CPU interruptions and with an Erlang-3 service time distribution of regular customers with Age Memory policy

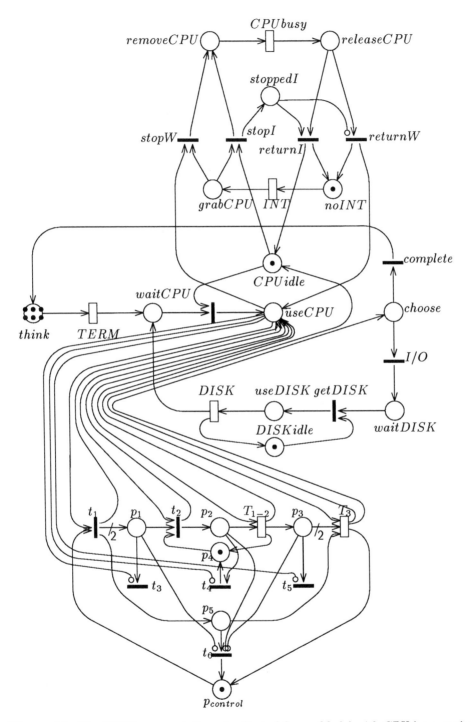

Figure 84   The GSPN representation of a Central Server Model with CPU interruptions and with an Erlang-3 service time distribution of regular customers with Enabling Memory policy

Table 19   Specification of the transitions of the Central Server Model of Fig. 83

transition	rate	semantics
$TERM$	0.1	infinite-server
T_{1-2}	3.0	infinite-server
T_3	3.0	infinite-server
$DISK$	0.8	infinite-server
INT	1.0	infinite-server
$CPUbusy$	1.0	infinite-server

transition	weight	priority	ECS
$getCPU$	1	1	1
$stopI$	1	1	1
$getDISK$	1	1	2
$complete$	1	1	3
I/O	9	1	3
$returnW$	1	1	4
$returnI$	1	1	5
$stopW$	1	1	6
t_1	1	1	6
t_2	1	1	6

Table 20   Initial marking of the Central Server Model of Fig. 83

place	initial marking
$think$	6
$CPUidle$	1
$DISKidle$	1
$noINT$	1
p_4	1
$p_{control}$	1

for the evaluation of the three models. All these models have the same mean firing delay for each CPU service. The difference is that in the model of Fig. 76 the second moment of the CPU service time is neglected, thus reducing the representation of the firing time to an exponential distribution. The models of Figs. 83 and 84 account instead for the second moment of the distribution. They differ because in Fig. 83 an age memory policy is assumed, while in the other case the memory policy is of the enabling type.

Table 23 reports some performance measures obtained from the evaluation of these models. The results focus on the effects that the different modelling assumptions have on the performance of the system as seen from the regular customers. The system throughput and response time computed with respect to place *think*, represent the

Table 21 Specification of the transitions of the Central Server Model of Fig. 84

transition	rate	semantics
$TERM$	0.1	infinite-server
T_{1-2}	3.0	infinite-server
T_3	3.0	infinite-server
$DISK$	0.8	infinite-server
INT	1.0	infinite-server
$CPUbusy$	1.0	infinite-server

transition	weight	priority	ECS
$getCPU$	1	1	1
$stopI$	1	1	1
$getDISK$	1	1	2
$complete$	1	1	3
I/O	9	1	3
$returnW$	1	1	4
$returnI$	1	1	5
$stopW$	1	1	6
t_1	1	1	6
t_2	1	1	6
t_3	1	3	7
t_4	1	3	8
t_5	1	3	9
t_6	1	2	10

Table 22 Initial marking of the Central Server Model of Fig. 84

place	initial marking
$think$	6
$CPUidle$	1
$DISKidle$	1
$noINT$	1
p_4	1
$p_{control}$	1

quantities that summarize the behaviour of the system as seen from the customers. The CPU utilization can instead be seen as an indication of system resource exploitation that is of some interest for a possible system manager. The numerical results show that the model with the negative exponential distribution provides performances that are bracketed by those of the other two models, the age memory being the policy that provides the best performance. It is interesting to observe that replacing in this model the exponential distribution of the CPU firing time with an Erlang-3 with

Table 23   Performance figures for the Central Server Models of Figs. 76, 83, and 84

CPU service time distribution	System throughput	System resp. time	CPU utilization
Erlang-3 with Age Memory	0.049082	112.2444	0.99874
Negative Exponential	0.047969	115.0805	0.97961
Erlang-3 with Enabling Memory	0.036253	155.4944	0.99670

age memory has only a marginal effect on the performance of the system (less than 2.5% improvement of the system throughput), while the assumption of an Erlang-3 distribution with enabling memory yields a considerable loss of performance from the point of view of the regular customers (about 25% decrease in system throughput). The fact that the CPU utilization increases when the Erlang-3 distribution is specified in the model can be explained by observing that in the case of the age memory policy the system is more efficient and an increase in throughput corresponds to a better system exploitation. In the case of the enabling memory policy, the increase in CPU utilization does not correspond to an improvement of the efficiency of the system because of the amount of work that is lost due to the interruptions.

This shows that in many situations the possibility of specifying timed transitions with non-exponential firing time distributions can be important and that confining the impact of this specification at the solution level is essential to keep under control the complexity of the analysis techniques used to study these models.

7.3   General Phase-Type Distributions

The basic idea used for developing a convenient representation of Erlang-r firing time distributions is exploited in [CBB89] to construct subnets whose passage times have general *PH* distributions still showing the property of being easy to embed in standard GSPN models with the same type of substitution rules sketched for the Erlang-3 distribution. In particular, all the expansions reported in [CBB89] present the important characteristic of being of the one-in/one-out type and of having a compact structure capable of accommodating distributions of the same type, but with different parameters within the same GSPN layout. This compact representation is especially important to allow the implementation of the memory policies in a self-contained manner.

With the use of this technique it is conceivable to devise algorithms that automatically perform the substitution of a standard timed transition with negative exponential firing time distribution, with a subnet implementing a general PH distribution, producing a detailed version of the model that is used for performance analysis, but is completely transparent to the user. In this way, the analyst could be relieved from the burden of understanding the meaning of the many arcs that must be added to implement the memory policies and could concentrate on the more important tasks of capturing the relevant feature of the system with the model and of interpreting the exact meanings of the results of the analysis.

8

MODELLING FLEXIBLE MANUFACTURING SYSTEMS

In this chapter we show that GSPNs represent a versatile tool for the modular construction of models that capture the most important features of the behaviour of Flexible Manufacturing Systems (FMSs).

In the last thirty years FMSs have emerged as a new strategic technology able to cope with the rapid changes in the market demand. In the design and construction of FMSs, a performance evaluation of the system is required at two different stages of development.

- At the beginning of the design of the system, when the machines, the layout, and the transport system are chosen and dimensioned. At this stage the performance estimates need not be particularly accurate; usually only the order of magnitude of the parameters of the system is known in this initial phase, and crudely approximated analytical methods are used.
- During the tuning phase of the system, when most of the parameters (the machines, the layout, etc.) have already been chosen, and only minor changes in the system (e.g. the size of buffers, or production mixes) can be introduced to optimize the overall throughput or the machine utilizations. For this purpose, an accurate performance evaluation of the system is required, usually obtained by developing complex simulation models.

In this chapter we will primarily address the first type of problem.

In Section 8.1 we give a very brief introduction to FMSs; for further details on automated manufacturing systems and related performance issues the reader may refer to [VN92]. In Sections 8.2 and 8.3 two FMS systems are modelled and analysed by means of GSPNs.

8.1 Flexible Manufacturing Systems

A Manufacturing System is a production system where (discrete) parts are machined and/or assembled. The oldest production system organization is the *production line*. It was optimized for mass production and was based on the synchronous operation of machines/workers performing repetitive tasks onto parts transported by a conveyor. Obviously this system can work only if the processing to be performed can be decomposed into a set of operations of identical duration.

A more flexible organization is the *flow shop*, where parts may by-pass some of the machines/workers on the conveyor path. This system allows the production of a family of slightly different products.

In the *job shop* organization, the production line doesn't exist any more. For each different kind of product a *working schedule* is defined, specifying the sequence (or alternative sequences) of machines the parts have to visit to complete their processing. The sequence of machines is not restricted by the physical layout of the machines. This organization is very flexible and allows the production of very different families of products, hence it easily adapts to changes in the market demand. The operation of this type of system is necessarily asynchronous; as a consequence, the machine utilization can be high only at the price of a very large in-process inventory, or using sophisticated machine scheduling algorithms.

FMSs were introduced as a trade-off between the efficiency of old production lines and the flexibility of job shop organizations. An FMS consists of a set of flexible machines, an automatic transport system, storage facilities, and a scheduling system capable of deciding at runtime which operation has to be done on each machine. The scheduling system must be able to deal with machine failures; it has the objective of maximizing machine utilizations and of meeting the production deadlines taking into account the limits of storage facilities. Usually, parts need to be loaded onto supports called *pallets* to be transported within the production system.

Due to the complexity of FMSs, scheduling decisions are distributed, and global coordination is achieved by communicating the local decisions upwards in a hierarchy of control levels. At a local level, scheduling rules implement one among several possible *inventory management strategies*. The *push* and *pull* inventory management strategies are based on two opposite ideas. In the *push* control an operation is started every time raw material is available and a machine is idle. When several operations may be performed at a given time, decisions are made based on priority and required production mixes. This approach leads to a production schedule that is driven by the *Material Requirement Planning*. Of course the Material Requirement Planning should be guided by some guess on the future demand; however, this may end up in large in-process inventories in case of an error in the demand forecast.

The *pull* strategies, on the contrary, are driven by the demand: every time the in-process inventory is lower than a given threshold, a request for new products is issued to the machine that feeds the inventory. This strategy gives good response time only if in-process inventory is large enough.

The *Just-In-Time* strategy belongs to the class of pull strategies, and has the additional constraint of keeping the in-process inventory as small as possible.

In [SV89] and [VN92] these and other aspects of FMSs are described, and several applications of PN theory in this framework are highlighted. In the following sections two examples will be developed that show how it is possible to model and analyse FMSs using GSPNs.

8.2 A Kanban System

The first example system we are going to consider is the so-called *Kanban*. The *Kanban* philosophy originated in Japanese industry; it is based on the *Just-In-Time* (JIT) control method. Kanban systems are a special kind of pull production systems designed to minimize the size as well as the fluctuation of in-process inventory. *Kanban* is the Japanese word for *card*: the flow of cards controls the flow of items in the production line. A *Kanban* system is a linear system of production cells; the demand for finished parts from a cell depends exclusively on the needs of the next cell that are communicated through cards posted on a bulletin board. As a result, each cell produces its parts *just-in-time* to meet the demand of succeeding cells, hence it is the final product demand that ultimately controls the system behaviour.

In Fig. 85 a block diagram model of a sequential Kanban system with a single type of cards is depicted. Each cell has a fixed number of cards (not necessarily the same number in each cell) that are initially posted in the bulletin board. Parts can be stored in the input and output buffers of each cell; every part has to be associated with a card from the pool of cards of that cell; hence at any time each cell contains at most as many parts as the number of cards it owns. If cell i has a finished part in its *output buffer* (observe that the part has to have an attached card k_i belonging to the pool of cards of cell i), and a card k_{i+1} is posted in the bulletin board of cell $i + 1$, then the part is transferred to the input buffer of cell $i + 1$ labelled with the card k_{i+1} while card k_i is detached from the part and posted in the bulletin board of cell i. A part in the input buffer of cell i is processed as soon as the machine is available, and is deposited in the output buffer when the processing is completed.

A simple GSPN model of cell i is depicted in Fig. 86; the same model was presented in [BF89, LBR89]. Tokens in place BB_i represent cards posted in the bulletin board. Places IB_i and OB_i represent the input and output buffers, respectively. A token in

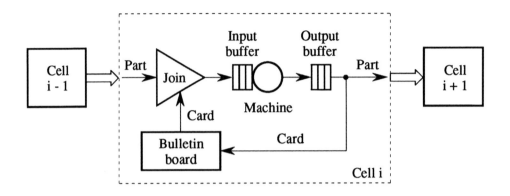

Figure 85   A Kanban cell and the parts and cards that flow into and out of it

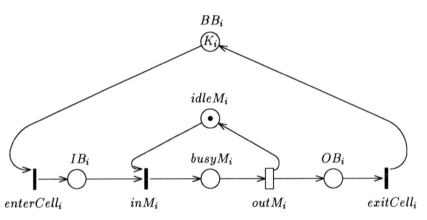

Figure 86   GSPN model of a single Kanban cell

place $idleM_i$ represents the condition "machine M_i is idle", while a token in place $busyM_i$ represents the condition "machine M_i is busy". The transitions represent the possible events that can cause the movement of parts and/or cards in the cell. An n-cell Kanban system is obtained by composing n such submodels by simply merging transition $exitCell_i$ and $enterCell_{i+1}$ as shown in Fig. 87. In the GSPN model of Fig. 87, an unlimited source of raw parts and an unlimited sink for finished products is implicitly assumed. For this reason places BB_1 and OB_n are never marked in any tangible marking.

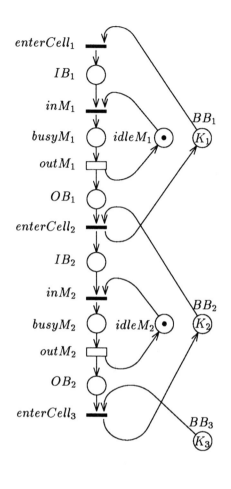

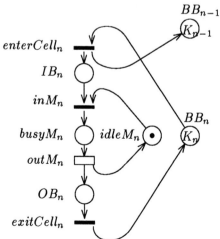

Figure 87   GSPN model of an n-cell sequential Kanban system

8.2.1 Structural analysis of the GSPN model of the Kanban system

In this section we show how structural analysis methods can be used to check whether the GSPN model correctly represents the studied system and whether the system behaviour is correct.

Structural analysis allows us to conclude that the GSPN model in Fig. 87 is bounded, since it is covered by P-semiflows.

The n-cell Kanban model of Fig. 87 has $2n$ minimal P-semiflows, whose associated P-invariants are:

$$\forall i, 1 \leq i \leq n:$$
$$M(BB_i) \quad + \quad M(IB_i) \quad + \quad M(busyM_i) \quad + \quad M(OB_i) \quad = \quad K_i$$
$$M(idleM_i) \quad + \quad M(busyM_i) \quad = 1$$

The former kind of P-invariant ensures that the number of parts in cell i is at most K_i, the number of cards in the cell; the latter instead ensures that each machine can process only one part at a time, and that places $idleM_i$ and $busyM_i$ are mutually exclusive, consistently with their intended interpretation.

All the transitions of the GSPN model are covered by a unique minimal T-semiflow. It represents the deterministic flow of the unique type of parts processed by the system. Observe that the net behaviour is deterministic: indeed, no structural conflicts exist, hence effective conflicts can never arise. Since confusion is a situation related to conflict resolution, this net is surely confusion-free.

Using P-invariants it is easy to prove that the GSPN model is live. Let us consider the model of cell i in isolation: it is trivial to show that due to the P-invariant

$$M(BB_i) \; + \; M(IB_i) \; + \; M(busyM_i) \; + \; M(OB_i) \; = \; K_i$$

at least one of the four transitions is enabled. Using the net structure it is possible to show that from any marking where at least one transition is enabled, markings in which any other transition in the cell model is enabled can be eventually reached.

When the cells are connected, however, we have to take into account some additional constraint. The transitions of the subnet representing cell i might all be disabled because $busyM_i$ is empty, IB_i is empty, and either BB_i contains some token, but OB_{i-1} is empty, or OB_i contains some token, but BB_{i+1} is empty.

If cell i is blocked because K_i tokens are in place BB_i but OB_{i-1} is empty, it is easy to see that OB_{i-1} will eventually receive a token so that $enterCell_i$ will become enabled (and hence also transitions inM_i and $outM_i$ will eventually become enabled). This can be proved by induction, showing that if OB_j is marked (for some $j : 1 \leq j < i-1$) then OB_{j+1} will eventually receive a token. Indeed, due to the P-invariant above, if OB_{j+1} is empty, then K_{j+1} tokens must be distributed into places BB_{j+1}, IB_{j+1} and $busyM_{j+1}$; since by hypothesis OB_j is marked, at least one token can eventually flow from any of the three places listed before, to place OB_{j+1}. Moreover, it is always possible to reach a marking in which OB_1 is marked due to the fact that transition $enterCell_1$ can fire as soon as BB_1 contains at least one token (the reader may easily convince him/herself that this statement is true by playing the token game on the GSPN model).

Hence, from a marking in which BB_i is marked, $\forall k : j < k \leq i-1, OB_k$ are empty and OB_j is not empty, it is eventually possible to reach a marking in which OB_{j+1} is marked; from here it is possible to reach a marking in which OB_{j+2} is marked, and so on until a marking is reached in which OB_{i-1} is marked, so that transition $enterCell_i$ may fire.

If the subnet of cell i is blocked because K_i tokens are in OB_i but BB_{i+1} is empty, then it is possible to show that transition $enterCell_{i+1}$ will eventually become enabled. In fact, it is easy to verify that if BB_{j+1} is marked (for some $j : i < j \leq n$) and BB_j is empty, then BB_j will eventually receive a token. Moreover, from a marking in which BB_n is empty, it is always possible to reach a marking in which BB_n is marked due to the fact that transition $exitCell_n$ can fire as soon as OB_n contains at least one token. Hence from a marking in which OB_i is marked, $\forall k : i+1 \leq k < j, BB_k$ are empty and BB_j is not empty, it is possible to reach a marking in which BB_{j-1} is marked. From here it is possible to reach a marking in which BB_{j-2} is marked, and so on, until a marking is reached in which BB_{i+1} is marked, so that transition $enterCell_{i+1}$ may fire.

8.2.2 Performance analysis of the Kanban system

In this section we summarize the results of the extensive performance evaluation study of a Kanban model presented in [LBR89]. The experiments have the objective of studying the performance and fault tolerance of a Kanban system with five cells. The studied system is highly homogeneous: all the cells have the same machining time (the rate of transitions $outM_i$ is 4.0) and the same number of cards K. A first set of experiments was performed to compute the average inventory of the input and output buffers of each cell (average number of tokens in places IB_i and OB_i). The results are summarized in Table 24. Observe that while the input inventory is fairly constant, the output inventory decreases as the cell position increases.

In a second set of experiments the system throughput (firing rate of transition $exitCell_5$) was computed as a function of the number of cards in the two cases of a fault free and a failure prone system. The fault tolerance was studied on two models: the former model represents a system in which all cells can fail, the latter represents a system in which only one out of five cells can fail.

The GSPN model in Fig. 88 represents a failure prone cell. The only difference with

Table 24   Input and output inventory in the cells of a Kanban system as a function of the number of cards

	Input buffer inventory			Output buffer inventory		
Cell	1 Card	2 Cards	3 Cards	1 Card	2 Cards	3 Cards
1	0.486	1.041	1.474	0.514	0.958	1.526
2	0.486	1.040	1.470	0.383	0.713	1.131
3	0.486	1.047	1.478	0.282	0.524	0.811
4	0.486	1.056	1.490	0.170	0.316	0.472
5	0.486	1.073	1.515	0.000	0.000	0.000

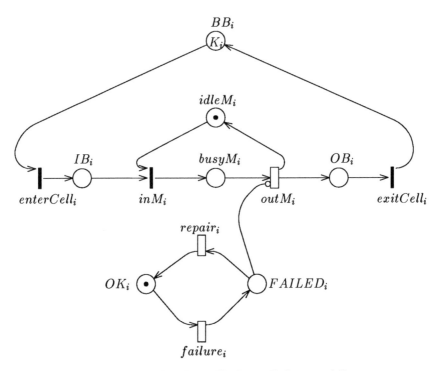

Figure 88   Model of a Kanban cell that can fail

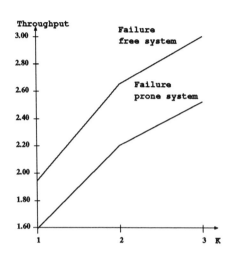

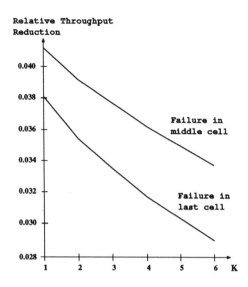

Figure 89 Throughput comparison between a failure free system and a system in which all cells can fail, as a function of the number of cards

Figure 90 Throughput comparison between a middle failing cell and a final failing cell (percentage reduction), as a function of the number of cards

respect to the model in Fig. 86 is the presence of the extra subnet composed of two places OK_i and $FAILED_i$ representing respectively the condition "cell i is working" and "cell i is out of order", and two transitions $failure_i$ and $repair_i$ representing the occurrence of a failure and the completion of a repair, respectively. The inhibitor arc from place $FAILED_i$ to transition inM_i has the effect of interrupting the service upon the occurrence of a failure.

The performance of the system is characterized by its throughput, which can be computed as the throughput of transition $exitCell_5$. In Fig. 89 the performance of the system without failure is compared to that computed when all cells can fail (the cells fail independently; the failure rate of each cell is 0.02, while the repair rate is 0.4).

The results of Table 24 show that even in a perfectly balanced Kanban system the cell performance is position-dependent. Hence, the influence of a single failure on the system performance depends on the failed cell position. This phenomenon was studied by comparing the throughput of a system in which only the middle cell can fail, against that of a system in which only the final cell can fail. The results are plotted in Fig. 90: observe that a failure in the last cell has a less severe impact on the throughput, with respect to a failure in the middle cell.

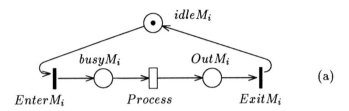

(a)

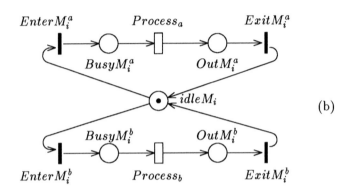

(b)

Figure 91   GSPN models of machines

8.3   Push Production Systems

The second system we are going to model is a *push* production system. It comprises a Load/Unload (*LU*) station, used to mount raw parts on "pallets" and unload finished parts from them, and three machines (M_1, M_2 and M_3) that are used to process two different kinds of parts. We consider two alternative transportation systems: the first one is a *continuous transportation system* (i.e., a conveyor) while the second is an Automated Guided Vehicle (AGV). Machines that process only one type of part are modelled as shown in Fig. 91(a) while machines that process two different types of parts are modelled as shown in Fig. 91(b). The reason for including in the model place $OutM_i$ and immediate transition $ExitM_i$ depends on the fact that an already processed part may have to stay in the machine because there is no space in the output buffer. If this is not the case, transition $ExitM_i$ can be merged with transition *Process* and place $OutM_i$ disappears.

A system using continuous transportation —   In this example we assume that type **a** parts must be processed by machine M_1 and machine M_2 in sequence, while

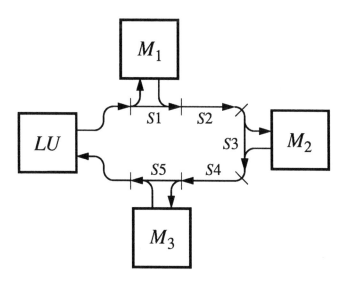

Figure 92   Schematization of a FMS with continuous transportation system

type **b** parts must be processed by machine M_2 and machine M_3 in sequence. We also assume that no I/O buffer exists; the parts waiting for a machine to become available queue up on the transport path. The continuous transport system allows the flow of parts from LU to the three machines in sequence and to LU again. When a part reaches the segment of transport positioned in front of a machine, it either waits in that position, if the service of that machine is required, or moves ahead. To model the transport system with a GSPN, it must first be discretized, i.e., divided into segments each capable of holding a pallet loaded with a part. A part can move from a segment to the following segment only if the latter is free. Each segment can thus be modelled by a place representing its availability, and by two places representing the presence of either a type **a** or a type **b** part in it. In Fig. 92 the continuous transport system is depicted: it has been divided into five segments, $S1, \ldots, S5$. Machines M_1, M_2 and M_3 can be accessed from segments $S1$, $S3$ and $S5$ respectively. Fig. 93 illustrates the GSPN submodel of the transport system: the submodels representing a segment in front of a machine contain one exiting arc towards the machine and one entering arc from the machine.

Composing the submodels in Figs. 91 and 93 we obtain the GSPN model of Fig. 94. An observation on this net is necessary: when a part leaves the system, its identity is forgotten and it is replaced by a new part of unknown type; the new part enters the system, and after its loading on a pallet, it probabilistically receives a type

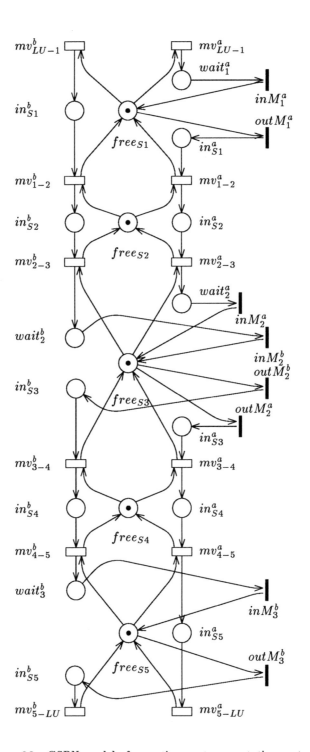

Figure 93   GSPN model of a continuous transportation system

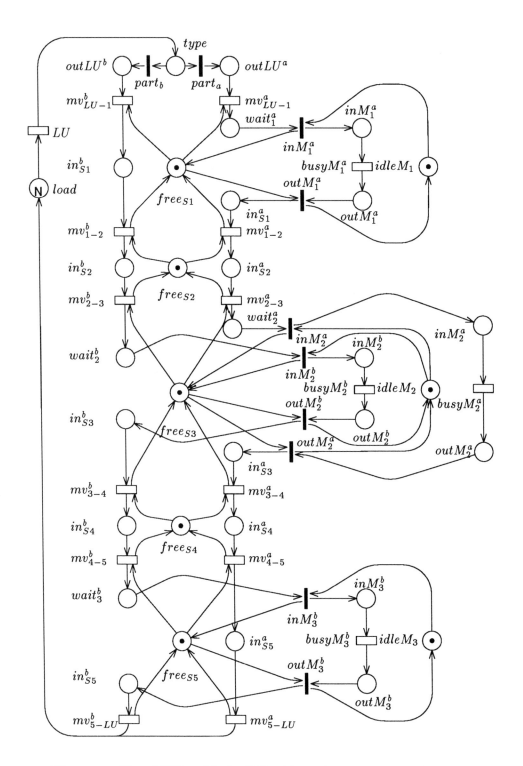

Figure 94   First GSPN model of a FMS with continuous transportation system

Table 25   Working schedules

Class	Required Production Mix	Process Number	Machining times (min)				
			M_1	M_2	M_3	AGV	LU
a	20%	1	10	15	−	2	4
		2	10	−	10	2	4
b	80%	1	−	20	−	2	4
		2	−	−	30	2	4

identification by firing either transition $part_a$ or transition $part_b$. This is a "compact" representation of the input policy: the probabilities associated with transitions $part_a$ and $part_b$ depend on the desired *production mix* (the proportion of produced parts of each type).

A system with AGV transportation —   We now consider a different FMS with the following new features: (1) the transportation system consists of a single AGV; (2) there are various alternative working schedules (i.e., machine processing sequences) for each part type, that are summarized in Table 25; (3) parts of each type have to be loaded onto pallets of corresponding type and there is a limited number of pallets of each type; the available number of pallets thus constrains the number of parts of the various types flowing through the system, and consequently affects the production mix.

The AGV used to transport the parts among the machines is a resource shared by all the parts in the system. Type **a** parts have two possible working schedules that involve the following movements:
- from LU to M_1;
- from M_1 to either M_2 or M_3;
- from M_2/M_3 to LU.

Type **b** parts have two possible working schedules involving the following movements:
- from LU to either M_2 or M_3;
- from M_2/M_3 to LU.

The transportation system in this case is modelled as shown in Fig. 95.   The machines are modelled as in the previous example, except for the presence of unlimited input/output buffers. The complete model is depicted in Fig. 96. Since the parts have alternative working schedules (both types of parts can choose between $M2$ and $M3$), a

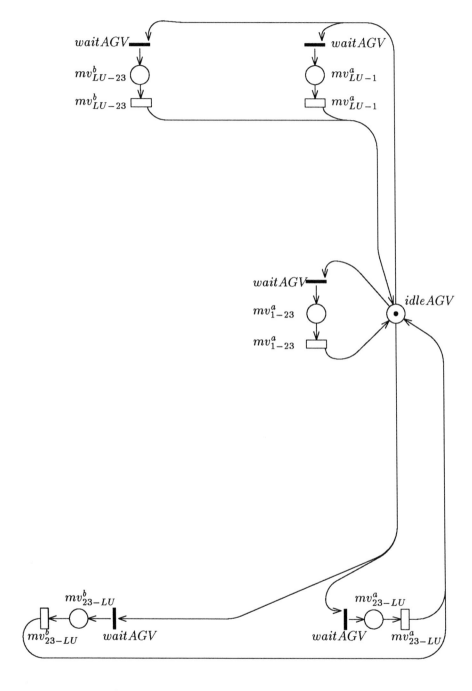

Figure 95 GSPN model of an AGV behaviour

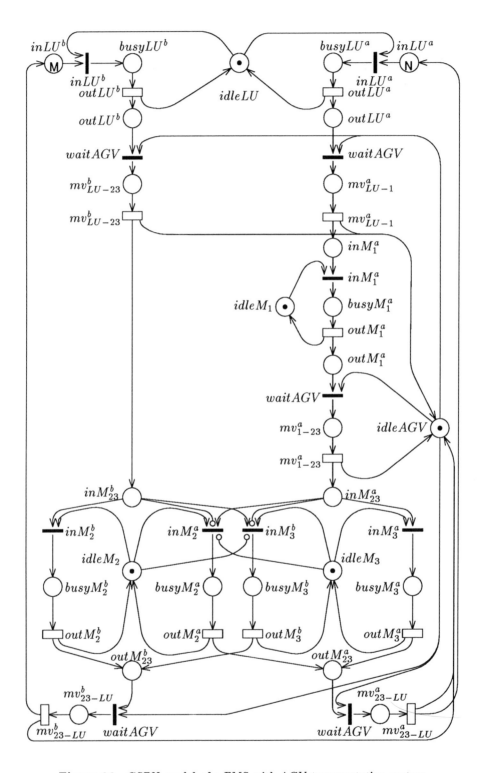

Figure 96   GSPN model of a FMS with AGV transportation system

policy is needed to select the machine to be used. The policy we have modelled is very simple: if both machines are free, the part chooses the fastest one, while if two types of parts are waiting for the same machine, the part with shortest machining time is selected to be processed on that machine. This is represented in the net by means of the four inhibitor arcs connected to transitions inM_3^a and inM_2^b.

8.3.1 Structural analysis of the push production systems

In this section we show how the structural analysis methods can be used to check whether the models correctly represent the studied systems and whether the system behaviour is correct.

P-invariant analysis allows us to conclude that both GSPN models built in this section are bounded, since both of them are covered by P-semiflows. Here we give a list of P-invariants for each model and provide their interpretation.

The GSPN model of Fig. 94 (continuous transport system) has nine minimal P-semiflows from which it is possible to derive the P-invariants listed in Table 26. The first three invariants ensure that each machine can process at most one part at a time. The following five invariants ensure that at most one part can be present in one section of the continuous transport system at any time. The last invariant ensures that the total number of parts circulating in the system is constant and equal to N. This is consistent with our approach of modelling a closed system: every time a part exits the system through the LU station, it is replaced with a raw part to be processed.

The model of Fig. 96 (AGV transport system) is covered by seven P-semiflows that allow the derivation of the P-invariants listed in Table 27.

The first four invariants ensure mutual exclusion for the usage of the three machines and the LU station. The fifth invariant ensures that only one transport can happen at a time (due to the presence of a unique AGV). The last two invariants mean that there is a fixed number (N) of type **a** parts and a fixed number (M) of type **b** parts in the system, respectively. Notice that in the previous model these two invariants are replaced by a unique invariant due to the fact that in the GSPN model of Fig. 94 when a part of any type exits the system, it is not necessarily replaced by a part of the same type due to the probabilistic choice implemented through the free-choice conflict comprising transitions $part_a$ and $part_b$.

Let's now discuss the T-invariants obtained for the two models.

The GSPN model of the continuous transport system is covered by two T-invariants, corresponding to the (deterministic) flow of parts of each type. The GSPN model of the AGV transport system is covered by four T-invariants, corresponding to the four working schedules (two for each part type) the parts can undergo.

Table 26   P-invariants of the GSPN model of Fig. 94

$M(idle M_1)$	$+$	$M(in M_1^a)$	$+$	$M(out M_1^a)$			$= 1$
$M(idle M_2)$	$+$	$M(in M_2^a)$	$+$	$M(in M_2^b)$	$+$	$M(out M_2^a)$	
					$+$	$M(out M_2^b)$	$= 1$
$M(idle M_3)$	$+$	$M(in M_3^b)$	$+$	$M(out M_3^b)$			$= 1$
$M(free_{S1})$	$+$	$M(wait_1^a)$	$+$	$M(in_{S1}^a)$	$+$	$M(in_{S1}^b)$	$= 1$
$M(free_{S2})$	$+$	$M(in_{S2}^a)$	$+$	$M(in_{S2}^b)$			$= 1$
$M(free_{S3})$	$+$	$M(wait_2^a)$	$+$	$M(wait_2^b)$	$+$	$M(in_{S3}^a)$	
					$+$	$M(in_{S3}^b)$	$= 1$
$M(free_{S4})$	$+$	$M(in_{S4}^a)$	$+$	$M(in_{S4}^b)$			$= 1$
$M(free_{S5})$	$+$	$M(wait_3^b)$	$+$	$M(in_{S5}^a)$	$+$	$M(in_{S5}^b)$	$= 1$
$M(load)$	$+$	$M(type)$	$+$	$M(out LU^a)$	$+$	$M(out LU^b)$	
	$+$	$M(wait_1^a)$	$+$	$M(in_{S1}^a)$	$+$	$M(in_{S2}^a)$	
	$+$	$M(wait_2^a)$	$+$	$M(in_{S3}^a)$	$+$	$M(in_{S4}^a)$	
	$+$	$M(in_{S5}^a)$	$+$	$M(out LU^b)$	$+$	$M(in_{S1}^b)$	
	$+$	$M(in_{S2}^b)$	$+$	$M(wait_2^b)$	$+$	$M(in_{S3}^b)$	
	$+$	$M(in_{S4}^b)$	$+$	$M(wait_3^b)$	$+$	$M(in_{S5}^b)$	
	$+$	$M(in M_1^a)$	$+$	$M(out M_1^a)$	$+$	$M(in M_2^a)$	
	$+$	$M(out M_2^a)$	$+$	$M(in M_2^b)$	$+$	$M(out M_2^b)$	
			$+$	$M(in M_3^b)$	$+$	$M(out M_3^b)$	$= N$

A GSPN model covered by T-invariants *may* be live for some initial marking, but some other analysis must be applied to ensure that the model does not deadlock for the set of initial markings defined by the parametric initial marking. Applying deadlock and trap analysis, it is possible to establish whether a model *is not* live. Indeed, a model may be live only if each minimal deadlock contains a trap marked in the (parametric) initial marking. In the AGV transport system model, every deadlock contains a trap that is marked in the parametric initial marking. The continuous transport system model instead has three deadlocks that do not contain any marked trap in the parametric initial marking. This implies that some transitions are not live; moreover this is a clue that the system may reach a dead marking. The three deadlocks that do not contain a marked trap are listed below:

1. $\{idle M_1, free_{S1}, in_{S1}^a, in_{S1}^b\}$
2. $\{idle M_2, free_{S3}, in_{S3}^a, in_{S3}^b\}$
3. $\{idle M_3, free_{S5}, in_{S5}^a, in_{S5}^b\}$

Using definition 2.5.2, it is easy to verify that the above sets of places are indeed

Table 27 P-invariants of the GSPN model of Fig. 96

$M(idle\,LU)$	$+$	$M(busy\,LU^a)$	$+$	$M(busy\,LU^b)$			$= 1$
$M(idle\,M_1)$	$+$	$M(busy\,M_1^a)$					$= 1$
$M(idle\,M_2)$	$+$	$M(busy\,M_2^a)$	$+$	$M(busy\,M_2^b)$			$= 1$
$M(idle\,M_3)$	$+$	$M(busy\,M_3^a)$	$+$	$M(busy\,M_3^b)$			$= 1$
$M(idle\,AGV)$	$+$	$M(mv_{LU-1}^a)$	$+$	$M(mv_{1-23}^a)$	$+$	$M(mv_{23-LU}^a)$	
			$+$	$M(mv_{LU-23}^b)$	$+$	$M(mv_{23-LU}^b)$	$= 1$
$M(in\,LU^a)$	$+$	$M(busy\,LU^a)$	$+$	$M(out\,LU^a)$	$+$	$M(mv_{LU-1}^a)$	
	$+$	$M(in\,M_1^a)$	$+$	$M(busy\,M_1^a)$	$+$	$M(out\,M_1^a)$	
	$+$	$M(mv_{1-23}^a)$	$+$	$M(in\,M_{23}^a)$	$+$	$M(busy\,M_2^a)$	
	$+$	$M(busy\,M_3^a)$	$+$	$M(out\,M_{23}^a)$	$+$	$M(mv_{23-LU}^a)$	$= N$
$M(in\,LU^b)$	$+$	$M(busy\,LU^b)$	$+$	$M(out\,LU^b)$	$+$	$M(mv_{LU-23}^b)$	
	$+$	$M(in\,M_{23}^b)$	$+$	$M(busy\,M_3^b)$	$+$	$M(out\,M_{23}^b)$	
					$+$	$M(mv_{23-LU}^b)$	$= M$

deadlocks. For example, the input set of the first deadlock is:

$$\{out\,M_1^a, mv_{1-2}^a, mv_{1-2}^b, mv_{LU-1}^b, in\,M_1^a\}$$

and it is contained into its output set

$$\{out\,M_1^a, mv_{1-2}^a, mv_{1-2}^b, mv_{LU-1}^a, mv_{LU-1}^b, in\,M_1^a\}$$

An interpretation of the three deadlocks above can be provided in terms of system states. Let us consider the first set of places, and try to understand whether a state where such places are all empty makes any sense: using the previously computed P-invariants we can deduce that if

$$M(idle\,M_1) + M(free_{S1}) + M(in_{S1}^a) + M(in_{S1}^b) = 0$$

then

1. machine M_1 is busy (due to the fact that $M(idle\,M_1) = 0$ and $M(idle\,M_1) + M(busy\,M_1^a) = 1$);
2. the transport segment in front of machine M_1 is occupied by a part (due to the fact that $M(free_{S1}) = 0$);

3. the part currently in segment $S1$ is a type **a** part that needs to be processed by M_1 (due to the fact that $M(free_{S1}) + M(in^a_{S1}) + M(in^b_{S1}) = 0$ and $M(free_{S1}) + M(wait^a_1) + M(in^a_{S1}) + M(in^b_{S1}) = 1$).

Thus, a dead state could be reached when a type **a** part is in the segment in front of machine M_1 wishing to enter it, and another part is being processed by machine M_1. This is a perfectly legal state according to our specification of the system. A similar argument applies to the other deadlocks. This problem can be solved by modifying the part movement control, introducing a test that prevents a part from entering the transport segment of a machine from which it requires processing if such machine is busy. This can be easily implemented in our model by adding a test arc from the "machine-free" place to the proper "enter segment" transition as shown in Fig. 97. For machine M_2, since every part entering its associated transport segment needs its processing, it is enough not to give back the "segment free" token when a part enters the machine.

Observe that we could have discovered this problem by means of reachability analysis for any $N \geq 2$; however, deadlock analysis helps in concentrating on the subnet that causes the problem; moreover, it allows to prove that a dead state can be indeed reached working at a parametric level, i.e., without instantiating a specific initial marking.

8.3.2 *Performance analysis of the system with AGV transport*

In this section we present the performance analysis results for the FMS with AGV transport.

We first study the throughput of the system as a function of the total number of parts circulating in it. To alleviate the state space growth problem, we show how the model can be transformed obtaining two new models with smaller state spaces, providing an upper and a lower bound on the throughput, respectively. The analysis is performed forcing the model to match the desired production mix: this is done by probabilistically choosing the type of a part at the instant of its arrival. A second study is then performed to determine how many pallets of each type are necessary to obtain the required production mix.

The model used to compute the system throughput with forced production mix is depicted in Fig. 98. Observe that this model has been obtained from the model in Fig. 96 by merging the subnets representing the flow of type **a** and type **b** parts into and out of the LU station to represent the probabilistic choice of the type of a raw part entering the system.

The throughput of the system corresponds to the throughput of transition mv_{23-LU}; it can be computed from the steady-state probability of the markings, multiplying

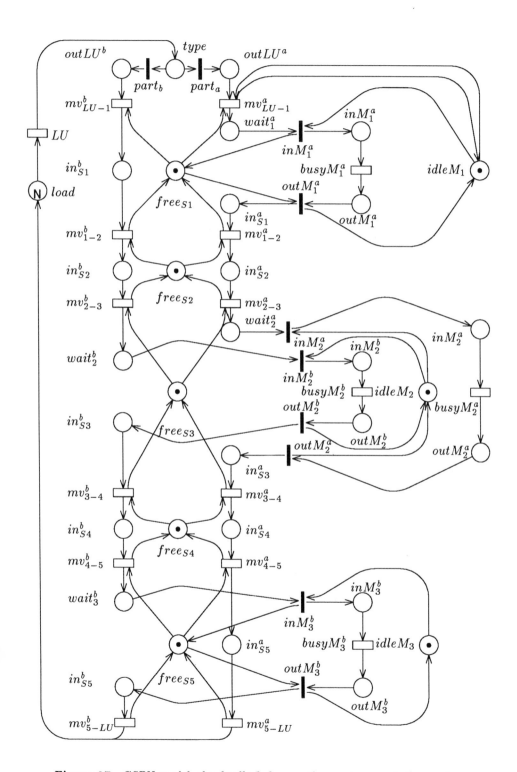

Figure 97 GSPN model of a deadlock-free continuous transportation system

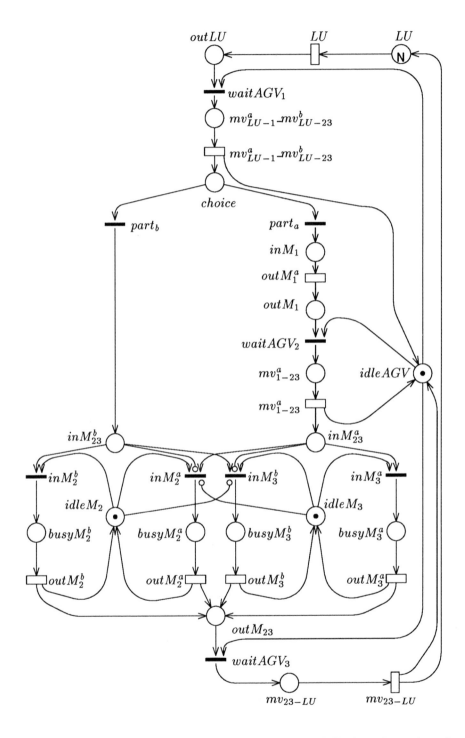

Figure 98   GSPN model used for the computation of the FMS throughput given the

production mix

Table 28 Specification of the transitions of the GSPN of Fig. 98

transition	rate	semantics
LU	0.25	single-server
mv^a_{LU-1}-mv^b_{LU-23}	0.5	single-server
$out M^a_1$	0.1	single-server
mv^a_{1-23}	0.5	single-server
$out M^b_2$	0.05	single-server
$out M^a_2$	0.0667	single-server
$out M^b_3$	0.0333	single-server
$out M^a_3$	0.1	single-server
mv_{23-LU}	0.5	single-server

transition	weight	priority	ECS
$wait AGV_1$	1	1	1
$wait AGV_2$	1	1	1
$wait AGV_3$	1	1	1
$part_a$	20	1	2
$part_b$	80	1	2
$in M^a_2$	1	1	2
$in M^b_2$	1	1	3
$in M^a_3$	1	1	4
$in M^b_3$	1	1	5

the firing rate of mv_{23-LU} by the probability of having at least one token in place mv_{23-LU}.

Table 28 contains the complete specification of each transition rate/weight, priority and ECS: five ECSs can be identified within this system. Three of them can be considered "degenerate" ECSs as they comprise only one transition (observe that transitions $in M^a_2$, $in M^b_2$, $in M^a_3$, and $in M^b_3$ are not in the same ECS because they are mutually exclusive with each other).

The ECS identified by number 1 comprises all the immediate transitions representing the acquisition of the AGV for a transport. They have equal weight, meaning that in case of conflict for the use of the AGV, the choice is performed using a uniform probability distribution. ECS number 2 is somehow unexpected: while it is natural to associate transitions $part_a$ and $part_b$ with a common ECS, and assign them a weight

Table 29   ECS definition of the model with modified priority definition

transition	weight	priority	ECS
$waitAGV_1$	1	1	1
$waitAGV_2$	1	1	1
$waitAGV_3$	1	1	1
$part_a$	20	2	2
$part_b$	80	2	2
inM_2^a	1	1	3
inM_2^b	1	1	4
inM_3^a	1	1	5
inM_3^b	1	1	6

according to the required production mix, it is annoying to have transition inM_2^a in the same ECS. However, this cannot be avoided since transition $part_b$ is in SC relation with transition inM_2^a due to the inhibitor arc from place inM_{23}^b (which is in the output set of $part_b$) to transition inM_2^a. ECS number 2 may cause confusion, indeed it is a non free-choice ECS and some immediate transitions exist that are in causal connection with the transitions in the ECS and have the same priority. For instance let us consider a marking with two tokens in place inM_{23}^a, one token in place *choice*, one token in place $idleM_3$, and one token in place $idleM_2$; the firing sequences $part_b$, inM_2^b, inM_3^a and inM_3^a, $part_b$, inM_2^b, lead to the same new marking, but the second sequence requires a conflict resolution between $part_b$ and inM_2^a that is not solved in the first sequence. The reason is that transition inM_3^a is in causal connection with inM_2^a.

As a matter of fact, such a situation can never arise, due to the parametric initial marking and the priority structure of the model: in this model, transitions $part_a$ and $part_b$ are never enabled together with transitions inM_2^a, inM_2^b, inM_3^a or inM_3^b. However, to eliminate any possibility for confusion to arise, the modeller might assign a higher priority level to $part_a$ and $part_b$. Table 29 shows the new ECS definition obtained from the modified model.

To reduce both the time and memory required to obtain the desired result, a new model has been devised that gives good upper and lower bounds on the system throughput and has a considerably reduced state space. The new GSPN model is depicted in Fig. 99. The lower bound net is obtained by merging in a unique transition three operations: the transport of a finished part to the LU station, its unloading, the loading of a raw piece and its transportation to the first machine in the working schedule: all these operations are performed never releasing the AGV thus reducing the potential concurrency in the model. The upper bound instead is obtained by assuming a 0 time duration for the load/unload operation. The structure of the upper/lower bound GSPN models is exactly the same; they only differ in the rate of transition mv_LU_mv. Observe that, as a consequence, the reachability graph must be built only once for a given value of N, then two different Markov chains are derived from the common tangible reachability graph using the different rates for transition mv_LU_mv. The bounds obtained from these two models are plotted in Fig. 100 and are compared with the throughput obtained solving the GSPN model of Fig. 98. In Fig. 101 the state space size of the model in Fig. 98 is compared with the state space size of the model in Fig. 99 for several values of the parameter N.

The second part of the analysis is performed using the model of Fig. 96. Several experiments are run for different values of the two parameters N and M. The results shown in Table 30 allow one to decide, for any given load (total number of pallets), how many pallets of each type should be available to obtain a production mix as close as possible to the required mix (20% of type **a** parts, and 80% of type **b** parts). From the table, it is possible to see that the mix can only be approximated, and that the global throughput of the system corresponding to the pair N, M that better approximates the required mix for a given load, doesn't match exactly the throughput plotted in Fig. 100.

Table 30　Study of the number of pallets needed to get the desired production mix

N	M	Load $(N+M)$	Type **a** parts Throughput	Type **b** parts Throughput	Total Throughput	Number of States
1	4	5	0.016510 (18.4%)	0.073446 (81.6%)	0.089560	539
2	3	5	0.033614 (35%)	0.062485 (65%)	0.096099	1327
1	5	6	0.015677 (17.1%)	0.076110 (82.9%)	0.091787	911
2	4	6	0.030478 (30.7%)	0.068784 (69.3%)	0.099262	2553
1	6	7	0.015365 (16.6%)	0.077222 (83.4%)	0.092587	1421
2	5	7	0.029228 (29%)	0.071547 (71%)	0.100775	4362
3	4	7	0.042504 (39.6%)	0.064823 (60.4%)	0.107327	8466
1	7	8	0.015245 (16.4%)	0.077682 (83.6%)	0.092927	2090
2	6	8	0.027896 (27.7%)	0.072742 (72.3%)	0.100638	6865
1	8	9	0.015197 (16.3%)	0.077870 (83.7%)	0.093067	2939
2	7	9	0.028521 (28%)	0.073258 (72%)	0.101779	10173
1	9	10	0.015178 (16.3%)	0.077946 (83.7%)	0.093124	3989
2	8	10	0.028435 (27.9%)	0.073478 (72.1%)	0.101913	14397
3	7	10	0.040261 (36.7%)	0.069345 (63.3%)	0.109606	34542

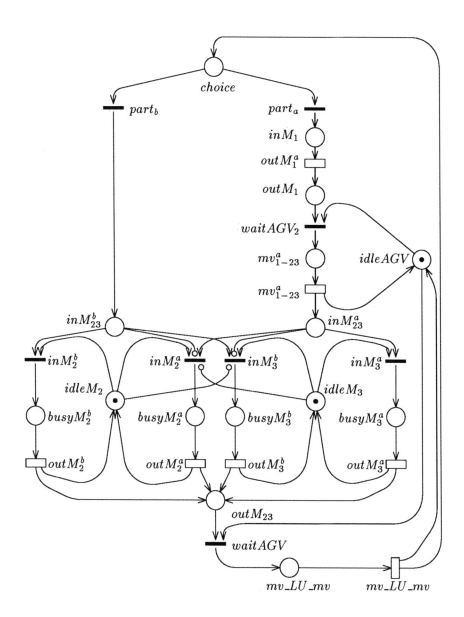

Figure 99   GSPN model used for the computation of the throughput bounds

N	Lower Bound	Exact Value	Upper Bound
5	0.082850	0.089363	0.092707
6	0.086305	0.089363	0.094580
7	0.088755	0.094143	0.095459
8	0.090531	0.095036	0.095847
9	0.091839	0.095036	0.096011
10	0.092816	0.095681	0.096079

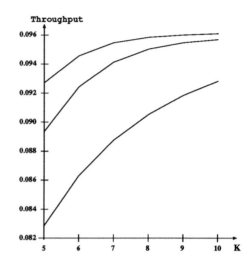

Figure 100   Throughput as a function of N compared with the lower and upper bounds

N	Bounds Model	Exact Model
5	275	1072
6	507	2397
7	873	4922
8	1421	9431
9	2207	17059
10	3295	29388

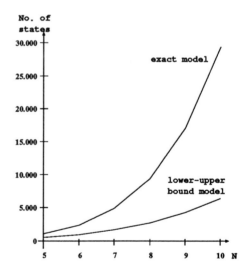

Figure 101   State space growth as a function of N for the two GSPN models of the FMS

9

COMPACT MODELS OF RANDOM POLLING SYSTEMS

The GSPN modelling paradigm is a versatile tool that can be used in many different ways. We saw in previous chapters that the GSPN approach allows the simple development of detailed, easy-to-understand models of complex systems. With some additional effort in the modelling process, GSPNs can also be used to develop compact, abstract models, where symmetries and other behavioural properties are exploited to reduce the number of places, transitions, and arcs with respect to the corresponding detailed models. The major benefit of this abstraction process consists in the reduction of the (tangible) reachability set, thus yielding much simpler analyses.

In this chapter we discuss the construction of compact GSPN models of a multiserver random polling system by progressively abstracting the description of the system behaviour. In this way we will show that the abstraction can yield very significant advantages in terms of the reduction of the size of the state space of the underlying CTMC, at the expense of the effort and ingenuity of the modeller. Moreover, as the abstraction process develops, the intermediate results help us to understand the fundamental laws that govern the behaviour of the system under investigation.

9.1 Polling Systems

The interest in polling systems has been steadily increasing over the last two decades, due to a very wide range of application fields for which they provide adequate descriptions and accurate performance estimates. Prominent application areas of polling models are the fields of telecommunications, computer science, and manufacturing. A comprehensive list of publications on polling models and their applications was collected by H.Takagi [Tak88a]. Good survey papers were published by H.Takagi [Tak86, Tak88b], and more recently by H.Levy and M.Sidi [LS90], and by D.Grillo [Gri90].

A single-server cyclic polling system (the simplest and most common polling system)

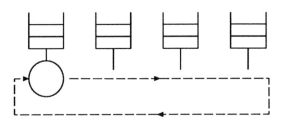

Figure 102   Queuing representation of a cyclic single-server polling system

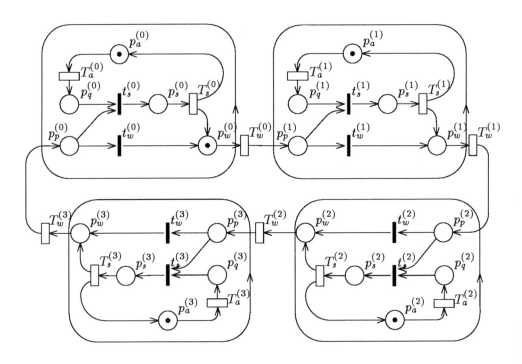

Figure 103   GSPN representation of a cyclic single-server polling system

comprises a set of waiting lines that receive arrivals from the external world, and one server that cyclically visits the queues, providing service to customers that afterwards depart from the system. The usual pictorial representation of this behaviour in queuing notation is shown in Fig. 102 in the case of four queues. The GSPN description of the same system is provided in Fig. 103.

It can be observed that the GSPN model in Fig. 103 comprises four replicas

Table 31 Characteristics of the timed transitions in the GSPN model of a cyclic single-server polling system ($q = 0, 1, 2, 3$)

transition	rate	semantics
$T_a^{(q)}$	$\lambda^{(q)}$	single-server
$T_s^{(q)}$	$\mu^{(q)}$	single-server
$T_w^{(q)}$	$\omega^{(q)}$	single-server

of the subnet that describes the internal organization of each individual queue (enclosed within ovals), interconnected by four replicas of the subnet that describes the movement of the server from a queue to the next one.

Transition $T_a^{(q)}$ models the customer arrival process at queue[1] q ($q = 0, 1, 2, 3$). Customers waiting for a server are queued in place $p_q^{(q)}$, while a token in place $p_p^{(q)}$ represents the server when polling queue q. The two immediate transitions $t_s^{(q)}$ and $t_w^{(q)}$ have priorities 2 and 1, respectively ($\Pi(t_s^{(q)}) = 2, \Pi(t_w^{(q)}) = 1$). Transition $t_s^{(q)}$ fires if the server finds a waiting customer when it polls the queue, so that service can be provided; if $t_s^{(q)}$ cannot fire when the queue is polled by a server, i.e., if the server finds no waiting customers, then $t_w^{(q)}$ fires, and the server moves to the next queue.

One token in place $p_s^{(q)}$ represents a customer of queue q being served, as well as the server when providing service at queue q. $T_s^{(q)}$ is timed with a delay equal to the customer service time.

The server moves to place $p_w^{(q)}$ at the end of the visit at queue q (after the service completion represented by the firing of $T_s^{(q)}$, if a waiting customer was found; after the firing of $t_w^{(q)}$ if no waiting customer was found). From $p_w^{(q)}$ the server walks to the next queue. Transition $T_w^{(q)}$ models the server walk time from queue q to the next queue in the cyclic schedule.

The characteristics of the timed and immediate transitions in the GSPN model in Fig. 103 are summarized in Tables 31 and 32, respectively.

The GSPN model in Fig. 103 provides a more detailed description of the system behaviour with respect to the queuing representation in Fig. 102: from the GSPN model we see that queues have finite capacity, that the server can serve at most one customer before leaving a queue (this is a specification of the *1-limited service discipline*); furthermore, the GSPN description makes it clear that the server does not stop at a queue if no service can be provided, and that the server movement consumes time.

---

[1] The superscript (q) indicates that the place (or transition) belongs to the model of queue q.

Table 32 Characteristics of the immediate transitions in the GSPN model of a cyclic single-server polling system ($q = 0, 1, 2, 3$)

transition	weight	priority	ECS
$t_s^{(q)}$	1	2	$q+1$
$t_w^{(q)}$	1	1	$q+5$

To completely specify the behaviour of a single-server polling system, it is necessary to define several parameters and operating rules:

- the *number of queues*
- the *storage capacity* at each queue, which can be either finite or infinite
- the customer *arrival process* at each queue
- the *queuing discipline* at each queue, which is normally assumed to be FCFS
- the customer *service times* at each queue, which can be random variables with general distributions
- the *service discipline* at each queue, which specifies the customers that can be served when a server visits a queue; the distinction among service disciplines is irrelevant for systems where the storage capacity at all queues is 1
- the *polling order*, which defines the sequence according to which the server visits the queues; the normal polling order is cyclic, but other polling orders are also interesting: for example, with the *random order*, the next queue to be visited is selected at random among all queues, including the one just visited
- the server *walk times* from one queue to the next, which can be random variables with general distributions

While traditional polling models consider the availability of only one server, a new emerging area of interest is the one of *multiserver* polling models, also called multiserver multiqueue (MSMQ) systems.

The description of the behaviour of a multiserver polling system requires the definition of the same elements that we listed above for single-server polling systems, together with some new aspects:

- the *number of servers*
- the *server utilization policy*, which defines the maximum number of servers that can be simultaneously attending a queue; the distinction among server utilization policies is irrelevant in the single-server case, as well as for systems where the storage capacity at all queues is 1

The research on MSMQ systems started only recently, so that the literature is rather scarce: some papers that deal with MSMQ systems, both from a theoretical and from an applicative point of view, are [MW84], [KH89], [Rai85], [YGB86], [CB88], [YP88], [AMDN90], [AMdDN90], [AMDN91]. Some of the first exact numerical results for MSMQ systems were obtained with GSPN models: for example, in [AMDN90], MSMQ systems with cyclic polling order were analysed.

Here we consider multiserver polling models where:

- the *number of queues* is equal to N (≥ 1)
- the *storage capacity* at each queue is equal to 1
- the customer *arrival process* at each queue is Poisson with rate λ, with interruptions due to the limited storage capacity
- the *number of servers* is equal to S ($1 \leq S \leq N$)
- at each queue, for each server, the customer *service times* are independent, exponentially distributed random variables with mean $1/\mu$
- the *polling order* is **random**; the next queue to be visited is selected according to a uniform distribution encompassing all queues, including the one just visited
- the server *walk times* from one queue to the next are independent, exponentially distributed random variables with mean $1/\omega$

The queuing discipline, the service discipline, and the server utilization policy need not be specified, due to the storage capacity limit of one customer.

A typical application area in which the single-buffer queue is required is that of machine repairman models, where machines are subject to faults and repairs (in this case a customer arrival corresponds to a fault, and a service models a repair). Also, most LAN interconnections of personal computers have interfaces that can store at most one data packet at a time, thus token passing PC LANs can be modelled with single-buffer polling schemes.

Single-server random polling systems were analysed in [KL88, BLW90]; some numerical results obtained with the GSPN models described in this chapter are presented in [AMDNR91], where the performance of MSMQ systems with random and cyclic polling orders is compared.

Typical aggregate performance figures of interest in the analysis of polling systems are the average customer delay, as well as the throughputs of the whole system, and of individual queues. We shall refer to these parameters in the analysis.

9.2 Modelling Random Polling the Easy Way

The simplest GSPN model of a random polling system comprising N queues is obtained by combining N replicas of the subnet that describes the operations within a single

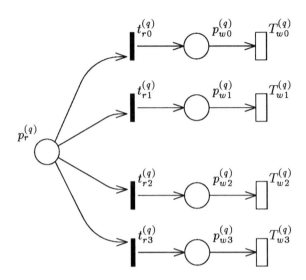

Figure 104   The subnet modelling the choice of the next queue and the server movement

queue with N replicas of the subnet that describes the movements of servers from one queue to the next.

The subnet modelling the internal queue operations is identical to that of Fig. 103, whereas the subnet modelling the server movements must now account for the different polling order. Fig. 104 shows the subnet describing the choice of the next queue to be visited and the movement towards that queue, assuming that the present queue is q and that the system comprises four queues ($N = 4$) numbered from 0 to 3.

A server that leaves queue q is modelled by a token in place $p_r^{(q)}$; the choice for the next queue is modelled by the four conflicting immediate transitions $t_{r0}^{(q)}, t_{r1}^{(q)}, t_{r2}^{(q)}$, and $t_{r3}^{(q)}$ which all have priority equal to 3. The firing of transition $t_{rp}^{(q)}$ corresponds to the selection of the queue with index p as the next queue to be visited. Since the next queue to be visited must be selected according to a uniform distribution encompassing all queues, the four immediate transitions have identical weights.

After the next queue has been selected, the server walks to the chosen queue. The timed transitions $T_{wp}^{(q)}, p = 0, 1, 2, 3$ model the walk times to reach queue p from queue q; therefore, in a marking M they are assigned a rate equal to $M(p_{wp}^{(q)})\omega$, where ω^{-1} is the mean walk time required to move from one queue to the next.

Table 33 Characteristics of the timed transitions in the first GSPN model of a multiserver random polling system $(p, q = 0, 1, 2, 3)$

transition	rate	semantics
$T_a^{(q)}$	λ	single-server
$T_s^{(q)}$	μ	single-server
$T_{wp}^{(q)}$	ω	multiple-server

Table 34 Characteristics of the immediate transitions in the first GSPN model of a multiserver random polling system $(p, q = 0, 1, 2, 3)$

transition	weight	priority	ECS
$t_s^{(q)}$	1	2	$q + 1$
$t_w^{(q)}$	1	1	$q + 5$
$t_{rp}^{(q)}$	1	3	$q + 9$

9.2.1 The first complete random polling model

Fig. 105 shows a GSPN model describing a multiserver random polling system with four queues. It is clearly composed of four replicas of the queue submodel, connected through the submodels describing the queue selection and the server walks. The initial marking (S tokens in place $p_p^{(0)}$ and one token in places $p_a^{(q)}$) defines the number of servers in the system, as well as their initial position and the initial states of the individual queues.

The characteristics of the timed and immediate transitions in the GSPN model in Fig. 105 are summarized in Tables 33 and 34, respectively.

The GSPN model in Fig. 105 comprises four ECSs of immediate transitions (counting only the ECSs that include more than one transition, and that may thus originate a conflict), corresponding to the choice of the next queue to be visited at the output of the four queues.

Five P-semiflows cover all the GSPN places. Four of them cover the triplets of places $p_a^{(q)}$, $p_q^{(q)}$, $p_s^{(q)}$, with $q = 0, 1, 2, 3$. The resulting P-invariants are $M(p_a^{(q)}) + M(p_q^{(q)}) + M(p_s^{(q)}) = 1$. This guarantees that places $p_a^{(q)}$, $p_q^{(q)}$, $p_s^{(q)}$, with $q = 0, 1, 2, 3$ are 1-bounded, as was expected, since the number of customers either waiting or being served at any queue cannot exceed one. The fifth P-semiflow covers places $p_p^{(q)}$, $p_s^{(q)}$,

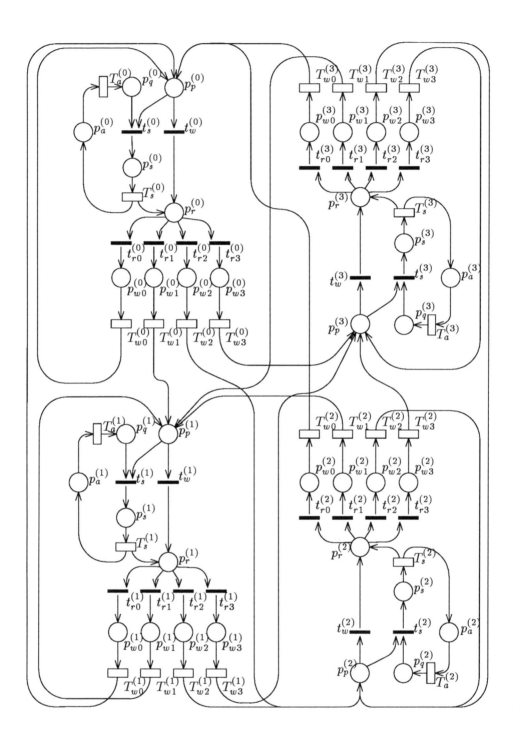

Figure 105   The first complete GSPN model of a multiserver random polling system

Table 35   Tangible state space cardinality for various GSPN models of a random polling
system with two servers and queue capacities equal to one

N	Fig.105	Fig.106	Fig.107	Fig.108	Fig.109	Fig.112
2	57	21	9	6	6	6
3	474	90	26	9	9	9
4	2712	312	72	12	12	12
5	12480	960	192	15	15	15
6	49776	2736	496	18	18	18
7	—	7932	1248	21	21	21
8	—	19200	3072	24	24	24
9	—	—	7424	27	27	27
10	—	—	17664	30	30	30
50	—	—	—	150	150	150
100	—	—	—	300	300	300

$p_r^{(q)}$, $p_{w0}^{(q)}$, $p_{w1}^{(q)}$, $p_{w2}^{(q)}$, $p_{w3}^{(q)}$, with $q = 0, 1, 2, 3$. The token count of the resulting P-invariant is S, since the P-invariant refers to the conservation of the number of servers in the system. As a result, the GSPN model is bounded, and thus the number of reachable states is finite. A number of T-semiflows (192) cover all transitions. The structural characteristics of the GSPN fulfil the necessary condition given in Chapter 2 for the model to be live and reversible. The reachability analysis shows that the GSPN model indeed is live and reversible.

Note that the GSPN model in Fig. 105 does not account for the system symmetries. Indeed, with such a PN structure, we might allow the queue parameters to be different for different queues, and the choice of the next queue to depend on both the queue that the server is leaving, and the one it is going to visit next. The price that has to be paid for this generality is a high number of reachable states: it can thus happen that in the case of large values of N, the complexity of the solution exceeds the capacity of existing software packages.

The second columns of Tables 35 and 36 show the number of tangible and vanishing states, respectively, for the model presented in Fig. 105 in the case of two servers ($S = 2$), for an increasing number of queues: only the entries for models with up to six queues were computed, because larger values of N lead to memory requirements that our computers[2] cannot satisfy.

---

[2] The GSPN models described in this chapter were implemented and solved by means of the GreatSPN [Chi91a] package on SUN4 workstations.

Table 36 Vanishing space cardinality for various GSPN models of a random polling system with two servers and queue capacities equal to one

N	Fig.105	Fig.106	Fig.107	Fig.108	Fig.109	Fig.112
2	62	34	24	8	5	0
3	384	141	80	12	7	0
4	1744	476	240	16	9	0
5	6640	1435	672	20	11	0
6	22560	4026	1792	24	13	0
7	—	10745	4608	28	15	0
8	—	27640	11520	32	17	0
9	—	—	28160	36	19	0
10	—	—	67584	40	21	0
50	—	—	—	200	101	0
100	—	—	—	400	201	0

9.3 Beginning to Exploit Symmetries

The symmetries of the random polling system considered in this chapter can be exploited in the development of abstract GSPN models. In this section we use symmetries to obtain simpler server routing subnets.

Since the server routing probabilities do not depend on the index of the queue the server is leaving, we need not provide separate submodels for the server routing after the visit at different queues; we can thus simplify the GSPN model as in Fig. 106, providing a more abstract view of the server routing process.

Note that the GSPN model in Fig. 106 is similar to that of Fig. 105, except for the server routing part. Indeed, in this case the server routing submodel is obtained by folding the four server routing submodels of Fig. 105 onto a single subnet. Place p_r is the folded equivalent of places $p_r^{(0)}, p_r^{(1)}, p_r^{(2)}$, and $p_r^{(3)}$, and each one of the four immediate transitions that in Fig. 106 represent the choice of the next queue, is obtained by folding four immediate transitions of Fig. 105; for instance, t_{r0} represents the choice of queue 0 and derives from the folding of $t_{r0}^{(0)}, t_{r0}^{(1)}, t_{r0}^{(2)}$, and $t_{r0}^{(3)}$. An analogous folding is done for timed transitions and places.

The GSPN model in Fig. 106 comprises only one non trivial ECS of immediate transitions, obtained from the folding of the four ECSs of Fig. 105. Five P-semiflows cover all the GSPN places, similarly to what happened in the GSPN of Fig. 105. Four of them refer to individual queues and have the same support as the first four

P-semiflows described for the GSPN in Fig. 105. The resulting P-invariants have a token count equal to one. This guarantees that places $p_a^{(q)}$, $p_q^{(q)}$, $p_s^{(q)}$, with $q = 0, 1, 2, 3$ are 1-bounded. The fifth P-semiflow covers places $p_p^{(q)}$, $p_s^{(q)}$, with $q = 0, 1, 2, 3$, and places p_r, p_{w0}, p_{w1}, p_{w2}, p_{w3}. The token count for the resulting P-invariant is S. As a result, the GSPN model is bounded. A number of T-semiflows cover all transitions, so that the structural characteristics of the GSPN fulfil the necessary condition given in Chapter 2 for the model to be live and reversible. The reachability analysis shows that the GSPN model indeed is live and reversible.

It should be emphasized that the GSPN model in Fig. 106 actually entails an abstraction with respect to the operations in the real system. Indeed, in the real system, servers do not join in a single place from which they are routed to the next queue to be visited; this feature is introduced in the model in order to obtain a simplified description (and thus a smaller number of states) that is equivalent to the detailed one from the point of view of the present study. It can be proven that this simplification does not alter customer delays, waiting times, and queue throughputs.

9.3.1 Walking before choosing?

In the GSPN model in Fig. 106, since the same exponentially distributed random variable with mean ω^{-1} can describe the walk times from any queue to any other queue, the timed transitions T_{w0}, T_{w1}, T_{w2}, and T_{w3} all have the same rate ω and the same infinite-server semantics.

We can now observe that a server arriving at place p_r in Fig. 106 makes a choice depending on the weights of the immediate transitions, and then, independently of the choice, walks for an amount of time that is exponentially distributed with parameter ω. Since the walk time is independent of the chosen queue, the choice can be postponed after the walk (we informally say that we "invert" the firing order of immediate and timed transitions). The resulting GSPN model is shown in Fig. 107.

If we interpret the inversion in terms of the model, it corresponds to the rather unrealistic situation of a multiserver random polling system where servers leaving a queue first walk, and then decide which queue they actually want to reach; in a system in which walk times are equal, choosing *before* a walk is equivalent to choosing *after* a walk. In other words, if the walk time is interpreted as a cost that the server must pay to move from the present queue to the next one, the fact that the cost is independent of the destination queue makes it possible to pay it before the selection of the next queue.

Again, the feature that we are introducing in the model has nothing to do with the actual system operations. It is instead an abstraction that is permitted by the symmetry in the model and that has the advantage of reducing the size of the state

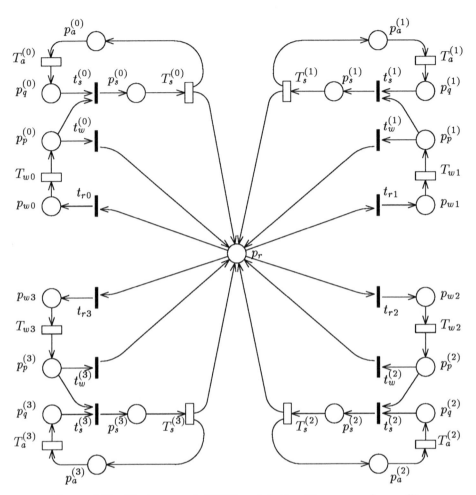

Figure 106   First compact GSPN model of multiserver random polling

space of the model. Moreover, the performance parameters that we declared of interest are not affected by the inversion. In fact, this abstraction is equivalent to a lumping of the state space of the underlying CTMC. To see this, note that the decision subnet of the GSPN model in Fig. 106 consists of one vanishing place p_r, and four tangible places, p_{w0}, p_{w1}, p_{w2}, and p_{w3}. In the decision subnet of the GSPN model in Fig. 107, the four tangible places are substituted by one tangible place p_w. All markings that in the GSPN in Fig. 106 contain the same sum of tokens in the four places p_{w0}, p_{w1}, p_{w2}, and p_{w3}, are grouped into a single marking of the GSPN model in Fig. 107.

The GSPN model in Fig. 107 comprises only one non trivial ECS of immediate transitions, that describes the selection of the next queue, like in the GSPN model

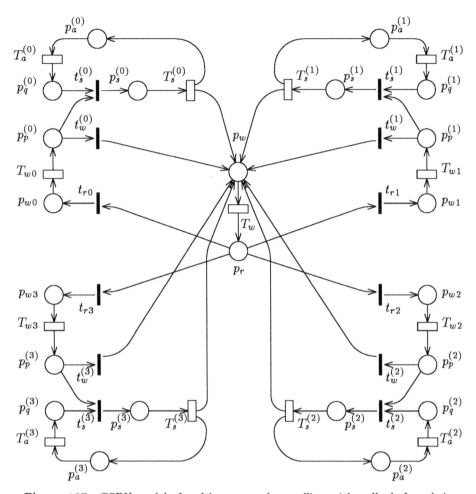

Figure 107   GSPN model of multiserver random polling with walks before choices

of Fig. 106. Five P-semiflows cover all the GSPN places, similarly to what happened in the GSPN of Fig. 106. As a result, the GSPN model is bounded. A number of T-semiflows cover all transitions, and the GSPN model is live and reversible.

9.3.2   Number of states and limitations of the model

The second, third, and fourth columns in Tables 35 and 36 show the cardinality of the tangible and vanishing state spaces for the three GSPN models in Figs. 105, 106, and 107, in the case of two servers $(S = 2)$ and for an increasing number of queues. Although in the three cases the growth of the total number of states with N is always combinatorial, the exploitation of symmetries yields very significant reductions, particularly for larger values of N (for $N = 6$ the reduction is more than one order of magnitude).

Note that all the models we have presented so far are parametric in S, the number of servers, but not in N, the number of queues in the system; indeed, in order to change the values of S we only need to change the initial marking, while in order to change the value of N, the structure of the net must be modified.

9.4   Abstracting from the Queue Identifiers

Since the system is completely symmetric, i.e., since all queues can be characterized with the same parameters, and the selection of the next queue is made on the basis of a uniform probability distribution, it is possible to produce a very abstract model in which queues are not modelled individually. This is a leap in the process towards abstraction, which produces a compact GSPN model featuring the remarkable property of being parametric with respect to the number of queues as well.

First of all, note that the total number of *customers* being served in the system equals the number of *queues* with a customer in service, and the total number of waiting *customers* equals the number of *queues* in which there is a customer waiting.

The latter observation may appear too trivial to be made, but it has far-reaching consequences, since it permits the global state of the system to be identified as the sum of the individual states of the queues.

The equally likely selection of the next queue to be visited allows the probability of providing service at the next queue to be written as:

$$\frac{N_q}{N} = \frac{C_q}{N} \tag{9.1}$$

where N_q and C_q are the number of queues with waiting customers, and the total number of waiting customers in the system, respectively.

Similarly, the probability of being unable to provide service at the next queue because a service is in progress can be written as:

$$\frac{N_s}{N} = \frac{C_s}{N} \tag{9.2}$$

where N_s and C_s are the number of queues with customers being served, and the total number of customers being served in the system, respectively.

Finally, the probability of being unable to provide service at the next queue because the buffer is empty can be written as:

$$\frac{N_a}{N} = \frac{C_a}{N} \tag{9.3}$$

where N_a and C_a are the number of queues with empty buffer and the total number of empty buffers in the system, respectively.

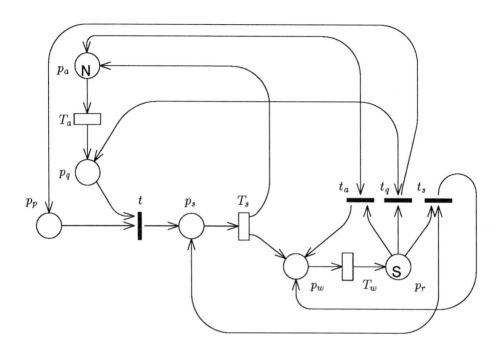

Figure 108   Abstract GSPN model of the symmetric multiserver random polling system

Table 37   Characteristics of the timed transitions in the abstract GSPN model of a
symmetric multiserver random polling system

transition	rate	semantics
T_a	λ	infinite-server
T_s	μ	infinite-server
T_w	ω	infinite-server

9.4.1   The abstract GSPN model

The abstract GSPN model of the symmetric multiserver random polling system with
N queues is depicted in Fig. 108. The characteristics of the timed and immediate
transitions in this GSPN model are summarized in Tables 37 and 38, respectively.

The global system state is defined by three quantities: the number of queues with
empty buffer (N_a), the number of queues with a waiting customer (N_q), and the
number of walking servers. Note that the number of queues being attended by a

Table 38 Characteristics of the immediate transitions in the abstract GSPN model of a symmetric multiserver random polling system

transition	weight	priority	ECS
t	1	4	1
t_a	$M(p_a)/N$	3	2
t_q	$M(p_q)/N$	3	2
t_s	$M(p_s)/N$	3	2

server (N_s) is simply the complement to N of the sum of the first two quantities ($N_s = N - N_a - N_q$), which also equals the number of busy servers.

These aggregate quantities are represented in the GSPN by the markings of places p_a, p_q, p_w and p_s. Tokens in place p_a represent queues with empty buffer ($M(p_a) = N_a$), tokens in place p_q represent queues with a waiting customer ($M(p_q) = N_q$), and tokens in place p_w represent walking servers. Tokens in place p_s model queues being served, as well as busy servers ($M(p_s) = N_s$).

Consequently, T_a is a timed transition with rate $M(p_a)\lambda$, modelling the superposition of the interrupted Poisson arrival processes, T_s has rate $M(p_s)\mu$, and models the $M(p_s)$ parallel service activities, and T_w has rate $M(p_w)\omega$ to model the server walks that are currently in progress.

Place p_r is the place where the decision about the queue to be visited next is made: the choice is implemented by firing one of the three conflicting immediate transitions t_a, t_q, or t_s (all with priority 3), corresponding to the choice of a queue with an empty buffer, of a queue with a waiting customer, or of a queue with a service in progress, respectively.

The initial parametric marking of a GSPN model of a multiserver random polling system with N queues and S servers has N tokens in place p_a and S tokens in place p_r.

The rationale of the model is as follows. When a server terminates a service at a queue (firing of T_s), it must execute a walk (firing of T_w) before choosing the next queue to visit. In this abstract model, queues are not modelled individually, so that instead of explicitly modelling the choice of the next queue to be visited, we model the causes and the consequences of the choice (this is the only relevant information from the point of view of the underlying stochastic model). A server chooses a queue with a waiting customer with the probability given in (9.1), which can be rewritten as $M(p_q)/N$.

This choice is conditioned on the existence of at least one queue with a waiting customer, and it is modelled in the GSPN by immediate transition t_q, whose weight (probability) is $M(p_q)/N$. As a consequence of this choice a customer will be served; therefore the number of waiting customers $M(p_q)$ is decremented by one, while the number of queues being served $M(p_s)$ is incremented by one (by the firing of the immediate transition t with priority 2), and a new service can start (timed transition T_s is enabled).

Alternatively, a server may choose a queue where the buffer is empty with the probability given in (9.3), which can be rewritten as $M(p_a)/N$, or it may choose a queue at which a service is in progress with the probability given in (9.2), which can be rewitten as $M(p_s)/N$.

The first choice is modelled by transition t_a, while the second is modelled by transition t_s. Again, both choices are conditioned on the presence of at least one queue in the required situation, i.e., on the presence of at least one token in the appropriate place, and this explains the presence of test arcs from t_a to p_a and from t_s to p_s (as well as from t_q to p_q).

The consequence of both choices is that the server must execute another walk (return to place p_w to execute T_w), and then repeat the choice of the next queue to be visited (coming back to the decision place p_r).

The GSPN model in Fig. 108 comprises only one non-trivial ECS of immediate transitions, with t_a, t_q, and t_r. Two P-semiflows cover all the GSPN places. The first P-semiflow covers places p_a, p_q, and p_s, and the resulting P-invariant is $M(p_a) + M(p_q) + M(p_s) = N$. The second P-semiflow covers places p_p, p_s, p_w and p_r. The resulting P-invariant is $M(p_p) + M(p_s) + M(p_w) + M(p_r) = S$. As a result, the GSPN model is bounded. Three T-semiflows cover all transitions, and the GSPN model is live, and reversible. The first two T-semiflows correspond to a walk that is not followed by a service: they cover T_w and either t_a or t_s. The third T-semiflow corresponds to a walk followed by a service: it covers T_w, t_q, t, T_s, and T_a.

9.4.2 Walking before choosing!

The abstract GSPN model presented in Fig. 108, like the GSPN model previously shown in Fig. 107, is such that servers first walk, and then decide which queue to visit next. Remember that this is just a simplification that we introduced in the model: in the real system, servers first randomly select the next queue to be visited and then walk towards it; the inversion of the two actions in the model is one of the results obtained by the exploitation of the symmetry in the model abstraction process.

There is an important difference in the inversion of walks and choices in the two models. Indeed, while for the GSPN model in Fig. 107 the inversion is optional, and was introduced only because it allows a reduction in the state space size (and because it permits the GSPN model in Fig. 108 to be more easily explained), for the GSPN model in Fig. 108 the inversion is mandatory.

This necessity stems from the fact that choices are modelled probabilistically, using information derived from the state of the system when servers visit the queues, and thus exactly when the decision is taken in the real system (the probabilities associated with immediate transitions t_a, t_q and t_s depend on the number of tokens in p_a, p_q and p_s). If the choices were made before the walk using the same probabilistic mechanism, it could happen that when the server reaches the chosen queue after the walk, the state of the system (and in particular the state of the chosen queue) has changed (because some other transition may have fired while the transition representing the walk was working), so that the choice would have been based on incorrect probability values.

To understand this incorrect behaviour, consider for example the case in which only one queue contains a waiting customer (only one token is in place p_q). Assume that a server chooses that queue (with probability $1/N$), and then starts walking towards it. Before the walk terminates, another server chooses the same queue (again with probability $1/N$) and starts walking. When the first walk ends, the service at the chosen queue begins, and no waiting customer remains in the system. Thus, at the end of the walk of the second server, no waiting customer will be found at the selected queue. This is because no coherence is guaranteed between the system state at the moment of the choice, and the system state at the end of the walk.

More subtle error situations can be easily devised. For example, a server may choose a queue with a customer waiting with probability $1/N$, if the number of tokens in place p_q at the time of the choice is equal to one; but it may be the case that when the server terminates its walk, there is more than one token in p_q (there are several queues with waiting customers in the system) so that the choice probability is incorrect.

The reason why this problem was not present in the GSPN model in Fig. 107 is that there queues had an identity, and servers chose according to this identity. The fact that the state of the chosen queue could change was irrelevant, because of the fact that the choice was not based on the queue state. Now, queues are identified only by their local state, but this local state changes in time, so that choices can only be based on the instantaneous situation.

9.4.3 Number of states and limitations of the model

The reduction in the state space size with respect to the models in which queues are individually described, is shown in Tables 35 and 36, in the case of two servers ($S = 2$), for an increasing number of queues.

The differences in the number of states become drastic for larger values of N, due to a linear growth with N, which can be expected by the elimination of the combinatorial growth of the possible symmetric combinations of individual queue states.

It is also interesting to note that the resulting model is parametric in both the number of queues and the number of servers. The parametrization is a result of the exploitation of the system symmetries.

9.5   From GSPNs to SPNs

The abstractions discussed so far have always been due to the ingenuity of the modeller. In Chapter 6 we briefly illustrated the rules for the structural reduction of GSPN models, aiming at the elimination of all immediate transitions from a GSPN, thus producing an equivalent SPN. We now apply those rules to the reduction of the abstract GSPN model of Fig. 108. It is worth mentioning at this point that in this particular case the reduction process not only eliminates all immediate transitions, and consequently induces a (consistent) reduction in the number of states, but also produces a model that is much simpler than the initial one, thus allowing a deeper understanding of the intrinsic system behaviour. Unfortunately, this is not always the case: in general, the elimination of immediate transitions is paid with the introduction of a large number of timed transitions, usually resulting in models that, although easier to solve, are more difficult to understand or to reason about.

Before applying the reduction algorithm, we can observe that in the GSPN model of Fig. 108 two immediate transitions always fire in a row: the firing of transition t_q is indeed always followed by that of transition t, because t_q is enabled only if p_q is marked (although the firing of t_q does not modify the marking of p_q), so that t is always enabled after the firing of t_q. As a consequence, p_p is a vanishing place. Fig. 109 shows, with a rearranged layout, the abstract GSPN model of Fig. 108 after t_q and t have been merged (the transition resulting from the combination was named t_q) and place p_p has been removed.

The net in Fig. 109 is covered by two P-semiflows. $M(p_a) + M(p_q) + M(p_s) = N$ is the P-invariant that represents the conservation of queues (a queue can be either empty $[p_a]$, or waiting for service $[p_q]$, or in service $[p_s]$). The P-invariant $M(p_s) + M(p_w) + M(p_r) = S$ represents the conservation of servers (a server may be either serving $[p_s]$, or walking $[p_w]$, or deciding which queue to visit next $[p_r]$).

We shall see that P-invariants are very useful for the reduction of the GSPN model.

A first consequence of the P-invariants is that place p_r is vanishing: the three immediate transitions (t_a, t_q, t_s) that remove tokens from p_r have two input places each: p_r and one among p_a, p_q, p_s; because of the P-invariant covering the three places, at least one of them is marked in any possible system state, so that at least one of the three immediate transitions is enabled when p_r is marked.

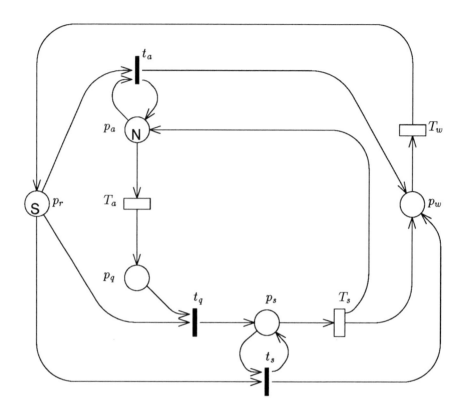

Figure 109   Abstract GSPN model obtained from that of Fig. 108 by eliminating one
immediate transition and one vanishing place

Since p_r is vanishing, T_w is the only timed transition in the model whose firing causes an immediate transition to become enabled. Indeed, when T_a (T_s) fires, t_q (t_a) is not enabled because p_r cannot be marked.

Since the reduction procedure outlined in Chapter 6 reduces a subnet of immediate transitions by including them into the timed transitions whose firing can cause that of an immediate transition in the subset, its application to our example would therefore require that t_a, t_q and t_s be included into T_a, T_s, and T_w, but considering that the firing of T_a and T_s cannot enable any immediate transition, as explained above, we only have to include t_a, t_q, and t_s into T_w.

Transitions t_a, t_q and t_s form a non-free-choice conflict, so that all possible combinations of enabled and disabled transitions must be considered, as described in Chapter 6.

If we concentrate on the firing of T_w followed by t_a, four cases are possible, that

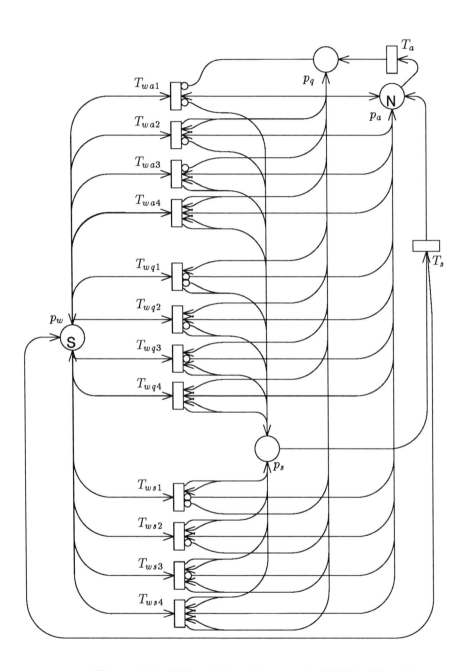

Figure 110 SPN model equivalent to the GSPN in Fig. 109

correspond to four new transitions whose names are in parentheses: t_a is the only enabled transition (T_{wa1}), t_a is enabled with t_q (T_{wa2}), t_a is enabled with t_s (T_{wa3}), and t_a is enabled with both t_q and t_s (T_{wa4}).

Similar sets of replicas exist for t_q and t_s.

The resulting net is shown in Fig. 110, where one timed and three immediate transitions have been replaced by twelve timed transitions, and the vanishing place p_r has been removed. The states of this SPN are isomorphic to the *tangible* states of the GSPN model in Fig. 109, so that the total number of states has been reduced at the price of cluttering the resulting SPN with timed transitions and arcs.

Fig. 110 is where the reduction algorithm leads us, but we can again exploit the modeller's ingenuity and familiarity with the model, and in particular the knowledge of P-invariants, to greatly simplify the net.

A first important observation is that all transitions in the same set of replicas modify the SPN marking in the same way, as they actually correspond to the firing of the same transition.

Let's write the rates of the transitions in the first set of replicas. Denoting by $W(T_x)$ the rate of transition T_x, we have

$$
\begin{aligned}
W(T_{wa1}) &= M(p_w)\,\omega\,\frac{M(p_a)}{M(p_a)} = \\[2mm]
&= M(p_w)\,\omega\,\frac{M(p_a)}{N} \\[3mm]
W(T_{wa2}) &= M(p_w)\,\omega\,\frac{M(p_a)}{M(p_a)+M(p_q)} = \\[2mm]
&= M(p_w)\,\omega\,\frac{M(p_a)}{N} \\[3mm]
W(T_{wa3}) &= M(p_w)\,\omega\,\frac{M(p_a)}{M(p_a)+M(p_s)} = \\[2mm]
&= M(p_w)\,\omega\,\frac{M(p_a)}{N} \\[3mm]
W(T_{wa4}) &= M(p_w)\,\omega\,\frac{M(p_a)}{M(p_a)+M(p_q)+M(p_s)} = \\[2mm]
&= M(p_w)\,\omega\,\frac{M(p_a)}{N}
\end{aligned}
$$

where $M(p_w)\omega$ is the firing rate of T_w, and the first expression provides the rates assigned by the algorithm, while the second is how the rate can be rewritten by exploiting P-invariants. For example, the first equation is true because T_{wa1} is enabled only when both t_q and t_s are not enabled, and therefore p_a must contain N tokens, so that $M(p_a)/N = 1$. Similar considerations hold for the other two sets of replicas.

This implies that each set of replicas comprises four mutually exclusive transitions with equal rate. We can therefore substitute the four transitions with just one, with

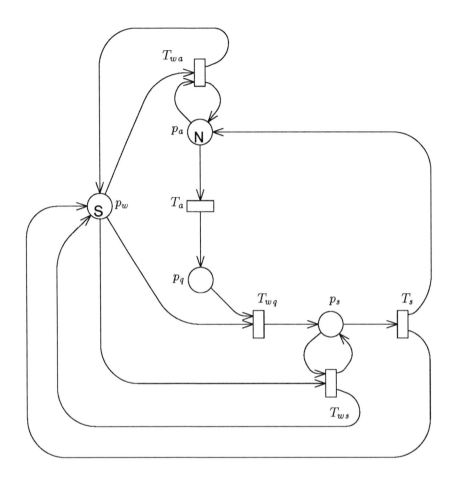

Figure 111   SPN model after the simplification of transition rates

the same rate. The SPN obtained with this substitution is shown in Fig. 111: it enjoys the two nice features of being graphically as simple as the original GSPN, and of producing a reduced number of states.

A further simplification of the SPN in Fig. 111 can be obtained by observing that the two timed transitions T_{wa} and T_{ws} have preconditions equal to the postconditions, so that their firing does not modify the SPN marking. They can therefore be removed from the model. We thus come to the net shown in Fig. 112(a).

The covering of the net by the two P-semiflows $p_a + p_q + p_s$ and $p_s + p_w$ is even clearer in this very compact model. P-invariants again help us to further simplify the model, producing the final SPN shown in Fig. 112(b). To make this final step we take advantage of the fact that the sum of tokens in p_s and p_w is always equal to S, so that

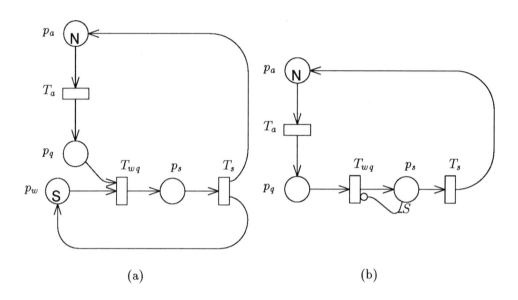

(a)   (b)

Figure 112   Two further simplifications of the SPN model

we can translate the test for at least one token in p_w (input arc from p_w to T_{wq}) into a test for less than S tokens in p_s (inhibitor arc with weight S from p_s to T_{wq}). The rate of transition T_{wq} is changed accordingly from $\frac{M(p_q)}{N}M(p_w)\omega$ to $\frac{M(p_q)}{N}[S-M(p_s)]\omega$. At this point both the enabling of T_{wq} and its firing rate are independent of the marking of p_w which can therefore be removed.

The striking simplicity of the final model in Fig. 112(b) deserves a few remarks. First of all, note that the SPN model is parametric both in N and in S, but the initial marking only comprises N tokens in place p_a: the dependency on S is embedded into the arc weights and transition rates. This embedding bears some resemblance to the embedding of the model characteristics into appropriate functions, typical of high-level SPNs [JR91]. Second, note that servers have disappeared from the model; the server utilization policy is not obvious, as it is not obvious that servers can perform several walks in a row. Third, note that we ended up with three transitions and three places arranged in a circle; that two of the transitions have infinite-server rates, while the rate of the third one is an infinite-server multiplied by a function that accounts for the number of servers in the system and the number of tokens in the transition output place.

Finally, a few words are needed to comment on the numerical results in Tables 35 and 36, which report the cardinality of the tangible and vanishing state spaces of the various GSPN models presented so far, in the case of two servers $(S = 2)$, for an increasing number of queues.

While a linear growth with N was already achieved with the model in Fig. 108, that already exhibits a tangible state space cardinality equal to $3N$, the reduction of immediate transitions allows the elimination vanishing markings, so that the cardinality of the whole state space of the final model equals $3N$. This is extraordinarily less than the number of states of the original simple GSPN model we started with!

10

MODELLING AND ANALYSIS OF CONCURRENT PROGRAMS

In this chapter we provide an example of how GSPNs can be used to evaluate and validate concurrent programs. Parallel programs are translated into GSPN models that are used to perform a static analysis yielding information on possible deadlocks, mutual exclusions, and resource utilizations, as well as a dynamic analysis to study performance. These models are useful to understand the overall behaviour of a concurrent program, to increase the confidence in its correctness, and to assess the efficiency of its implementation. The example of this chapter shows a class of GSPN models that do not require any ingenuity from the modeller to be built, as they are obtained through an *automatic* translation process.

The usefulness of Petri net models for the static analysis of concurrent programs was pointed out in [Tay83] for programs written in languages such as Ada [SC87] and Occam [DB91], while relations between Petri nets and other concurrent languages and paradigms such as CCS [Mil89] and CSP [Hoa78] have been widely studied in the literature [GR84].

10.1 Introduction to the Static Analysis of Concurrent Programs

Static analysis is a method that draws conclusions on the qualitative behaviour of a program by "simply" looking at its code without requiring any execution (that is to say, at compile time). The classical approach of static analysis is to derive from the program a formal model that is subsequently studied to infer the properties of the program. Since during static analysis nothing is known about the run-time behaviour of the program (for example its input data), no assumption is made about which of the possible execution paths is actually followed by the program. Static analysis thus tends to account also for many program behaviours that would never occur in real executions, but all possible run time behaviours are surely included. Three types of anomalies may be detected by static analysis in a distributed/concurrent environment [SW89]: unconditional faults, conditional faults, and nonfaults. Unconditional faults correspond to errors that will definitely occur during program executions. Conditional faults represent instead errors whose occurrence depends either on nondeterministic choices or on specific sets of input data. Nonfaults, finally, are errors which are reported by the static analyser although they will never occur during program executions: nonfaults are detected when the correct behaviour of programs is ensured by control variables that are ignored during static analysis. Static analysis thus provides a pessimistic picture of program behaviour: a measure of goodness of a static analyser is its ability to eliminate (or at least to reduce) the number of nonfaults.

Once a concurrent program is determined to be correct it must also be fast. A common way of analysing the performance of concurrent programs is to construct appropriate queuing network models of the application, which account for the structure of the program and of the hardware of the application and in which parameters and delay centres are carefully chosen to characterize the application being modelled. This approach requires considerable ingenuity. Moreover little relation exists between these models and those used for validation purposes.

GSPNs can be considered as a formalism capable of representing both the characteristics of the architecture (the hardware) and the peculiarities of the program (the software) of a concurrent computer in such a way that both validation and performance evaluation can be performed using basically the same model. In principle, GSPNs can thus be used to prove the correctness of a concurrent program as well as the efficiency of its implementation: for an example the reader may refer to [BCBC92], where a mutual exclusion algorithm is first proved correct and subsequently evaluated to characterize the range of applications for which it can be considered efficient. It is often the case, however, that a complete assessment of the correctness and of the efficiency of a program is not feasible with theoretical/analytical approaches, due to the dimension of the state space. In these cases, GSPNs still play a relevant role, as they allow the programmer to reason about program behaviours using a formal specification, and make objective statements about their properties and about their performances. In these cases the simulation of the evolution of the model is particularly important. Indeed, GSPN models can aid the user in visualizing the many possible execution sequences of the program. Being able to actually see the *dynamic* behaviour of a concurrent program provides the implementor with a powerful debugging tool: observe that this is the dynamic behaviour of the static model and therefore summarizes all possible run time behaviour of the program. Moreover, measurements performed on these sample executions allow the probability distributions of model states to be estimated.

10.2 The Automatic Translation from Programs to GSPNs

PN models can be obviously utilized to describe the control flow (flowchart) of a program. For example the model depicted in Fig. 113 represents the following piece of C-like code:

```
if (cond1)
    A
else
    do B while (cond2)
```

Observe that all decisions are represented as nondeterministic choices between two conflicting transitions (t_{cond1} and $t_{\sim cond1}$ on one side, and t_{cond2} and $t_{\sim cond1}$ on the other), while, of course, at run time choices are deterministically based on the evaluation of conditions $cond1$ and $cond2$.

PN models can also faithfully represent many constructs proper of concurrency and communication: for example, we have already seen in Chapters 1, 5, and 6 how to model a fork and join construct. In this chapter we shall explain how it is possible to compile a concurrent application into a GSPN system: to do this we need first to define the language of the application and then to illustrate the translation process.

10.2.1 Languages of interest

The class of concurrent programs that we consider for the automatic translation conforms to a CSP style: a typical application is organized as a set of processes that include statements of type **SEQ** (sequence of statements), **ALT** (nondeterministic choice among a set of possible communications), **PAR** (parallel activation of processes), **if**, **while (repeat, for)**, **?** and **!**. The two operators **?** and **!** are used to indicate inputs and outputs on a channel. Communications are of the rendez-vous style, i.e. both partners of a communication need to be ready to exchange the data (one ready for an input and one for an output) before the communication can actually take place. Communication among processes is assumed to happen through declared common channels. This is the mechanism provided by Occam [INM84] and it represents a generalization of the basic mechanism of CSP.

We assume that there is a process that initiates the concurrent execution of a certain number of processes. This is the equivalent of the **PLACED PAR** instruction

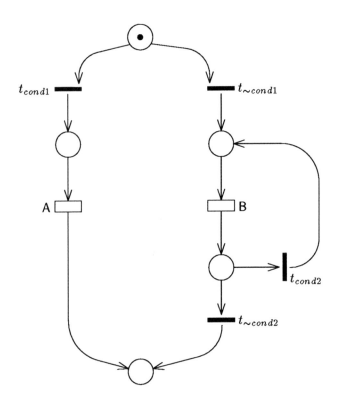

Figure 113   A do-while statement nested inside an if-then-else

in Occam. Processes can be activated by a **PLACED PAR** instruction or by any **PAR** instruction contained in an already activated process. In the command **PAR** A B **ENDPAR**, A and B are names of processes and the execution of the command corresponds to instantiating and activating a copy of each process.

Having discussed the type of languages we are interested in, we must decide which features of a program we want to represent in the model. It is important to remark that GSPNs could account for all the details of a real concurrent program. This approach would lead to enormous nets, cluttered with lots of details, and with huge reachability graphs. These models would be difficult to analyse and their results problematic to interpret. The choice of what to model must be driven by the type of results we want to obtain. Each program can be represented with different levels of abstraction, yielding different consequences in terms of complexity and accuracy of their analysis: in particular, it is clear that, if we want to study deadlocks, all process synchronizations must be carefully described.

10.2.2   The translation procedure

A possible choice for the abstraction level to be used in the translation is that of including only process activation and communication statements in the model control flow [Tay83, SC87, Fer89, DB91]. In particular we model every single communication statement as well as each **PAR**, **SEQ**, **ALT**, **if**, and **while (repeat, for)** statement that includes in its body a communication or a process activation (i.e. an **ALT**, **PAR**, a ! or a ?). A sequence of statements that does not include any of these instructions is represented in the GSPN system as a timed transition whose associated delay depends on its length.

Using this level of abstraction, concurrent programs are translated into GSPN systems according to the following procedure.

1. From each process we obtain a process schema by coalescing into single macro-statements all those sequences of instructions that do not include any communication or any **PAR**.
2. Each process schema yields a GSPN system in which processes activated by a **PAR** are represented by single transitions (i.e., they are not substituted by their translation), communication statements are represented as immediate transitions (thus disregarding the explicit representation of the communication partner, as well as the synchronization aspect of the rendez-vous), and macro-statements are substituted by timed transitions (whose associated delay is an estimate of their execution time).
3. Starting from the initial process, all process activation statements of the type **PAR** $A_1, A_2, \ldots, A_n$ are expanded with a copy of the GSPN systems of the process schemas of $A_1, A_2, \ldots, A_n$. Since each A_i can activate other processes in the same manner, the substitution continues in depth-first mode until all the transitions that represent the activation of a process have been replaced.
4. Pairs of communication transitions that belong to different processes and that represent their (mutual) communication are fused to concretely represent the synchronization deriving from the rendez-vous protocol.

Let us now describe each single step in more detail.

Step 1 consists of generating the process schema. This task requires an abstraction phase that eliminates all the parts that are irrelevant with respect to control. This can be a by-product of the compilation of the program, or a specific compiler can be produced for this task, whose complexity is substantially reduced, considering that many of the activities of a regular compiler are of no interest in this setting.

Step 2 consists of producing a GSPN structure for each process schema. The basic translation rules are shown in Fig. 114 (the sequential constructs), and Fig. 115 (the concurrent construct). A, B and A_i are used to indicate process names, and τ indicates

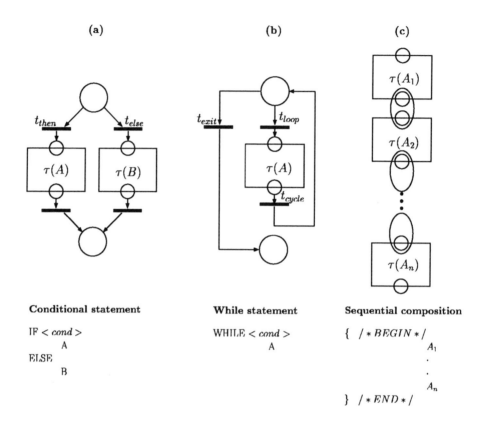

Figure 114   Translation rules for sequential constructs

the translation function. Each process can be characterized by a GSPN with one input place and one output place; the same is true for any construct of our CSP-like applications.

A sequence of statements, none of which is modelled explicitly, is simply represented by a timed transition with one input and one output place. Fig. 114(a) depicts the translation of an **if** statement: the two alternatives are represented by a nondeterministic choice (two immediate transitions with a common input place). If nothing is known about the relative frequencies of the outcomes of the condition evaluation, equal weights are assigned to the two immediate transitions. The **case** statement can be translated in the same way, yielding a structure with as many parallel sequences as there are cases. The **while** statement is instead shown in Fig. 114(b); the same discussion as for the **if** statement applies; the translation of the **while true** statement, not shown in the figure, is a simplification of the translation of the regular

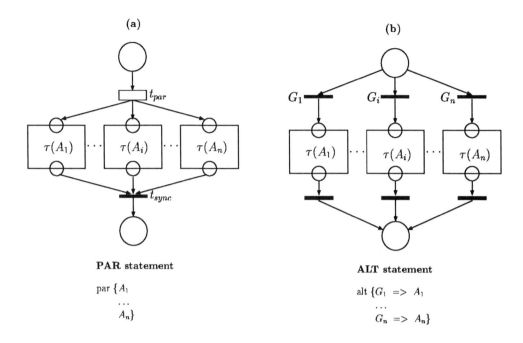

Figure 115   Translation rules for concurrent constructs

while that is obtained by eliminating the exit arc out of the decision place[1]. The translation of the **SEQ** statement is shown in Fig. 114(c): the output place of the translation of A_i is superposed with the input place of the translation of A_{i+1}.

For what concerns concurrent statements, communications (either ! or ?) are simply represented (for the moment) by an immediate transition with a single input and a single output place. This is a reasonable choice considering that we are modelling each process in isolation, and therefore communication is seen as an action that involves no delays. A process activation statement is translated into a timed transition, again with one input and one output place. The translation of the **PAR** statement is shown in Fig. 115(a): the timed transition represents the time needed to activate the single branches of the **PAR**. The final transition represents the fact that the **PAR** completes its execution only when this is true for all branches: it is an immediate transition because it expresses a logical condition (there is no time involved, as the delay is caused by the reciprocal wait and not by the action *per se*). The translation of the **ALT** statement (Fig. 115(b)), is modelled instead as a nondeterministic choice among possible communications; the G_i are communication statements (input guards) or simple conditions and are thus represented as immediate transitions.

---

[1] Observe that in this case there is no direct path between the input place and the output place.

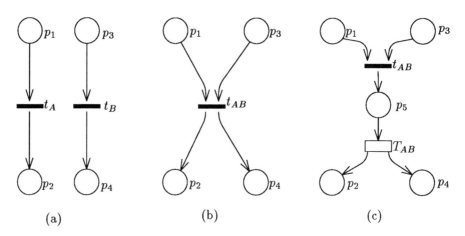

(a)   (b)   (c)

Figure 116   Rendez-vous and communication, simple case

The automatic implementation of these rules is quite straightforward as it corresponds to simple modifications of any algorithm that translates a program into a flowchart. Applying these translation rules mechanically, many useless immediate transitions and places are generated: they can be partially removed, since all sequences of immediate transitions of the 1-in 1-out type can be collapsed into a single one (of course this is not true if a transition represents communication, as it will be manipulated during the fourth step of the procedure). Removing these useless transitions corresponds to the application of well-known reduction techniques [Sil85, CDF91].

Step 3 consists of replacing all transitions that represent named processes with their net representations. The substitution can be easily performed by superimposing the input (output) place of the process equivalent subnet with the input (output) place of the transition that represents the named process.

Step 4 consists of implementing the rendez-vous. In a CSP-like language, a rendez-vous is caused by any pair of input and output (communication) statements. Indeed a process that executes an input (output) command is blocked if its partner is not ready to execute the complementary statement: when both processes are ready the communication takes place and the blocked process resumes execution. Observe Fig. 116(a): if the meaning of t_A (t_B) in the translation of process A (B) is that of requiring a rendez-vous with B (A), then the superposition of t_A with t_B is all what we need (Fig. 116(b)). Moreover, the actual communication requires the logical action of the rendez-vous plus the time for transmission. This is reflected in the GSPN by expanding the immediate transition into the sequence immediate transition – place

– timed transition, as shown in Fig. 116(c); the delay associated with the transition depends on the estimated amount of exchanged information.

When several input (?) and output (!) statements on the same channel exist in the code of the concurrent program, they can yield many rendez-vous. Without making any assumption on the program behaviour, we can only say that each input statement on a channel x can represent a rendez-vous with any output statement on the same channel x. Therefore, we need to superpose each transition that represents an input from x with *all* transitions which represent an output on x. In terms of PNs this operation is a superposition of nets on transitions [DCDMPS82] and it leads to as many transitions as the product of the input and output statements. Each immediate transition is then expanded into the sequence immediate transition – place – timed transition, as in the previous case. Fig. 117 shows a case of this more complex situation. Part (a) shows two processes that communicate on a single channel. Transitions i_1 and i_2 represent input from the channel and o_1 and o_2 represent output on the channel. Part (b) shows the two processes with the rendez-vous modelled explicitly. Since either of the two inputs can be combined with either of the two outputs, we obtain four possible combinations represented by transitions $i_1o_1, i_1o_2, i_2o_1, i_2o_2$. Each transition is then expanded as in Fig. 116(c).

Let us make a few comments on the difficulties of this translation procedure. The first step requires a preprocessor that produces the process schemas: this is already a standard feature of many compilers. The second step requires a simple translator based on the rules of Figs. 114 and 115. The first two steps can thus be easily automated.

The third step can be problematic if the language allows direct or indirect recursion of processes within a **PAR** construct, i.e., if the language allows dynamic instantiation of processes, which is not the case for Occam. The fourth step is simple and can be easily automated, but the nets produced in this manner can be cluttered with arcs if there are many inputs and outputs on the same channel.

10.3   An Example of Translation

We now introduce an example program to illustrate the translation process. The program realizes a "printer spooler" that accepts the print requests of two user programs P_1 and P_2. The structure of the spooler and of the user programs P_1 and P_2 is depicted in Fig. 118, where $Chan_1$ and P_1Sp ($Chan_2$ and P_2Sp) are the channels used for communication between the process *Spooler* and process P_1 (P_2).

The corresponding Occam-like code is presented in Fig. 119. Process P_1 (P_2) executes a loop of computation and requests the results to be printed. If process P_1 (P_2) wants to send a sequence of packets for printing to the spooler, it first sends

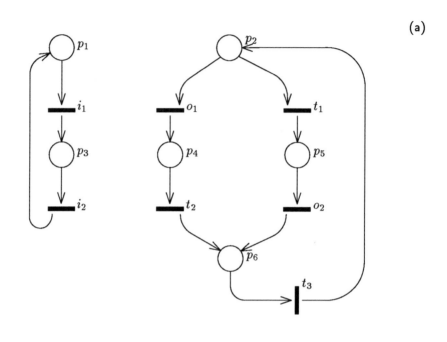

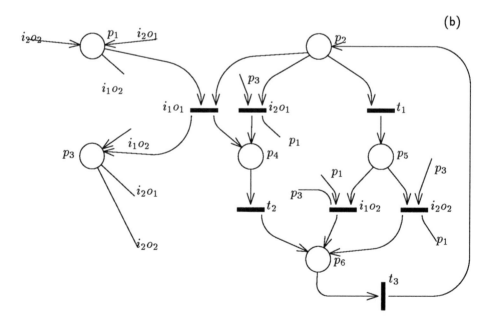

Figure 117   Rendez-vous and communication, complex case

Figure 118   A spooler system

Spooler	**P_1**
while true	while true
ALT	$\langle P_1$ computes pckt[1..k] $\rangle$
$Chan_1$? x :	$Chan_1$! k
for i=x-1 downto 0	for i=k-1 downto 0
P_1Sp? pckt	P_1Sp! pckt[i]
$\langle$ Print pckt $\rangle$	endfor
endfor	endwhile
$Chan_2$? x :	
for i= x-1 downto 0	**P_2**
P_2Sp? pckt	while true
$\langle$ Print pckt $\rangle$	$\langle P_2$ computes pckt[1..n] $\rangle$
endfor	$Chan_2$! n
endwhile	for i=n-1 downto 1
	P_2Sp! pckt[i]
	endfor
	endwhile

Figure 119   A spooler system code

a message on channel $Chan_1$ ($Chan_2$) containing a request to transmit k (n) packets and then enters a loop where at each iteration it sends one of the k (n) packets on channel P_1Sp (P_2Sp). Process *Spooler* executes a loop (the external one) in which it is willing to receive the first available request to print from either one of the two channels (ALT command). If it receives a request for $k(n)$ packets from $Chan_1$ ($Chan_2$), it will then enter a loop of reception of $k(n)$ messages from P_1Sp (P_2Sp).

The code presented in Fig. 119 is already in a form in which only control structures that include PAR and communications have been kept. All other operations are summarized within angle brackets. Fig. 120(a,b,c) presents the results of the translation of each single process (P_1, *Spooler*, and P_2, respectively). Observe how the **for** has been translated: since the static analysis doesn't include any variable,

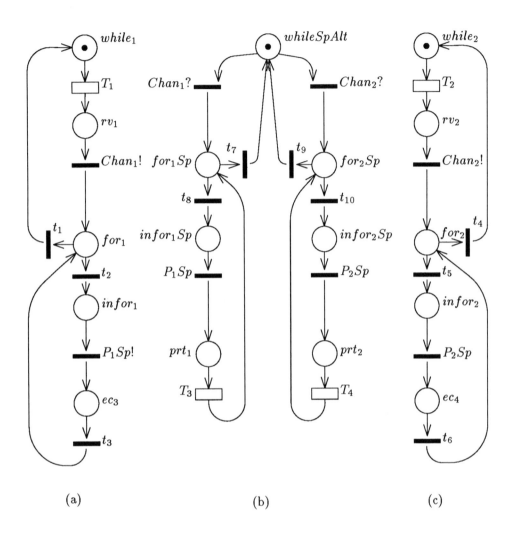

Figure 120   The GSPN system of each process schema

the exit from the **for** is probabilistically controlled. The *Spooler* code consists of a **while true**, an **ALT** and two **for**, one on each branch of the **ALT**. Communications statements have been translated as immediate transitions whose tags are obtained from the concatenation of the name of the channel with the type of input/output operation (? or !).

Fig. 121 presents the result of the complete translation of the program of Fig. 119. The centre portion of the net represents the spooler process, while the left and right portions represent processes P_1 and P_2, respectively. The **ALT** statement, which

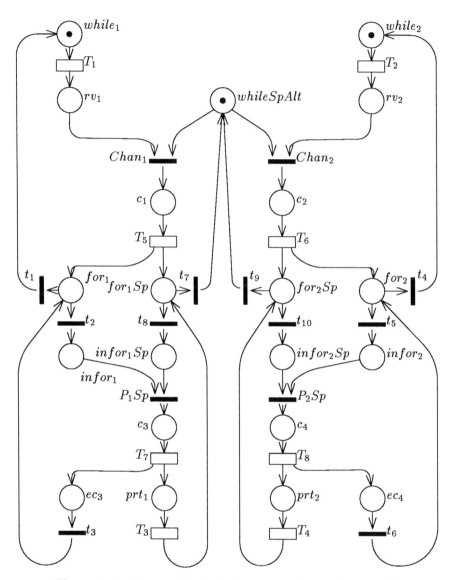

Figure 121 The complete GSPN system of the spooler example

is represented in the translation rule as a free-choice subnet, after the inclusion of the complete communication model becomes a non-free-choice conflict among communications on the two channels $Chan_1$ and $Chan_2$.

The structural analysis applied to the net of Fig. 121 indicates three minimal P-semiflows, all with a token count of one: each P-semiflow identifies one of the three processes. The three P-semiflows originate the following P-invariants.

$M(while_1)$	$+$	$M(rv_1)$	$+$	$M(c_1)$	$+$	$M(for_1)$	$+$		
	$+$	$M(infor_1)$	$+$	$M(c_3)$	$+$	$M(ec_3)$		$=$	1
$M(while_2)$	$+$	$M(rv_2)$	$+$	$M(c_2)$	$+$	$M(for_2)$	$+$		
	$+$	$M(infor_2)$	$+$	$M(c_4)$	$+$	$M(ec_4)$		$=$	1
$M(whileSpAlt)$	$+$	$M(c_1)$	$+$	$M(for_1Sp)$	$+$				
	$+$	$M(infor_1Sp)$	$+$	$M(c_3)$	$+$	$M(prt_1)$	$+$		
	$+$	$M(c_2)$	$+$	$M(for_2Sp)$	$+$				
	$+$	$M(infor_2Sp)$	$+$	$M(c_4)$	$+$	$M(prt_2)$		$=$	1

The token position inside each process represents the current state of the process. Observe that places $c_1 and c_3 (c_2 and c_4)$ are common to P_1 (P_2) and to *Spooler*, as they represent the action of communicating after the rendez-vous.

The analysis shows also that all transitions are covered by some T-semiflow, and that there are four minimal T-semiflows that represent the four possible behaviours of the loops. The following two minimal T-semiflows refer to the processes *Spooler* and P_1, and represent a run on the outer loop without entering the inner loop, and a single run of the inner loop, respectively.

T_1	$+$	$Chan_1$	$+$	T_5	$+$	t_1	$+$	t_7		
t_2	$+$	t_3	$+$	P_1Sp	$+$	T_7	$+$	t_7	$+$	T_3

Other two specular minimal T-invariants exist for processes *Spooler* and P_2.

The reachability graph analysis detects the following five deadlock states expressed as (P_1 + *Spooler* + P_2): ($while_1$ + $infor_1Sp$ + $while_2$), ($while_1$ + $infor_2Sp$ + $while_2$), ($while_1$ + $infor_1Sp$ + $infor_2$), ($infor_1$ + $infor_2Sp$ + $while_2$), ($infor_1$ + $whileSpAlt$ + $infor_2$). As we have already mentioned in Section 10.1, deadlock states detected by the static analysis do not necessarily mean deadlocks of the program, and this must be carefully verified *case by case*.

As an example let us check the state with places $while_1, while_2$ and $infor_1Sp$ marked. Processes P_1 and P_2 are in places $while_1$ and $while_2$ waiting to start a communication on channels $Chan_1$ and $Chan_2$, respectively; *Spooler* is waiting for an input from P_1Sp. This is clearly a deadlock since all processes are blocked. We can observe that the model can reach this state starting from a marking with process P_1 in place for_1 and *Spooler* in place for_1Sp. Indeed, since the number of iterations of the **for** is modelled probabilistically and since there is no relation in the net among the two **for** statements, process P_1 may decide to exit the for, while process *Spooler* may decide to do one more loop! These decisions are perfectly legal in the GSPN system, but do not correspond to a possible action of the program where the two **for** statements will execute the same number of loops since they are controlled by two variables whose values have been set equal prior to the beginning of the communication. This feature of the real program is not captured by the model that can thus enter an "illegal" situation.

In this simple case it is not too difficult to understand that the deadlock detected by the static analysis is a nonfault. This is not always the case, as it may be necessary to trace the model execution from the deadlock state back to the initial state: this may lead to many execution paths whose testing can be very tedious and error prone even in the presence of proper supporting tools.

10.4   Modelling Control Variables to Reduce Nonfaults

As we remarked at the beginning of this chapter, Petri nets have the capability of modelling a program in great detail. In this section we shall partially profit from this ability by including control variables into the model: we call control variables those that appear in a test explicitly included in the model. The goal is that of decreasing the number of anomalies detected by the analysis which are actually nonfaults.

There is a standard way to represent a variable in a Petri net model: a place is inserted in the net for each possible value of the variable; at most one of these places can be marked in a state, representing the value of the variable. Testing and assigning values to the variables is relatively simple, but the net becomes cluttered with arcs and places when the range of the variable is large.

Another possible solution is that of introducing one place per variable: the number of tokens in the place indicates the value of the variable. We may need two places if a variable can assume also negative values. If the variable can assume an infinite number of values we still have a Petri net with a finite number of places, but now the net may be unbounded. Testing the value of a variable is simple, while the assignment of a value requires extra arcs, places and transitions.

A simple modification of the GSPN of Fig. 121 is shown in Fig. 122, where the control variables are modelled using the second approach. Tags of places and transitions not shown in this figure are the same as in Fig. 121. The three control variables x, n and k are modelled by places p_x, p_n and p_k respectively. After communication on $Chan_1$ ($Chan_2$) the variables p_x and p_k (p_n) are initialized with the same constant value k (n); at each **for** iteration the transition that enters the loop decrements by one the corresponding control variable; the end of loop is deterministically implemented with a test for zero on the control variable place. In this net we have assumed that the values of n and k are known and are represented in the GSPN by assigning the corresponding multiplicity to the arcs from T_5 (T_6) to p_k (p_n) and p_x. In this case we can notice that the actual value of k (n) is not essential for capturing all the important aspects of the

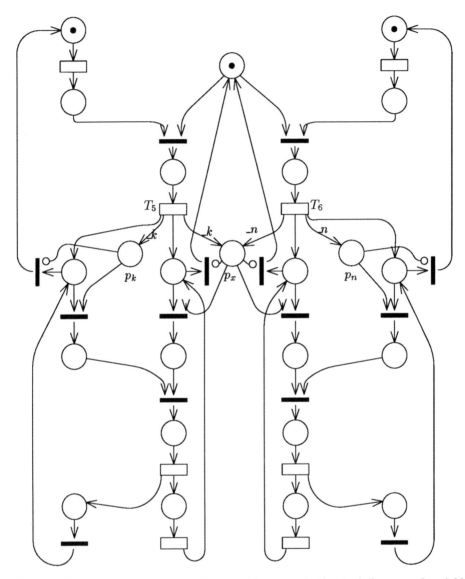

Figure 122   The GSPN system of the spooler example that includes control variables

qualitative behaviour of the net. It follows that the value of k (n) can be randomly generated each time the **for** loop starts (to mimic the variability of real messages that have different lengths), or be kept constant to a "typical value".

The structural analysis of the model of Fig. 122 reveals the same three P-semiflows obtained for the model of Fig. 121: places representing control variables are, of course, not included in any invariant.

No deadlock states are identified, i.e. the static analysis performed on this modified model of the program does not detect any nonfault. Indeed, by modelling the control variables we have forced the model to choose deterministically whether to enter or exit a loop, and this choice is not done independently by the processes (as in the previous model), but it is based on information exchanged between *Spooler* and the two processes P_1 and P_2. Moreover all transitions are live, meaning that we have not modelled impossible events.

The results are independent of the actual values of k (n). The size of the state space of the model of Fig. 122, however, grows linearly with the sum of n and k. The reason for introducing the control variables into the model was that of limiting the number of detected anomalies which are actually nonfaults. The price paid for obtaining such a result is an increased complexity of the graphical layout of the net as well as of its state space.

10.5   Stochastic Analysis

The previous subsections showed how to translate a program into a GSPN system. However, a complete definition of a GSPN system also requires that rates are associated with timed transition and weights are assigned to immediate transitions.

The rates associated with timed transitions that represent a PAR statement can be obtained from measurements on a real system. This is not true, instead, for the other timed transitions of the model as they may depend on input data. Consider for example the case of a timed transition that represents a whole sequence of statements; we can have two cases: either the number of executed statements is fixed (the sequence does not include any branching) or it is not. In the first case it is possible to estimate the execution time; in the second case some information is needed to estimate the mean number of times a loop is executed. If this is not possible, the only solution is to perform an analysis that depends on the mean values of the inputs. Similar problems exist for the assignment of weights to immediate transitions. It should be clear by this quick introduction to the problem that the assignment of weights and rates to transitions is an important step in the quantitative analysis, and it cannot be completely automated.

We shall use the example of Fig. 122 to show the type of results that can be derived from the GSPN system.

Probability of two communications at the same time — The CTMC derived from the GSPN system provides the probability that there is more than one communication place marked at the same time. The possibility of concurrent communication is given by: $P\{M(c_1)+M(c_2)+M(c_3)+M(c_4) > 1\}$. This probability is identically equal to zero, which is not surprising if we consider that c_1, c_2, c_3 and c_4 are part of the *Spooler* process and therefore are covered by a P-semiflow with token count equal to one. An analogous relation, based on the P-invariants of processes P_1 and P_2, holds for c_1, c_3 and c_2, c_4 considered two at a time: this indicates that the same channel can be used for transmitting the number of packets and the packets themselves, and, more importantly, that even if we want to keep the two channels separate for clarity, they can nevertheless be mapped on the same physical link without affecting the system performance.

Joint distribution of p_k and p_n — We want to study the probability of having $k = \alpha$ and $n = \beta$ where α and β are natural numbers. From the solution of the model we get the distribution of tokens in the different places, and we can compute all the desired joint probabilities. For our example we have obtained: $P\{M(p_k) > 0 \land M(p_n) > 0\} = 0$ and in a similar way $P\{M(p_k) > 0 \land M(p_x) = 0\} = 0$. This result confirms what was remarked about the dependence of the two variables.

Throughput — The comparison of throughputs of transitions representing a rendez-vous provides an indication of how often different processes need to synchronize. Assuming that all transition rates are identically equal to 1, and $n = k = 1$, then all transitions of the net have the same throughput (equal to 0.165468): this is due to the symmetry of P_1 and P_2 and to the fact that there are only two T-invariants: one for P_1 and one for P_2, and that all transitions in the invariants have multiplicity 1. We can destroy the symmetry by having P_2 requesting *Spooler* to print more than one packet (e.g. $n = 10$). As a consequence the throughputs of the transitions of P_1 are all the same (0.43274) and they differ from those of P_2. In particular the throughput for the transitions of P_2 inside the **for** loop is 10 times higher than the throughput of those outside the loop (0.413923 vs 0.041392). This is not surprising since process P_1 is now covered by a T-invariant where transitions belonging to the **for** loop have weight 10.

Mutual exclusion — If we define a process as "active" when it is not in a state in which it is waiting for a rendez-vous, then the probability that the two processes P_1 and P_2 are active at the same time is given by $P\{P_1 \text{ active} \land P_2 \text{ active}\}$ which in terms of distribution of tokens in places is given by:

$$P\{ \ M(while_1) + M(c_1) + M(for_1) + M(c_3) + M(ec_3) + M(while_2) + \\ + M(c_2) + M(for_2) + M(c_4) + M(ec_4) > 1\}$$

The value of this probability is a function of the transition rates, but it is always greater than zero, meaning that the two processes are not mutually exclusive, i.e. they can be doing useful work at the same time, and therefore it may be convenient to allocate them on two different processors.

11

MODELS OF CONCURRENT ARCHITECTURES

This chapter describes the GSPN-based performance evaluation of a parallel MIMD architecture with mesh interconnection scheme. The analysis considers regular computational structures in which data exchange and inter-process synchronization require communication only among processors that are physically connected. The effectiveness of the GSPN modelling technique for this class of architectures is shown through examples considering both the effect of the interaction policies among processes and the benefit of multitasking on the global efficiency of the architecture. The main value of this example is the modular construction of the GSPN model and the possibility of developing complex models starting from simple basic building blocks.

11.1 Concurrent Architectures

We consider MIMD architectures that use regular interconnection patterns and distributed memory schemes [Sei84]. The advantage and the success of this class of architectures are related to the availability of VLSI subsystems that can be used as building blocks of powerful massively parallel structures. In particular, different kinds of Transputer-based architectures, using this interconnection scheme, are now available as commercial products [INM89]. Moreover, most of the recently introduced massively parallel architectures are based on this paradigm (see for example the CM-5 from Thinking Machines Co. based on SPARC processing units and using a *fat tree* interconnection scheme and the T3D from Cray Research Co. based on DEC Alpha microprocessors using a torus interconnection network) [Hwa93].

In Fig. 123 a 3 × 3 regular mesh of processing elements is shown in which each processor is directly connected to its local neighbours. GSPN models for this class of architectures are developed under the assumptions that the workload is evenly distributed across all the processing elements and the computations assigned to each

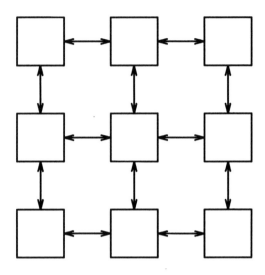

Figure 123   Regular mesh of processing elements

processor entail interactions with the local neighbours only (thus, we neglect any routing problem).

The first step of the modelling procedure is the development of basic GSPN models of the behaviour of a single processing unit. Models for multiprocessor architectures will be obtained combining such basic building blocks, according to the specific interconnection topology.

The computation assigned to each processor is modelled, in general, as a set of concurrent tasks performing cyclic activities. These activities include a local operation phase, whose duration is modelled by a stochastic variable, exponentially distributed with parameter λ, followed by a request for service addressed with equal probability to one of the neighbours. Service time is modelled by a stochastic variable, exponentially distributed with parameter μ. Thus, each processor must provide service to requests coming from any of its immediate neighbours. In these models we do not explicitly represent communication activities: the time required to perform sending and receiving operations is considered part of the service requesting and service providing tasks.

11.2   Single Processor Model

The basic structure of the GSPN model of each processing unit is shown in Fig. 124. It is composed of two different subnets. The first one, labelled (a), describes the local

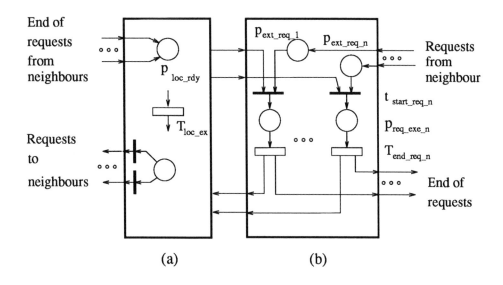

Figure 124   Basic model of the processing elements

activity of the task (modelled by the timed transition T_{loc_ex} with rate λ) along with the issuing of the service requests towards the neighbours. The second subnet (b), models the service provided by the processor to requests coming from neighbours.

In subnet (b), for any direct neighbour the model must include a place to describe the pending requests ($p_{ext\_req\_n}$ for the nth neighbour), an immediate transition ($t_{start\_req\_n}$) to model the granting operation, and a place ($p_{req\_exe\_n}$) followed by a timed transition ($T_{end\_req\_n}$) with rate μ describing the service operation. Once service has been completed, a token is returned to the requesting neighbour, where the task is inserted in the ready-task pool (place p_{loc_rdy} of subnet (a)).

The specific process interaction and scheduling policies determine whether a local computation is resumed or further external requests (if pending) are served next. These policies are modelled by subnet (a) (not yet specified) and by the priority of transitions $t_{start\_req\_n}$. In any case, the activity of each processor alternates between execution of local tasks (subnet (a)) and service of external requests (subnet (b)).

Two basic interaction policies will be considered in the following:

- *preemptive interaction*: requests coming from the neighbours are served with higher priority with respect to a local activity, i.e., requests are preemptive;
- *non-preemptive interaction*: requests are not preemptive, but are served at the end of the local operation.

All models in this section refer, for ease of representation, to a processor with

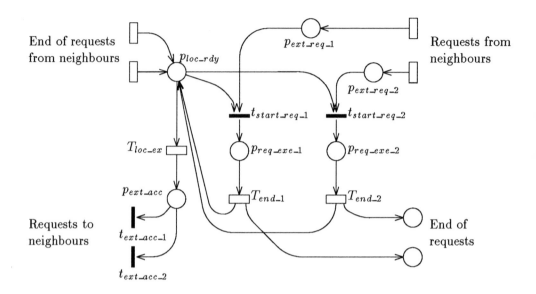

Figure 125   Simplified GSPN model of the behaviour of a processor in the case of preemptive interaction and no multitasking

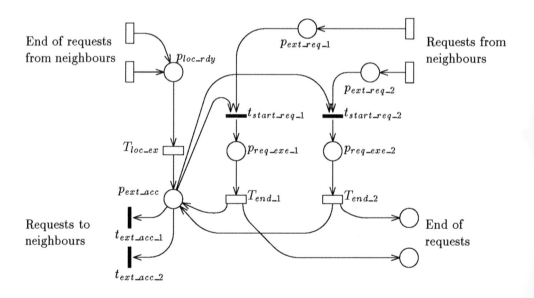

Figure 126   Simplified GSPN model of the behaviour of a processor in the case of non-preemptive interaction and no multitasking

two neighbours. We first discuss two simplified models considering only one task per processor. Fig. 125 shows the GSPN model of the behaviour of a processor in the case in which the requests are preemptive, whereas Fig. 126 depicts the case in which requests are not preemptive. In both cases the local computation is modelled by a place p_{loc_rdy} and a transition T_{loc_ex} with rate λ, the completion of the local computation is modelled by place p_{ext_acc}, and the request for service towards the neighbours is modelled by the transitions $t_{ext\_acc\_1}$ and $t_{ext\_acc\_2}$.

Under the preemptive policy (Fig. 125), the external requests are immediately served (firing of transition $t_{start\_req\_1}$ or $t_{start\_req\_2}$), preempting any local computation. The local computation may resume only when no further external requests are pending.

In the non-preemptive case (Fig. 126), service is given to neighbours only at the end of the local computation. In this case, at the end of the local operation, priority is given to accepting and serving requests from the neighbours rather than to issuing the local request. The priority of immediate transitions $t_{start\_req\_1}$ and $t_{start\_req\_2}$ is higher than that of immediate transitions $t_{ext\_acc\_1}$ and $t_{ext\_acc\_2}$. If the two groups of transitions have the same priority a deadlock may occur. Consider the case with two processors and assume both executing local activities (places p_{loc_rdy} of both processors have a token). When T_{loc_ex} of processor 1 fires a token is moved to p_{ext_acc} and transition $t_{ext\_acc\_2}$ of the same processor is enabled and its firing submits a request to processor 2. If the next transition to fire is T_{loc_ex} of processor 2 transition $t_{ext\_acc\_1}$ of processor 2 will be enabled together with transition $t_{ext\_req\_1}$ when T_{loc_ex} of processor 2 fires. If now transition $t_{ext\_acc\_1}$ is chosen to fire the net reaches a condition on which no transition is enabled.

11.3   Single Processor Model with Multitasking

Models in Figs. 125 and 126, though fairly intuitive, fail to appropriately distinguish between *processor* state and *task* state. As a consequence, when a task has completed its local execution phase and has been dispatched to one of the neighbours by the owner processor, the processor is not able to provide service to incoming requests. In actual concurrent architectures, efficiency in use of the processing power dictates the following constraints for any reasonable scheduling policy:

1. if no external request is pending and the ready-task pool is not empty, a local task is immediately scheduled for execution;
2. if the ready-task pool is empty but there are external requests pending, service of an external request is immediately scheduled for execution;
3. if the ready-task pool is not empty and there are external requests pending, either a local task or service of an external request is immediately scheduled for execution.

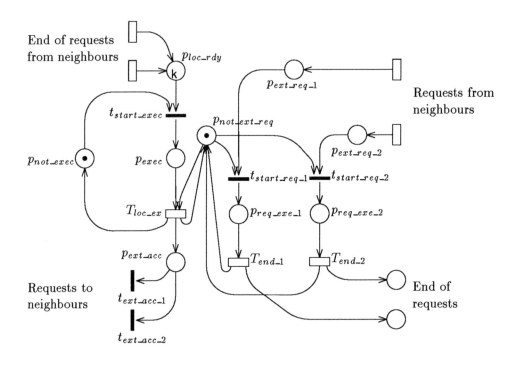

Figure 127   GSPN model of the behaviour of a processor in the case of preemptive
interaction and multitasking

The more elaborate GSPN models in Fig. 127 and 128 show the behaviour of a
processor taking into account multitasking and efficient use of the processing power.
Fig. 127 represents the case in which requests are preemptive, whereas Fig. 128
represents the case in which requests are not preemptive. It can be seen that both
these models satisfy the constraints on the scheduling policy mentioned before: when
a task terminates its local activity and sends a service request to a neighbour, the
processor is immediately free to serve incoming requests or to execute another task.

In Fig. 127 the local computation is modelled by place p_{exec} and transition T_{loc_ex}
with rate λ. The completion of the local computation moves a token in p_{not_exec},
and the requests for service towards the neighbours are modelled by the transitions
$t_{ext\_req\_1}$ and $t_{ext\_req\_2}$. The parametric initial marking of place p_{loc_rdy} (k) expresses
the number of tasks active on the processor (multitasking level). A token in place
$p_{not\_ext\_req}$ indicates that either the processor is executing a local task or it is idle.
Since the described policy is preemptive, in both cases an external request may be
immediately served. Multiple incoming requests are not allowed to preempt each other.

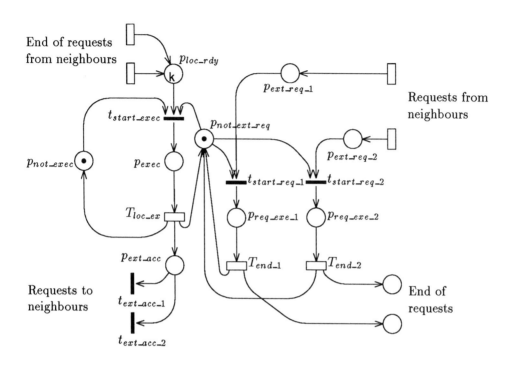

Figure 128 GSPN model of the behaviour of a processor in the case of non-preemptive interaction and multitasking

The following two P-invariants can be computed:

$$M(p_{not\_ext\_req}) + M(p_{ext\_req\_1}) + M(p_{ext\_req\_2}) = 1$$

$$M(p_{not\_exec}) + M(p_{exec}) = 1$$

These relationships imply that the processor can be in one out of six different states that can be classified according to the following scheme:

- executing a local task: $[M(p_{not\_ext\_req}) = 1] \wedge [M(p_{exec}) = 1]$,
- idle: $[M(p_{not\_ext\_req}) = 1] \wedge [M(p_{not\_exec}) = 1]$,
- serving an external request: $[M(p_{ext\_req\_1}) = 1] \vee [M(p_{ext\_req\_2}) = 1]$.

It must be observed that the last condition groups together four different states, being independent from the second P-invariant.

The model of Fig. 128 shows the case of a non-preemptive interaction. Firing of transition T_{loc_ex}, which as in the previous case models task execution, moves a token into both places $p_{not\_ext\_req}$ and p_{ext_acc}. The token in place $p_{not\_ext\_req}$ enables transition t_{start_exec}, thus making active a ready task. Pending requests of service from neighbours have priority over the execution of new local tasks, thus transitions $t_{start\_req\_1}$ and $t_{start\_req\_2}$ have higher priority than transition t_{start_exec}.

The following P-invariant can be computed:

$$M(p_{exec}) + M(p_{not\_ext\_req}) + M(p_{ext\_req\_1}) + M(p_{ext\_req\_2}) = 1$$

. This relationship implies that the processor is in one of the following states:

- executing a local task: $M(p_{exec}) = 1$,
- idle: $M(p_{not\_ext\_req}) = 1$,
- serving an external request: $[M(p_{ext\_req\_1}) = 1] \vee [M(p_{ext\_req\_2}) = 1]$.

11.4 Models of Mesh Structures

Once the behaviour of each processor has been defined by a suitable GSPN submodel, the GSPN model of a complete MIMD architecture can be obtained by proper interconnection of these submodels. GSPN analysis can now be applied to assess deadlock potential and other structural properties, along with performance measures such as processor idle time and overall processing power. We report results for both the cases of single task and multitask activities within each processor.

11.4.1 Mesh models without multitasking

Meshes of size 2×2, 2×3, and 3×3 were analysed considering both the simplified processor models (Figs. 125 and 126) and the more detailed ones (Figs. 127 and 128) with k set to 1. Structural analysis shows that, in all models, all places are covered by P-invariants so that the net is bounded. Furthermore, the number of T-invariants is given by the sum over all processors of the number of neighbours and all transitions are covered by T-invariants. This last result is a necessary condition for liveness and reversibility of bounded nets.

Table 39 reports the number of tangible states for the simplified models in Figs. 125 and 126, whereas Table 40 reports the number of states for the models in Figs. 127 and 128 with $k = 1$. With the simpler model, reachability graph construction for the 3×3 mesh with non-preemptive interaction among processors takes about 1 hour of CPU time on a SUN4 SPARCstation 1+ equipped with 16 Mbyte RAM, thus approaching the computational limits of GreatSPN on this workstation. With the more elaborate model, the analysis of the 3×3 mesh exceeds these limits.

Tables 41 and 42 show some performance figures obtained from the quantitative analysis assuming $\lambda = 1$ and $\mu = 10$. For all these models we can distinguish

Table 39 Number of tangible states for different mesh sizes and interaction policies (simplified models)

Mesh size and interaction policy	No. of states
2×2, preemptive	57
2×3, preemptive	833
3×3, preemptive	58681
2×2, not preemptive	117
2×3, not preemptive	2176
3×3, not preemptive	215712

Table 40 Number of tangible states for different mesh sizes and interaction policies (models in Figs. 127 and 128 with $k = 1$)

Mesh size and interaction policy	No. of states
2×2, preemptive	57
2×3, preemptive	939
3×3, preemptive	81893
2×2, not preemptive	189
2×3, not preemptive	4692
3×3, not preemptive	$\gg 300000$

Table 41 Performance results: idle time and effective processing power (simplified models)

Mesh size and interaction policy	processing power	idle time		
		2-neigh. pr.	3-neigh. pr.	4-neigh. pr.
2×2, preemptive	3.64(90.95%)	9.0%	-	-
2×3, preemptive	5.46(90.93%)	9.3%	8.9%	-
3×3, preemptive	8.16(90.67%)	9.6%	9.1%	9.2%
2×2, not preempt.	1.70(42.62%)	57.4%	-	-
2×3, not preempt.	2.44(40.67%)	60.1%	57.8%	-
3×3, not preempt.	3.54(39.33%)	58.6%	56.0%	55.6%

Table 42   Performance results: idle time and effective processing power

Mesh size and interaction policy	processing power	idle time		
		2-neigh. pr.	3-neigh. pr.	4-neigh. pr.
2×2, preemptive	3.66(91.52%)	8.5%	-	-
2×3, preemptive	5.49(91.47%)	8.7%	8.2%	-
3×3, preemptive	8.23(91.43%)	9.0%	8.2%	8.4%
2×2, not preempt.	2.66(66.39%)	33.6%	-	-
2×3, not preempt.	3.96(66.03%)	34.6%	32.7%	-

the processor performance figures according to the number of neighbours. Given the uniform workload, within each model, all processors with the same number of neighbours exhibit the same performance figures. Specifically, the idle time (time spent by the processors waiting for service) is reported in Tables 41 and 42, along with the overall effective processing power. In all models each processor can be in one of the following states:

- active executing its local computation
- active serving a request from one of the neighbours
- idle, with the local task waiting for service from a neighbour
- idle, but with the local task being served by a neighbour

Only the active states of the processors are considered in the computation of the effective processing power index reported in Tables 41 and 42.

The results in Tables 41 and 42 confirm that non-preemptive interaction policies achieve a low throughput if multitasking is not allowed, whereas preemptive interrupt-like policies are an effective replacement for multitasking. Thus, in this (unfair) comparison the preemptive interaction policy is dramatically more efficient than the non-preemptive one.

11.4.2   Mesh models with multitasking

Fig. 129 shows the model of a 2×2 concurrent architecture with preemptive interaction policy when the multitasking behaviour of Fig. 127 is adopted on each processor. The model of the processing element is sligthly simplified with respect to that of Fig. 127: places p_{exec} and $p_{not\_ext\_req}$ are merged, but the behaviour of the net is the same. Fig. 130 shows the model of an architecture with the same topology when the behaviour of each processor is modelled as in Fig. 128.

Tables 43 and 44 report some results that can be obtained by the GSPN analysis of these architectures for different values of the multitasking level. The throughput

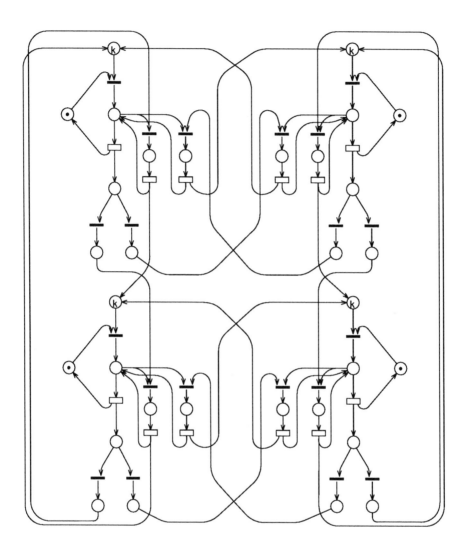

Figure 129   GSPN model of a 2 × 2 mesh in the case of preemptive interaction and multitasking

indicates the number of tasks that are executed by each processor per time unit. This performance parameter is obtained (with reference to Figs. 127 and 128), multiplying the rate of transition T_{loc_ex} by the probability that $M(p_{exec}) \geq 1$. In the case of preemptive interaction, considering the values of λ and μ used to derive the results, the asymptotic throughput is quickly reached with a multitasking level of only 3 tasks per processor. When a non-preemptive policy is used, the performance obtained at

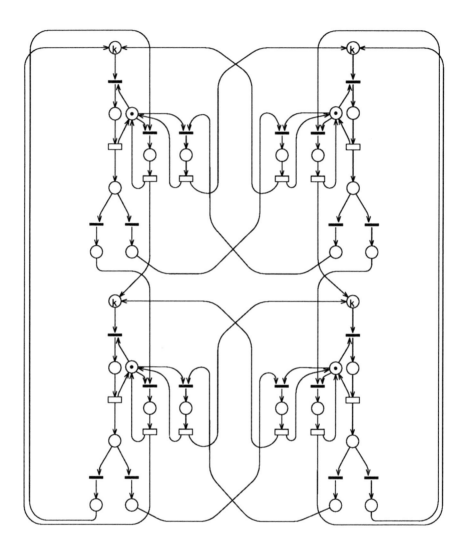

Figure 130   GSPN model of a 2 × 2 mesh in the case of non-preemptive interaction and
multitasking

a reasonable multitasking level (4) is very close to the asymptotic value (96.7%).
Therefore, multitasking allows this simpler policy to be adopted with a minimal
penalty on performance.

The cycle time in Tables 43 and 44 is simply the reciprocal of the throughput and
is reported for sake of clarity and to derive task latency. Latency represents the time
between two successive reschedulings of a given task and is computed by multiplying

Table 43   Performance results: 2×2 mesh, preemptive interaction with multitasking

multitasking level (k)	throughput	cycle time	%busy	latency	number of states
1	0.827	1.209	91.0%	1.209	57
2	0.903	1.107	99.3%	2.214	461
3	0.909	1.100	99.9%	3.300	1837
4	0.909	1.100	99.9%	4.400	5147
5	0.909	1.100	100%	5.500	11681

Table 44   Performance results: 2×2 mesh, non-preemptive interaction with multitasking

multitasking level (k)	throughput	cycle time	%busy	latency	number of states
1	0.604	1.657	66.4%	1.657	189
2	0.756	1.324	83.1%	2.648	5327
3	0.838	1.193	92.2%	3.579	37527
4	0.879	1.138	96.7%	4.552	141537

the cycle time by the number of tasks. Latency corresponds to the total delay that a task experiences in the following steps: execution on its local processor, waiting for service from the remote processor, receiving service from the remote processor, waiting in the ready-task queue until the next rescheduling. Individual waiting times may also be readily computed by applying Little's formula, since the mean number of tokens in each place and the throughput of transitions can be directly computed by GreatSPN.

The analysis of the 2×2 models seems to reach the computational limits of the available tools when the multitasking level is in the range of 4 to 5 (see Table 44), therefore the direct analysis of meshes with larger dimensions does not seem feasible with the present tools. However, the analysis of the single task models shows that the results obtained in the case of the 2×3 and 3×3 architectures do not differ significantly from the results obtained in the 2×2 case.

Appendix A

STOCHASTIC PROCESS FUNDAMENTALS

In this appendix we briefly summarize the basic results and definitions concerning the classes of stochastic processes produced by the execution of GSPNs.

The stochastic processes on which we mostly focus our attention are Markovian processes with finite state spaces (finite Markov chains), and their generalizations (Markov reward processes, and semi-Markov processes).

The goal of this appendix is not to provide a complete, rigorous, and formal treatment of the whole subject, which well deserves a book by itself, rather to introduce the notation used in the book, and to develop in the reader some intuition about the structure and the dynamics of the stochastic processes of interest.

Readers who desire a more formal and complete treatment of the theory of stochastic processes are referred to the vast literature that exists on this subject.

A.1 Basic Definitions

Stochastic processes are mathematical models useful for the description of random phenomena as functions of a parameter which usually has the meaning of time.

From a mathematical point of view, a *stochastic process* is a family of random variables $\{X(t), t \in T\}$ defined over the same probability space, indexed by the parameter t, and taking values in the set S. The values assumed by the stochastic process are called *states*, so that the set S is called the *state space* of the process.

Alternatively, we can view the stochastic process as a set of time functions, one for each element of the probability space. These time functions are called either *sample functions*, or sample paths, or realizations of the stochastic process.

The probabilistic description of a stochastic process is given by means of either the joint *probability distribution function*[1] (PDF – also known as the cumulative

---

[1] Note that throughout the book we use the notation $P\{A\}$ to indicate the probability of event A, and boldface to denote row vectors and matrices.

distribution function) of the random variables $\{X(t_i), i = 1, 2, \cdots, n\}$,

$$F_{\boldsymbol{X}}(\boldsymbol{x}; \boldsymbol{t}) = P\left\{X(t_1) \leq x_1, X(t_2) \leq x_2, \cdots, X(t_n) \leq x_n\right\} \tag{A.1}$$

or, alternatively, their joint *probability density function* (pdf),

$$f_{\boldsymbol{X}}(\boldsymbol{x}; \boldsymbol{t}) = \frac{\delta F_{\boldsymbol{X}}(\boldsymbol{x}; \boldsymbol{t})}{\delta \boldsymbol{x}} \tag{A.2}$$

The complete probabilistic description of the process $X(t)$ requires the specification of either one of these two functions for all values of n, and for all possible n-tuples $(t_1, t_2, \cdots, t_n)$.

The state space of the process can be either discrete or continuous. In the former case we have a *discrete-space* stochastic process, often referred to as a *chain*. In the latter case we have a *continuous-space* process. The state space of a chain is usually the set of natural integers $I\!N = \{0, 1, 2, \cdots\}$, or a subset of it.

If the index (time) parameter t is continuous, we have a *continuous-time* process. Otherwise the stochastic process is said to be a *discrete-time* process, and is often referred to as a stochastic *sequence*, denoted as $\{X_n, n = 0, 1, 2, \cdots\}$.

In this appendix we are interested in stochastic processes with a discrete state space, both in continuous and in discrete time. For the sake of simplicity, the results of this appendix only refer to the case of finite state spaces.

Possible sample functions of discrete-space stochastic processes are shown in Figs. 131(a) and 131(b) in the continuous- and discrete-time cases, respectively. The process is observed to spend a random time in each state before a transition to a new one. Note that in the continuous-time case the sample functions are assumed to be right-continuous.

A.2 Markov Processes

Markov processes owe their name to the Russian mathematician A.A.Markov, who studied the class of stochastic processes whose conditional PDF is such that

$$P\left\{X(t) \leq x \mid X(t_n) = x_n, X(t_{n-1}) = x_{n-1}, \cdots, X(t_0) = x_0\right\} \tag{A.3}$$

$$= P\left\{X(t) \leq x \mid X(t_n) = x_n\right\} \qquad t > t_n > t_{n-1} > \cdots > t_0$$

The above condition is known as the *Markov property*. A stochastic process $\{X(t), t \in T\}$ for which the above condition holds is said to be a *Markov process*. For the sake of simplicity we assume that T is the set of real nonnegative numbers,

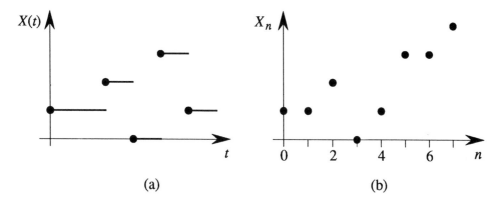

Figure 131   Possible sample functions of discrete-space stochastic processes:
(a) continuous-time; (b) discrete-time

i.e., $T = I\!R^+ = [0, \infty)$. [2]

In this appendix we consider only discrete-space Markov processes, known as *Markov chains* (MCs). MCs can be either continuous-time, or discrete-time, depending on the values that the index parameter t can assume. We thus consider both *discrete-time Markov chains* (DTMCs), and *continuous-time Markov chains* (CTMCs).

The application areas that we consider in this book allow a further assumption on the conditional PDF to be made. Indeed, we can assume that the behaviour of the systems that we study does not depend on the time of observation. We can thus arbitrarily choose the origin of the time axis. Hence it is possible to state that

$$P\{X(t) \le x \mid X(t_n) = x_n\} = P\{X(t - t_n) \le x \mid X(0) = x_n\} \qquad (A.4)$$

An MC for which the above condition holds is said to be (time) *homogeneous*.

In this appendix we restrict our presentation to homogeneous (and finite) MCs.

The Markov property can be intuitively explained by saying that the future evolution of the process, from the instant t_n on, is independent of the past history of the process; i.e., the state $X(t_n)$ contains all relevant information about the past process history. For a homogeneous MC it is not necessary to know t_n, and we can thus say that the future of the process is completely determined (in a probabilistic

---

[2] With the notation $[x, y)$ we indicate the real interval from x to y, including x but excluding y. Other authors indicate the same interval with the notation $[x, y[$.

sense) by the knowledge of the present state.

An important implication of the Markov property is that the distribution of the *sojourn time* in any state must be memoryless. Indeed, if the future evolution depends on the present state only, it cannot depend on the amount of time already spent by the process in the state. This, coupled with the observation that for a continuous random variable X the only pdf that satisfies the memoryless property

$$P\{X \geq t + \tau \mid X \geq t\} = P\{X \geq \tau\} \tag{A.5}$$

is the negative exponential

$$f_X(x) = a\, e^{-ax} \qquad x \geq 0 \tag{A.6}$$

leads to the conclusion that sojourn times in CTMC states must be exponentially distributed random variables.

Similarly, in the case of DTMCs, sojourn times in states must be geometrically distributed random variables: denoting by SJ the sojourn time in an arbitrary state,

$$P\{SJ = i\} = p^{i-1}(1-p) \qquad i = 1, 2, 3, \cdots \tag{A.7}$$

The importance of the memoryless distribution of the times spent in states can be better understood by noting that to check whether a stochastic process satisfies the Markov property, it suffices to check whether the distributions of sojourn times are memoryless, and whether the probabilities of going from one state to another depend only on the state the process is leaving and on the destination state.

The memoryless property of the exponential pdf can be visualized by observing its shape, depicted in Fig. 132. If we refer this distribution to a sojourn time, the original curve (solid line in Fig. 132) describes the probability density of the sojourn duration, at the instant when the state is entered.

After t units of time have elapsed without a change of state, we know that the sojourn time will not be less than t. The uncertainty about the sojourn time duration at this point is thus described by the tail of the exponential pdf at the right of the abscissa t (shaded area in Fig. 132). However, to obtain a valid pdf, it is necessary to rescale the tail so that it integrates to one. By so doing, we obtain the dashed line in Fig. 132, that is identical to the original curve, except for a translation to the right of t time units. This translation reflects the fact that, after t time units have been spent in the state, the sojourn time is made of a constant part (the time that already elapsed, equal to t) and a variable part (the time that will be further spent in the state, called the residual sojourn time), whose pdf is obtained by translating the dashed line in Fig. 132 to the left by t time units. The final result is thus that the residual sojourn time in a state at any instant always has the same pdf as the entire sojourn time.

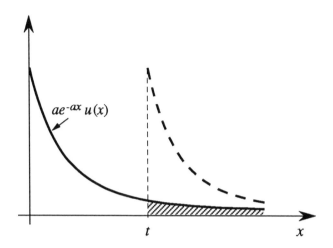

Figure 132 The negative exponential pdf and its memoryless characteristics

A.3 Discrete-Time Markov Chains

By specializing the Markov property to the discrete-time, discrete-space case we obtain the definition of a DTMC.

DEFINITION

The stochastic sequence $\{X_n, n = 0, 1, 2, \cdots\}$ is a DTMC provided that

$$
\begin{aligned}
P\{X_{n+1} = x_{n+1} \mid X_n = x_n, \ X_{n-1} = x_{n-1}, \cdots, \ X_0 = x_0\} \\
= P\{X_{n+1} = x_{n+1} \mid X_n = x_n\}
\end{aligned}
\tag{A.8}
$$

$\forall n \in \mathbb{N}$, and $\forall x_k \in S$.

The expression on the right-hand side of the above equation is the (one-step) *transition probability* of the chain, and it denotes the probability that the process goes from state x_n to state x_{n+1} when the index parameter is increased from n to $n + 1$. We use the following notation:

$$
p_{ij}(n) = P\{X_{n+1} = j \mid X_n = i\}
\tag{A.9}
$$

Since we consider only homogeneous DTMCs, the above probabilities do not depend on n, so that we may simplify the notation by dropping the variable n, and thus denote transition probabilities as

$$
p_{ij} = P\{X_{n+1} = j \mid X_n = i\}
\tag{A.10}
$$

This quantity provides the probability of being in state j at the next step, given that the present state is i. Note that summing the probabilities p_{ij} over all possible states j in the state space S, the result is 1.

The probability that the process is in state i at a given step n is denoted as

$$\eta_i(n) = P\{X_n = i\} \tag{A.11}$$

and it can be evaluated from the knowledge of the transition probabilities and of the initial PDF at time 0.

Moreover, in the case of DTMCs, the probabilistic behaviour of the process is completely described by the initial distribution and by the one-step transition probabilities.

A.3.1 Steady-state distribution

An important problem arising in the study of DTMCs concerns the existence and the evaluation of the steady-state distribution.

To present the main results concerning the steady-state analysis of DTMCs we must introduce several definitions concerning the chain and its states.

Let

$$f_j^{(n)} = P\{\text{first return in state } j \text{ occurs } n \text{ steps after leaving it}\} \tag{A.12}$$

and

$$f_j = \sum_{n=1}^{\infty} f_j^{(n)} = P\{\text{ever returning in state } j\} \tag{A.13}$$

A state j is said to be *transient* if $f_j < 1$, i.e., if there is a nonzero probability of never returning to state j after leaving it. A state j is said to be *recurrent* if $f_j = 1$, i.e., if the process returns to state j with probability one after leaving it.

Define the *period* of a state j, d_j, as the greatest common divisor of all positive integers n such that it is possible to reach state j from state j in n steps. A recurrent state j is said to be *periodic* with period d_j, if $d_j > 1$, and *aperiodic* if $d_j = 1$.

A state j is said to be *absorbing* if $p_{jj} = 1$. An absorbing state is recurrent.

For a recurrent state j define the *mean recurrence time* M_j as

$$M_j = \sum_{n=1}^{\infty} n\, f_j^{(n)} \tag{A.14}$$

The mean recurrence time is the average number of steps needed to return to state j for the first time after leaving it.

Recurrent states for which $M_j < \infty$ are said to be *recurrent nonnull*. Recurrent states for which the mean recurrence time is infinite are said to be *recurrent null*. In the case of DTMCs with finite state space (finite DTMCs), recurrent states cannot be null. Since we consider only the finite state space case, we shall use the term recurrent implying recurrent nonnull.

A subset A of the state space S is said to be *closed* if no transition is possible from states in A to states in $\bar{A}$ (the complement of set A), i.e., if

$$\sum_{i \in A} \sum_{j \in \bar{A}} p_{ij} = 0 \tag{A.15}$$

A DTMC is said to be *irreducible* if no proper subset of S is closed. This implies that every state of the chain can be reached from every other state.

It can be shown that all states of a finite and irreducible DTMC are recurrent. Note that an irreducible chain cannot comprise absorbing states. Moreover, either all states are aperiodic, or they all have the same period d. In the former case the chain itself is said to be aperiodic, while it is said to be periodic with period d in the latter case.

A distribution $\{z_i , i \in S\}$ defined on the DTMC states is said to be *stationary* if

$$z_i = \sum_{j \in S} z_j \, p_{ji} \quad \forall i \in S \tag{A.16}$$

that is if, once this distribution is reached, then for all successive steps this is the distribution of the process.

Define the *limiting probabilities* $\{\eta_j, \ j \in S\}$ as

$$\eta_j = \lim_{n \to \infty} \eta_j(n) \tag{A.17}$$

It can be shown that for all finite, aperiodic, homogeneous DTMCs the above limits exist. Moreover, if the DTMC is irreducible, the limits are independent of the initial distribution $\{\eta_j(0), j \in S\}$, and since all states are recurrent,

$$\eta_j > 0 \quad \forall j \in S \tag{A.18}$$

and the limiting probabilities $\{\eta_j, j \in S\}$ form a stationary distribution.

In this case all states are said to be *ergodic,* and the DTMC itself is said to be ergodic; moreover the limiting probabilities $\{\eta_j, j \in S\}$ are unique. They can be obtained by solving the system of linear equations

$$\eta_j = \sum_{i \in S} \eta_i \, p_{ij} \quad \forall j \in S \qquad \text{(a)}$$

$$\sum_{j \in S} \eta_j = 1 \qquad \text{(b)} \tag{A.19}$$

Furthermore, in this case a very simple relation exists between the state limiting probabilities and the state mean recurrence times:

$$\eta_j = \frac{1}{M_j} \tag{A.20}$$

The limiting probabilities af an ergodic DTMC are often called also equilibrium or steady-state probabilities.

The average time spent by the process in state j in a period of fixed duration τ at steady-state, $v_j(\tau)$, can be obtained as the product of the steady-state probability of state j times the duration of the observation period:

$$v_j(\tau) = \eta_j \, \tau \qquad (A.21)$$

The average time spent by the process in state i at steady-state, between two successive visits to state j, v_{ij}, can be shown to equal the ratio of the steady-state probabilities of states i and j:

$$v_{ij} = \frac{\eta_i}{\eta_j} \qquad (A.22)$$

The term *visit* can be explained as follows. We say that the process visits state i at time n if $X_n = i$. The quantity v_{ij} is called *visit ratio* since it indicates the average number of visits to state i between two successive visits to state j.

A.3.2 *Matrix formulation*

The use of a matrix notation can be particularly convenient, since it simplifies many of the above results. Define the transition probability matrix $\boldsymbol{P} = [p_{ij}]$, whose entries are the transition probabilities, as well as the vector $\boldsymbol{\eta} = [\eta_i]$, whose entries are the limiting probabilities.

If the finite DTMC is ergodic, the steady-state probability distribution can be evaluated from the matrix equation:

$$\boldsymbol{\eta} = \boldsymbol{\eta} \, \boldsymbol{P} \qquad (A.23)$$

that is the matrix form of (A.19a). As before, the normalizing condition (A.19b) must be used in conjunction with (A.23) to identify the unique steady-state probability distribution.

As a final comment on the properties of DTMCs, we remark that, as said before, the sojourn time in state i is a geometrically distributed random variable SJ_i with parameter p_{ii}

$$P\{SJ_i = k\} = p_{ii}^{k-1} \, (1 - p_{ii}) \qquad k = 1, 2, \cdots \qquad (A.24)$$

Indeed, given that the process is in state i, at each step the probability of leaving state i is $(1 - p_{ii})$, and the choice is repeated independently at each step.

The average number of steps spent in state i before going to another state each time the process enters state i is then:

$$E[SJ_i] = \frac{1}{1 - p_{ii}} \qquad (A.25)$$

A.3.3   Example

Consider a two-processor system comprising two CPUs with their own private memories, and one common memory which can be accessed only by one processor at a time.

The two CPUs share the same clock, and they execute in their private memories for a random number of cycles before issuing a common memory access request. Assume that this random number of cycles is geometrically distributed with parameter p, so that for a processor executing in its private memory at each cycle the probability of a common memory access request is p, and the average number of cycles between two common memory access requests is $(1-p)^{-1}$.

The common memory access duration is also assumed to be a geometrically distributed random variable with parameter q, so that, when a common memory access is in progress, the probability of completing an access to the common memory at each cycle is q, and the average duration of the common memory access is $(1-q)^{-1}$ cycles.

To start with the simplest possible environment, assume that only one processor is operational. In this case the system can only be in one of two states:

1. the processor is executing in its private memory;
2. the processor is accessing the common memory.

The system behaviour can thus be modelled by a two-state discrete-time process. The assumptions introduced on the system workload are such that the system dynamics satisfy the memoryless property, so that the behaviour is Markovian.

We can thus describe the system operations with a 2-state DTMC with transition probability matrix

$$\begin{bmatrix} 1-p & p \\ q & 1-q \end{bmatrix}$$

Alternatively, the 2-state DTMC can be characterized with the graph shown in Fig. 133. This graph conveys the same information as the transition probability matrix. Indeed, each of the two representations can be derived from the other. The graphical representation is often called the state (transition) diagram of the DTMC.

This 2-state DTMC is obviously irreducible and aperiodic, provided that p and q are larger than zero and smaller than one. Hence, under the same assumption, the model is ergodic, so that the steady-state distribution can be found by solving the system of linear equations,

$$\begin{aligned}
\eta_1 &= (1-p)\,\eta_1 + q\,\eta_2 \\
\eta_2 &= p\,\eta_1 + (1-q)\,\eta_2 \\
1 &= \eta_1 + \eta_2
\end{aligned}$$

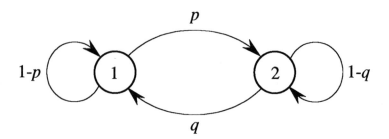

Figure 133 State transition diagram of the single processor model

Note that the first two equations are linearly dependent, so that one can be discarded.

The steady-state distribution can immediately be found to be:

$$\eta = \left(\frac{q}{p+q} \, , \, \frac{p}{p+q} \right)$$

This means that the steady-state probability of the processor executing in its private memory is $\frac{q}{p+q}$, that the mean recurrence time of state 2 is $\frac{p+q}{p}$ cycles, and that the average number of common memory access cycles between two consecutive private memory accesses is $\frac{p}{q}$.

Let us now return to the two-processor system: name the two processors A and B, and characterize the workloads of the two processors similarly to what was done above, adding subscripts to identify the two processors (i.e., use p_A to denote the common memory access probability of processor A, and so on).

The system can now be in the following five states:

1. both processors are executing in their private memories;
2. processor B is executing in its private memory, and processor A is accessing the common memory;
3. processor A is executing in its private memory, and processor B is accessing the common memory;
4. processor B is waiting for the common memory, and processor A is accessing the common memory;
5. processor A is waiting for the common memory, and processor B is accessing the common memory.

The system behaviour can thus be modelled by a five-state discrete-time process. Again, the assumptions introduced on the system workload are such that the system dynamics satisfy the memoryless property, so that the behaviour is Markovian.

We can thus describe the system operations with a five-state DTMC with transition probability matrix

$$
\boldsymbol{P} = \begin{bmatrix}
\overline{p_A}\,\overline{p_B} & p_A\,\overline{p_B} & \overline{p_A}\,p_B & p_A\,p_B & 0 \\
q_A\,\overline{p_B} & \overline{q_A}\,\overline{p_B} & q_A\,p_B & \overline{q_A}\,p_B & 0 \\
\overline{p_A}\,q_B & p_A\,q_B & \overline{p_A}\,\overline{q_B} & 0 & p_A\,\overline{q_B} \\
0 & 0 & q_A & \overline{q_A} & 0 \\
0 & q_B & 0 & 0 & \overline{q_B}
\end{bmatrix}
$$

where $\overline{p_A} = (1 - p_A)$, $\overline{p_B} = (1 - p_B)$, $\overline{q_A} = (1 - q_A)$, and $\overline{q_B} = (1 - q_B)$.

Note that in the case of two simultaneous common memory access requests, priority is given to processor A.

The chain is irreducible and aperiodic, hence ergodic, under the condition that p_A, p_B, q_A, and q_B are all greater than zero and smaller than one.

A.4 Continuous-Time Markov Chains

By specializing the Markov property to the continuous-time, discrete-space case we obtain the definition of a CTMC.

DEFINITION
The stochastic process $\{X(t), t \geq 0\}$ is a CTMC provided that

$$
P\{X(t_{n+1}) = x_{n+1} \mid X(t_n) = x_n, X(t_{n-1}) = x_{n-1}, \cdots, X(t_0) = x_0\}
\tag{A.26}
$$

$$
= P\{X(t_{n+1}) = x_{n+1} \mid X(t_n) = x_n\} \qquad t_{n+1} > t_n > \cdots > t_0
$$

$\forall n \in \mathbb{N}$, $\forall x_k \in S$, and all sequences $\{t_0, t_1, \cdots, t_{n+1}\}$ such that $t_0 < t_1 < \cdots < t_{n+1}$.

This definition is the continuous-time version of (A.8), and also in this case the right-hand side of the equation is the transition probability of the chain.

We use the notation

$$
p_{ij}(t, \theta) = P\{X(\theta) = j \mid X(t) = i\}
\tag{A.27}
$$

to identify the probability that the process be in state j at time θ, given that it is in state i at time t, assuming $\theta > t$. When $\theta = t$ we define

$$
p_{ij}(t, t) = \begin{cases} 1, & i = j \\ 0, & \text{otherwise} \end{cases}
\tag{A.28}
$$

If the CTMC is time-homogeneous, the transition probabilities depend only on the time difference $\tau = \theta - t$, so that we can simplify the notation by writing

$$p_{ij}(\tau) = P\{X(t + \tau) = j \mid X(t) = i\} \qquad (A.29)$$

to denote the probability that the process be in state j after an interval of length τ, given that at present it is in state i.

Also in this case, summing $p_{ij}(\tau)$ over all possible states j in the state space S we must obtain as a result 1 for all values of τ.

It can be shown that the initial distribution, together with the transition probabilities, allows the computation of the joint PDF of any set of random variables extracted from the process. This implies that the complete probabilistic description of the process depends only on the initial distribution and on the transition probabilities.

A.4.1 Steady-state distribution

Let $\eta_i(t) = P\{X(t) = i\}$, and define the limiting probabilities $\{\eta_j, j \in S\}$ as

$$\eta_j = \lim_{t \to \infty} \eta_j(t) \qquad (A.30)$$

The conditions for the existence of the steady-state distribution depend, as in the discrete-time case, on the structure of the chain and on the classification of states.

Define

$$q_{ij} = \lim_{\Delta t \to 0} \frac{p_{ij}(\Delta t)}{\Delta t} \qquad i \neq j$$

$$q_{ii} = \lim_{\Delta t \to 0} \frac{p_{ii}(\Delta t) - 1}{\Delta t} \qquad (A.31)$$

Such limits can be shown to exist under certain regularity conditions. The intuitive interpretation of the above two quantities is as follows. Given that the system is in state i at some time t, the probability that a transition occurs to state j in a period of duration Δt is $q_{ij} \Delta t + O(\Delta t)$. The rate at which the process moves from state i to state j thus equals q_{ij}. Similarly, $-q_{ii} \Delta t + O(\Delta t)$ is the probability that the process moves out of state i towards any other state in a period of duration Δt. Thus, $-q_{ii}$ is the rate at which the process leaves state i. We shall assume that q_{ij} is finite $\forall i, j \in S$. Note that

$$\sum_{j \in S} q_{ij} = 0 \qquad \forall i \in S \qquad (A.32)$$

Define h_j to be the *first hitting time* of state j, i.e., the instant in which the process enters state j for the first time after leaving the present state. Moreover let

$$f_{ij} = P\{h_j < \infty \mid X(0) = i\} \qquad (A.33)$$

A state j is said to be transient if $f_{jj} < 1$, i.e., if there is a positive probability that the process never returns to state j after leaving it. A state j is said to be recurrent if $f_{jj} = 1$, i.e., if the process returns to state j in a finite time with probability 1. A state i is said to be absorbing if $q_{ij} = 0$ for all $j \neq i$, hence if $q_{ii} = 0$. A subset A of the state space S is said to be closed if

$$\sum_{i \in A} \sum_{j \in \bar{A}} q_{ij} = 0 \qquad \text{(A.34)}$$

In this case $p_{ij}(t) = 0$ for all $i \in A$, all $j \in \bar{A}$, and all $t > 0$. The states in $\bar{A}$ are thus not reachable from states in A.

A CTMC is said to be irreducible if no proper subset of S is closed, hence if every state of S is reachable from any other state.

It can be shown that for all finite, irreducible, homogeneous CTMCs the limiting probabilities exist, are independent of the initial distribution $\{\eta_j(0), j \in S\}$, and form the steady-state distribution, which can be computed by solving the system of linear equations

$$\sum_{j \in S} q_{ji}\eta_j = 0 \qquad \forall i \in S \qquad \text{(A.35)}$$

together with the normalization condition

$$\sum_{i \in S} \eta_i = 1 \qquad \text{(A.36)}$$

In this case the states of the CTMC are ergodic, so that the chain itself is said to be ergodic.

The mean recurrence time for a state j, M_j, is defined as the average time elapsing between two successive instants at which the process enters state j. It can be shown that

$$M_j = -\frac{1}{\eta_j \, q_{jj}} \qquad \text{(A.37)}$$

A.4.2 Matrix formulation

Define the transition probability matrix $\boldsymbol{P}(t)$ as:

$$\boldsymbol{P}(t) = [p_{ij}(t)], \quad \boldsymbol{P}(0) = \boldsymbol{I} \qquad \text{(A.38)}$$

and define the matrix

$$\boldsymbol{Q} = [q_{ij}] \qquad \text{(A.39)}$$

that is called either the *infinitesimal generator* of the transition probability matrix $\boldsymbol{P}(t)$, or the *transition rate matrix*.

The matrix equation defining the steady-state distribution of an ergodic CTMC together with (A.36) is

$$\boldsymbol{\eta}\, \boldsymbol{Q} = 0 \tag{A.40}$$

where $\boldsymbol{\eta}$ is the vector

$$\boldsymbol{\eta} = \{\eta_1, \eta_2, \cdots\} \tag{A.41}$$

A.4.3 Sojourn and recurrence times

Sojourn times in CTMC states are exponentially distributed random variables, as was previously noted. In particular, denoting by SJ_i the sojourn time in state $i \in S$, it can be shown that

$$f_{SJ_i}(\tau_i) = -q_{ii}\, e^{q_{ii}\tau_i} \qquad \tau_i \geq 0 \tag{A.42}$$

The average sojourn time in state i is thus

$$E\,[SJ_i] = -\frac{1}{q_{ii}} \tag{A.43}$$

Moreover, if we define the *forward recurrence time* at time t, $\phi(t)$, as the amount of time that the process will still spend in the state occupied at t, or equivalently, as the length of the time period from t to the next change of state, i.e.

$$\phi(t) = \min\{\theta > 0 : X(t+\theta) \neq X(t)\} \tag{A.44}$$

due to the memoryless PDF of sojourn times in states, it is possible to show that

$$P\,\{\phi(t) > x \mid X(t) = i\} = e^{q_{ii}\, x} \qquad x \geq 0 \tag{A.45}$$

Hence the forward recurrence time is exponentially distributed with the same PDF as the sojourn time.

The same can be shown to be true for the *backward recurrence time,* defined as the time the process has already spent in the present state at time t, provided that the set T in which the parameter t takes values is $T = (-\infty, \infty)$. The distribution of the backward recurrence time is instead a truncated exponential in the usual case $T = [0, \infty)$. In any case, both the forward and the backward recurrence times are exponentially distributed in the limit for $t \to \infty$.

A.4.4 The embedded Markov chain

Consider the sample function of the CTMC $\{X(t), t \geq 0\}$ shown in Fig. 134. The stochastic sequence $\{Y_n, n \geq 0\}$ is a DTMC, and it is called the *embedded Markov chain* (EMC) of the process $X(t)$.

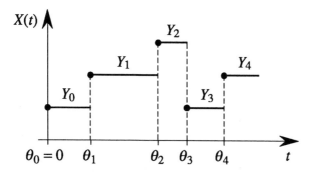

Figure 134   Possible sample function of a CTMC (or SMP) from which an EMC can be derived

The transition probabilities of the EMC, r_{ij}, are defined as

$$r_{ij} = P\{Y_{n+1} = j \mid Y_n = i\} \tag{A.46}$$

Note that, for all times t,

$$r_{ij} = P\{X[t + \phi(t)] = j \mid X(t) = i\} \tag{A.47}$$

Using the properties of CTMCs it is easy to show that

$$P\{Y_{n+1} = j, \theta_{n+1} - \theta_n > \tau \mid Y_n = i\} = r_{ij}\, e^{q_{ii}\tau}, \qquad \tau \geq 0 \tag{A.48}$$

and that the transition probabilities r_{ij} can be obtained as a function of the transition rates q_{ij}. Indeed, in the case of an ergodic CTMC,

$$r_{ij} = \begin{cases} -q_{ij}/q_{ii} & i \neq j \\ 0 & i = j \end{cases} \tag{A.49}$$

If the CTMC $\{X(t), t \geq 0\}$ is ergodic, then the DTMC $\{Y_n, n \geq 0\}$ is irreducible recurrent (possibly periodic), and the steady-state distribution of the process $X(t)$ can be determined from the *stationary* distribution of the sequence Y_n. Let

$$\eta_j^{(X)} = \lim_{t \to \infty} P\{X(t) = j\} \tag{A.50}$$

and let the quantities $\eta_j^{(Y)}$ be obtained by solving the system of linear equations that gives the stationary distribution for the DTMC $\{Y_n, n \geq 0\}$

$$\eta_j^{(Y)} = \sum_{i \in S} \eta_i^{(Y)} r_{ij} \tag{A.51}$$

$$\sum_{i \in S} \eta_i^{(Y)} = 1 \tag{A.52}$$

The steady-state probabilities for the CTMC $X(t)$ can then be shown to be

$$\eta_j^{(X)} = \frac{\left(\eta_j^{(Y)} / - q_{jj} \right)}{\sum_{i \in S} \left(\eta_i^{(Y)} / - q_{ii} \right)} \tag{A.53}$$

or, equivalently,

$$\eta_j^{(X)} = \frac{(1 / - q_{jj})}{\sum_{i \in S} \left(\eta_i^{(Y)} / \left[-q_{ii} \, \eta_j^{(Y)} \right] \right)} = \frac{E \left[SJ_j^{(X)} \right]}{\sum_{i \in S} v_{ij} \, E \left[SJ_i^{(X)} \right]} \tag{A.54}$$

where $E \left[SJ_j^{(X)} \right]$ is the average sojourn time in state j measured on the process $X(t)$, and the v_{ij} are the visit ratios relative to the EMC. Thus the steady-state probability of any state j in a CTMC can be evaluated as the ratio of the average sojourn time in state j to the sum of the products of the average sojourn times in all states i in the state space S multiplied by the visit ratios v_{ij}, i.e., by the average number of times that the process visits state i between two successive visits to state j. Note that we are considering a portion of the process that begins with the entrance into state j and ends just before the next entrance into state j. Call this portion of process a *cycle*. The steady-state probability of state j is obtained by dividing the average amount of time spent in state j during a cycle by the average cycle duration.

A.4.5 Example

Consider the continuous-time version of the two-processor system that was considered as an example of a DTMC model. We again have two CPUs with their own private memories, and one common memory that can be accessed by only one processor at a time.

The two CPUs execute in their private memories for a random time before issuing a common memory access request. Assume that this random time is exponentially distributed with parameter λ, so that the average time spent by each CPU executing in private memory between two common memory access requests is λ^{-1}.

The common memory access duration is also assumed to be an exponentially distributed random variable, with parameter μ, so that the average duration of the common memory access is μ^{-1}.

Also in this case, let us initially assume that only one processor is operational. Again the system can be in only one of two states (the same two states as in the discrete-time case):

1. the processor is executing in its private memory;

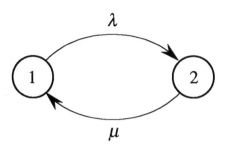

Figure 135   State transition rate diagram of the single processor model

2. the processor is accessing the common memory.

The system behaviour can thus be modelled with a two-state continuous-time process. Also in this case, the assumptions introduced on the system workload are such that the system dynamics satisfy the memoryless property, so that the behaviour is Markovian.

We can thus describe the system operations with a 2-state CTMC with infinitesimal generator:

$$Q = \begin{bmatrix} -\lambda & \lambda \\ \mu & -\mu \end{bmatrix}$$

Alternatively, the 2-state CTMC can be characterized with the graph shown in Fig. 135, called the state transition rate diagram of the CTMC.

The steady-state distribution of the 2-state DTMC can be found by solving the system of linear equations

$$
\begin{aligned}
0 &= -\lambda\, \eta_1 + \mu\, \eta_2 \\
0 &= \lambda\, \eta_1 - \mu\, \eta_2 \\
1 &= \eta_1 + \eta_2
\end{aligned}
$$

Note that the first two equations are linearly dependent, so that one can be discarded.
The steady-state distribution can be found to be

$$\eta = \left(\frac{\mu}{\lambda + \mu} , \ \frac{\lambda}{\lambda + \mu} \right)$$

This means, for example, that the steady-state probability of the processor executing in its private memory is $\dfrac{\mu}{\lambda + \mu}$.

Coming now to the two-processor system, we name the two processors A and B, and characterize the workload parameters with the appropriate subscripts. We can observe that the system can be in the same five states already identified in the discrete-time model:

1. both processors are executing in their private memories;
2. processor B is executing in its private memory, and processor A is accessing the common memory;
3. processor A is executing in its private memory, and processor B is accessing the common memory;
4. processor B is waiting for the common memory, and processor A is accessing the common memory;
5. processor A is waiting for the common memory, and processor B is accessing the common memory.

The system behaviour can thus be modelled with a five-state continuous-time process. Again, the assumptions introduced on the system workload are such that the system dynamics satisfy the memoryless property, so that the behaviour is Markovian.

We can thus describe the system operations with a five-state CTMC with infinitesimal generator

$$
Q = \begin{bmatrix}
-\lambda_A - \lambda_B & \lambda_A & \lambda_B & 0 & 0 \\
\mu_A & -\mu_A - \lambda_B & 0 & \lambda_B & 0 \\
\mu_B & 0 & -\lambda_A - \mu_B & 0 & \lambda_A \\
0 & 0 & \mu_A & -\mu_A & 0 \\
0 & \mu_B & 0 & 0 & -\mu_B
\end{bmatrix}
$$

Alternatively, the five-state CTMC can be characterized with the state transition rate diagram shown in Fig. 136.

It is interesting to note that now the model description is simpler than it was in the discrete-time case. This is due to the fact that the use of continuous random variables for the durations of execution and access times makes the probability of two simultaneous events go to zero. In the construction of the continuous-time model thus we just have to describe the events relating to the individual processor activities, without worrying about the possibility of two (or more) events happening at the same time. In particular, it is not necessary to give priority to processor A when both processors simultaneously request access to the common memory, since this event has probability zero.

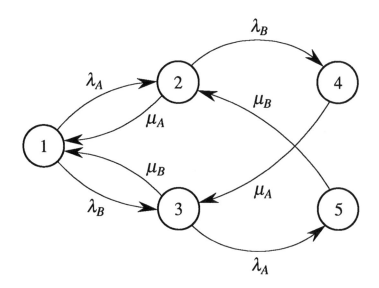

Figure 136   State transition rate diagram of the two-processor model

A.5   Aggregation of States in Markov Chains

Often, Markovian models of real systems comprise quite a large number of states, so that the numerical evaluation of the steady-state distribution is computationally expensive, in some cases infeasible.

On the other hand, the equilibrium solution is often used to derive specific quantities by performing a weighted summation of steady-state probabilities. In most cases, many states have the same weights, so that the same result could be achieved by solving a reduced problem in which the model comprises fewer macrostates, each macrostate containing all (or some) of the states for which the associated performance measure is the same.

In this section we address this problem by giving conditions for the existence of a compact aggregate Markovian model.

A.5.1   Aggregation in discrete-time Markov chains

Consider first a finite, ergodic DTMC $\{X_n, n = 0, 1, \cdots\}$ with state space $S = \{1, 2, \cdots, N\}$, transition probability matrix P, state distribution $\eta(n)$, and steady-

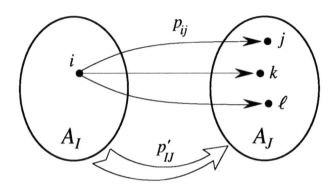

Figure 137   Transition probabilities between states and macrostates

state distribution η.

Define a partition of S by aggregating states into macrostates A_I such that

$$S = \bigcup_{I=1}^{M} A_I \quad \text{and} \quad \forall I \neq J \quad I, J \in (1, 2, \cdots, M) \quad A_I \cap A_J = \emptyset \qquad \text{(A.55)}$$

A new stochastic sequence $\{Y_n, n = 0, 1, \cdots\}$ can be defined on the set of macrostates, with state space $S' = \{A_1, A_2, \cdots, A_M\}$. To determine whether this new stochastic sequence is an ergodic DTMC, it is necessary to examine the conditional probabilities

$$P\{Y_{n+1} = A_J \mid Y_n = A_I, Y_{n-1} = A_K, \cdots, Y_0 = A_L\} \qquad \text{(A.56)}$$

If such conditional probabilities only depend on the most recent macrostate A_I, we recognize that $\{Y_n, n \geq 0\}$ is a DTMC, with transition probabilities (see Fig. 137)

$$p'_{IJ}(n) = P\{Y_{n+1} = A_J \mid Y_n = A_I\}$$

Summing over all states i in A_I and all states j in A_J, we obtain

$$p'_{IJ}(n) = \sum_{i \in A_I} \sum_{j \in A_J} p_{ij} \, \nu_{i|I}(n) \qquad \text{(A.57)}$$

where

$$\nu_{i|I}(n) = \frac{\eta_i(n)}{\sum_{k \in A_I} \eta_k(n)} \qquad \text{(A.58)}$$

represents the conditional probability of being in state $i \in A_I$ given that the process is in macrostate A_I at step n. Note that a necessary and sufficient condition for the process $\{Y_n, n \geq 0\}$ to be an ergodic DTMC is that

$$\sum_{j \in A_J} p_{ij} = p'_{IJ}(n) \tag{A.59}$$

for all $i \in A_I$, and for all n. Indeed, in this case the conditional probabilities (A.56) depend only on the present (macro)state, and the dependence on n in (A.57) and (A.58) disappears.

Condition (A.59) is the *lumpability condition* of the DTMC $\{X_n, n \geq 0\}$ with respect to the partition S'. The DTMC $\{Y_n, n \geq 0\}$ is then called the *lumped* Markov chain.

If only the steady-state behaviour is of interest, it is possible to write for the DTMC $\{X_n, n \geq 0\}$

$$\eta_j = \sum_{i \in S} \eta_i \, p_{ij} \qquad \text{(a)}$$

$$\hspace{6cm} \tag{A.60}$$

$$\sum_{j \in S} \eta_j = 1 \qquad \text{(b)}$$

Summing (A.60a) over all states j in macrostate A_J, we obtain

$$\eta'_J = \sum_{A_I \in S'} \eta'_I \, p'_{IJ} \tag{A.61}$$

for all $A_J \in S'$, and also

$$\sum_{A_J \in S'} \eta'_J = 1 \tag{A.62}$$

where

$$\eta'_J = \lim_{n \to \infty} P\{X_n \in A_J\} = \sum_{j \in A_J} \eta_j \tag{A.63}$$

$$p'_{IJ} = \sum_{i \in A_I} \sum_{j \in A_J} p_{ij} \, \nu_{i|I} \tag{A.64}$$

$$\nu_{i|I} = \frac{\eta_i}{\sum_{k \in A_I} \eta_k} \tag{A.65}$$

Note that equations (A.60) to (A.65) hold for all DTMCs, regardless of the fulfilment of the lumpability condition, so that it is possible to evaluate the steady-state distribution over macrostates from (A.61) and (A.62), provided that we can evaluate the quantities p'_{IJ} from (A.64) and (A.65). Obviously, we do not want to evaluate the steady-state distribution of the process $\{X_n, n \geq 0\}$ and then substitute the result into (A.64) and (A.65), since the reason to aggregate states into macrostates is exactly to avoid the solution of (A.60) due to the large number of states. In some cases, however, it is possible to evaluate the p'_{IJ} without solving for the η_i.

The lumpability condition (A.59) is sufficient to obtain the p'_{IJ} without solving for the η_i. In this case, (A.61) becomes

$$\eta'_J = \sum_{A_I \in S'} \eta'_I \sum_{j \in A_J} p_{ij} \qquad i \in A_I \tag{A.66}$$

A.5.2   Aggregation in continuous-time Markov chains

Consider a finite, ergodic CTMC $\{X(t), t \geq 0\}$ with state space $S = \{1, 2, \cdots, N\}$, infinitesimal generator $\boldsymbol{Q}$, transition probability matrix $\boldsymbol{P}(t)$, state distribution $\boldsymbol{\eta}(t)$, and equilibrium distribution $\boldsymbol{\eta}$.

Define also in this case a partition of S by aggregating states into macrostates A_I such that (A.55) holds.

A new stochastic process $\{Y(t), t \geq 0\}$ can be defined on the set of macrostates, with state space $S' = \{A_1, A_2, \cdots, A_M\}$. It can be shown that the condition for this new process to be an ergodic CTMC is

$$\sum_{j \in A_J} q_{ij} = q'_{IJ} \qquad \forall i \in A_I \tag{A.67}$$

The q'_{IJ} are the entries of the infinitesimal generator $\boldsymbol{Q}'$ of the process $\{Y(t), t \geq 0\}$. This equation represents the lumpability condition of the CTMC $\{X(t), t \geq 0\}$ with respect to the partition S'. This condition also implies that

$$\sum_{j \in A_J} p_{ij}(t) = p'_{IJ}(t) \qquad \forall i \in A_I \tag{A.68}$$

where the $p'_{IJ}(t)$ are the elements of the transition probability matrix $\boldsymbol{P}'(t)$ of the process $\{Y(t), t \geq 0\}$.

If we are only interested in the analysis of the steady-state probabilities of macrostates defined as

$$\eta'_I = \lim_{t \to \infty} P\{X(t) \in A_I\} = \sum_{i \in A_I} \eta_i \tag{A.69}$$

we can, as in the discrete-time case, write the following equation for the process $\{X(t), t \geq 0\}$:

$$\sum_{i \in S} \eta_i \, q_{ij} = 0 \tag{A.70}$$

for all $j \in S$, and

$$\sum_{i \in S} \eta_i = 1 \tag{A.71}$$

Summing (A.70) over all states $j \in A_J$ we obtain

$$\sum_{A_I \in S'} \eta'_I \, q'_{IJ} = 0 \tag{A.72}$$

for all $A_J \in S'$, and

$$\sum_{A_I \in S'} \eta'_I = 1 \tag{A.73}$$

where

$$q'_{IJ} = \sum_{i \in A_I} \sum_{j \in A_J} q_{ij} \, \nu_{i|I} \qquad (A.74)$$

and $\nu_{i|I}$ is as in (A.65). Also in this case, equations (A.69)–(A.74) hold, regardless of the fulfilment of the lumpability condition, so that we can directly evaluate the steady-state distribution of macrostates from (A.72) provided that we can evaluate the q'_{IJ} from (A.74) without solving for the steady-state distribution of the CTMC $\{X(t), t \geq 0\}$.

If the CTMC $\{X(t), t \geq 0\}$ is lumpable with respect to the partition S', then (A.67) holds, and (A.72) reduces to

$$\sum_{A_I \in S'} \eta'_I \sum_{j \in A_J} q_{ij} = 0 \qquad i \in A_I \qquad (A.75)$$

A.6 Semi-Markov Processes

Consider the stochastic process sample function shown in Fig. 134. Assume that the process $\{X(t), t \geq 0\}$ is a finite-state continuous-time homogeneous process which changes state at instants θ_n, $n = 0, 1, \cdots$, and assumes the value Y_n in the interval $[\theta_n, \theta_{n+1})$, and such that

$$P\{Y_{n+1} = j, \theta_{n+1} - \theta_n \leq \tau \mid Y_0 = k, \cdots, Y_n = i, \theta_0 = t_0, \cdots \theta_n = t_n\}$$
$$\qquad (A.76)$$
$$= P\{Y_{n+1} = j, \theta_{n+1} - \theta_n \leq \tau \mid Y_n = i\} = H_{ij}(\tau)$$

and let

$$p_{ij} = \lim_{\tau \to \infty} H_{ij}(\tau) \qquad (A.77)$$

In this stochastic process, sojourn times in states can be arbitrarily distributed; moreover their PDF may depend on the next state as well as on the present one. This class of stochastic processes is called semi-Markov processes (SMPs).

The PDF of the time spent in state i given that the next state is going to be j is given by

$$G_{ij}(\tau) = \begin{cases} H_{ij}(\tau)/p_{ij} & p_{ij} > 0 \\ 0 & p_{ij} = 0 \end{cases} \qquad (A.78)$$

The stochastic sequence $\{Y_n, n \geq 0\}$ is a DTMC and is called the EMC of the SMP $\{X(t), t \geq 0\}$.

The transition probabilities of the EMC are defined as in (A.46). It can be shown that

$$r_{ij} = p_{ij} \qquad (A.79)$$

with p_{ij} given by (A.77).

In this case, it is not necessary to exclude the possibility of a transition from state i to itself, hence not necessarily $r_{ii} = 0$.

The classification of the states of the process $\{X(t), t \geq 0\}$ can be done by observing whether the DTMC $\{Y_n, n \geq 0\}$ comprises either transient or recurrent states. Also the irreducibility question can be answered by observing the EMC. The periodicity of the process $\{X(t), t \geq 0\}$ is, instead, to be examined independently from the periodicity of the EMC. A state i of the SMP is said to be periodic if the process can return to it only at integer multiples of a given time δ. The maximum such $\delta > 0$ is the period of the state. Note that a state may be aperiodic in the SMP and periodic in the EMC, and vice versa.

Assume, for simplicity, that all states of the SMP $\{X(t), t \geq 0\}$ are recurrent aperiodic. The average sojourn time in state i can then be found as

$$E[SJ_i] = \int_0^\infty \left[1 - \sum_{k \in S} H_{jk}(t) \right] dt \qquad (A.80)$$

Define the quantities $\eta_j^{(Y)}$ as being the stationary probabilities of the EMC $\{Y_n, n \geq 0\}$, defined as in (A.51) and (A.52). The limiting probabilities of the SMP $\{X(t), t \geq 0\}$, defined as in (A.50) can be found as:

$$\eta_j^{(X)} = \frac{\eta_j^{(Y)} E[SJ_j]}{\sum_{k \in S} \eta_k^{(Y)} E[SJ_k]} \qquad (A.81)$$

which is analogous to (A.53). The EMC technique thus allows the steady-state analysis of a broader class of stochastic processes than was previously considered, namely of SMPs.

The mean recurrence time of state j, defined as the average time elapsing between two successive visits to state j, is

$$M_j = \frac{E[SJ_j]}{\eta_j^{(X)}} \qquad (A.82)$$

Note that also this equation is an extension of (A.37).

The class of SMPs comprises the class of MCs, but SMPs themselves are a subset of a more general class of stochastic processes named semi-regenerative processes. We shall not venture into the analysis of semi-regenerative processes, but it is useful to derive one result that, obviously, is valid for all SMPs and MCs as well.

Consider the SMP sample function shown in Fig. 134. From (A.76) it follows that the time instants at which a jump occurs are such that the future evolution of the process is independent of the past, given the present state, even if the sojourn time in the present state is not an exponentially distributed random variable. This is sufficient to recognize that the process is a semi-regenerative stochastic process.

In this case the characteristics of the process can be determined from the behaviour in the period comprised between two instants at which jumps occur. This time period is called a cycle. The cycle duration is a random variable CY whose average is

$$E\left[CY\right] = \sum_{j \in S} \eta_j^{(Y)} E\left[SJ_j\right] \tag{A.83}$$

Indeed, the cycle duration equals the sojourn time in state j provided that the state at the beginning of the cycle is j. Using the total probability theorem we obtain (A.83).

The limiting state probabilities of a semi-regenerative process can be found as the ratio of the average time spent in a state in a cycle divided by the average cycle duration. This provides another method for the derivation of (A.81).

The cycle analysis can also be performed in a slightly different manner. Consider as initial cycle times the instants at which the process enters state j. In this case the average cycle duration is obtained as

$$E\left[CY_j\right] = \sum_{k \in S} v_{kj} E\left[SJ_k\right] = \sum_{k \in S} \frac{\eta_k^{(Y)}}{\eta_j^{(Y)}} E\left[SJ_k\right] \tag{A.84}$$

where v_{kj} gives the average number of visits to state k between two successive visits to state j, and is given by (A.22). The average time spent in state j in a cycle is obviously equal to $E\left[SJ_j\right]$, so that we again find the result (A.81).

Note that in this latter case the future evolution of the process given that we are at the beginning of a cycle is independent of the past history, and of the present state. The process is thus said to be regenerative with respect to these new cycle starting instants.

The cycle analysis described above can be used to evaluate the steady-state distribution of regenerative stochastic processes; (A.84) can be applied for the computation of the average cycle time, and the steady-state probabilities of the process can be computed using (A.81).

A.7 Semi-Markov Reward Processes

A semi-Markov reward process is obtained by associating with each state $i \in S$ of a semi-Markov process $X(t)$ a real-valued *reward rate* r_i.

The semi-Markov reward process $R(t)$ is then defined as:

$$R(t) = r_{X(t)} \tag{A.85}$$

Assume, for the sake of simplicity, that the semi-Markov process state space is finite. Denote with $\boldsymbol{\eta}$ the steady-state distribution of the SMP, and with $\boldsymbol{r}$ the row vector of the reward rates. The expected reward rate in steady-state, R, can be obtained as:

$$R = \sum_{i \in S} r_i \eta_i = r \, \eta^{\mathrm{T}} \tag{A.86}$$

where η^{T} is the column vector obtained by transposing the row vector η.

The expected reward accumulated in a period of duration τ at steady-state can then be simply obtained as $R \, \tau$.

Markov reward processes (MRPs) are obtained in the special case in which the process $X(t)$ is a continuous-time Markov chain.

The definition of a (semi-)Markov reward process model is often interesting, because it normally happens that aggregate performance parameters are computed with a weighted summation of the probabilities resulting from the steady-state solution of the stochastic process. These weights can be interpreted as rewards, so that a clear abstract framework can be formulated.

Appendix B

GLOSSARY

AGV	automatic guided vehicle
$Bag(P)$	a multiset of elements from P
$\mathbf{C}$	the incidence matrix of a Petri net
$C(p,t)$	the entry of the incidence matrix corresponding to place p and transition t; the change of marking in p due to the firing of t
CPU	central processing unit
$CS(t_i)$	the conflict set comprising transition t_i
CTMC	continuous-time Markov chain
$CY(M_i)$	the cycle time relative to marking M_i
DTMC	discrete-time Markov chain
$E[.]$	the statistical average operator
$E(M)$	the set of enabled transitions in marking M
$E[M(p_i)]$	the average steady-state number of tokens in place p_i
$E_j(M_i)$	the set of transitions enabled in M_i whose firing produces M_j
$ECS(t_i)$	the extended conflict set comprising transition t_i
$ED(t,M)$	the enabling degree of transition t in marking M
EMC	embedded Markov chain
η	the vector of the steady-state probabilities
η_i	the ith entry of the vector of the steady-state probabilities; the steady-state probability of the ith state or marking
f_i	the probability of ever returning to state i after leaving it
FIFO	first-in-first-out
FMS	flexible manufacturing system
GSPN	generalized stochastic Petri net

H	the inhibition function defined on the set of transitions; the set of inhibitor arcs
$\boldsymbol{H}(t)$	the vector whose entries are the multiplicities of the inhibitor arcs from the various places to transition t
$H(t,p)$	the multiplicity of the inhibitor arc from place p to transition t
I	the input function defined on the set of transitions; the set of input arcs
$\boldsymbol{I}(t)$	the vector whose entries are the multiplicities of the input arcs from the various places to transition t
$I(t,p)$	the multiplicity of the input arc from place p to transition t
JIT	just-in-time
LAN	local area network
L-RRG	the reduced reachability graph at priorities greater than or equal to L
M, M'	markings
M_0	the initial marking
$M(p)$	the number of tokens in place p in marking M
$M(t)$	the marking stochastic process as a function of time
$\mathcal{M}$	a Petri net model
$\mathcal{M}_\pi$	a Petri net model with priority
$\mathcal{M}_{\text{GSPN}}$	a GSPN model
$M[t\rangle M'$	marking M' is immediately reachable from marking M by firing transition
$M[\sigma\rangle M'$	marking M' is reachable from marking M by firing the transition sequence
$\langle M_i, M_j, t\rangle$	the arc in the reachability graph from M_i to M_j, labelled t
MC	Markov chain
MIMD	multiple-instruction-multiple-data
MP	the parametric marking of a GSPN model
MRP	Markov renewal process
$\mathcal{N}$	a Petri net
$\mathcal{N}_\pi$	a Petri net with priority
$\mathbb{N}$	the set of natural numbers: $\{0, 1, 2, 3, \cdots\}$
O	the output function defined on the set of transitions; the set of output arcs
$\boldsymbol{O}(t)$	the vector whose entries are the multiplicities of the output arcs from transition t to the various places
$O(t,p)$	the multiplicity of the output arc from transition t to place p

P the set of places

$P\{T_k \mid M_i\}$ the probability that in marking M_i transition T_k wins the race and fires

PAR the set of parameters in the definition of a GSPN model

pdf   probability density function

PDF   probability distribution function

PH   phase-type (distribution)

PI_i the ith place invariant

PN   Petri net

$PRED$ the set of predicates in the definition of a GSPN model

PS_i the ith place semiflow

Π the priority function defined on transitions

$\Pi(t)$ the priority of transition t

π_i the priority of transition t_i (shorthand)

Q the infinitesimal generator of a continuous-time Markov chain

q_{ij} the entry in row i and column j of matrix Q;

        the transition rate from state i to state j, for $i \neq j$

q_{ii} the opposite of the total transition rate out of state i; $q_{ii} = -\sum\limits_{j \in S, j \neq i} q_{ij}$

q_i the total transition rate out of state i; $q_i = \sum\limits_{j \in S, j \neq i} q_{ij} = -q_{ii}$

R the average steady-state reward

$r(M)$ the reward rate in marking M

REMC   reduced embedded Markov chain

$RG(M_0)$ the reachability graph originating from the initial marking M_0

RS   reachability set

$RS(M_0)$ the reachability set originating from the initial marking M_0

$RS(M)$ the reachability set originating from marking M

$\mathcal{S}$ a Petri net system

$\mathcal{S}_\pi$ a Petri net system with priority

SJ_i the sojourn time in state i

SMP   semi-Markov process

SPN   stochastic Petri net

σ a transition sequence

T	the set of transitions
$t^\bullet$	the output set of transition t;
	the set of places connected to t with output arcs
$^\bullet t$	the input set of transition t;
	the set of places connected to t with input arcs
$^\circ t$	the inhibitor set of transition t;
	the set of places connected to t with inhibitor arcs
$t_1 CC(M) t_2$	in marking M, transition t_1 is causally connected with transition t_2
$t_1 EC(M) t_2$	in marking M, transition t_1 is in effective conflict with transition t_2
$t_1 HMEt_2$	transition t_1 is in structural mutual exclusion
	with transition t_2 due to inhibitor arcs
$t_1 IEC(M) t_2$	in marking M, transition t_1 is in indirect effective conflict with transition t_2
$t_1 ISCt_2$	transition t_1 is in indirect structural conflict with transition t_2
$t_1 MMEt_2$	transition t_1 is in mutual exclusion with transition t_2 due to marking
$t_1 \Pi MEt_2$	transition t_1 is in mutual exclusion with transition t_2 due to priority
$t_1 SCt_2$	transition t_1 is in structural conflict with transition t_2
$t_1 SCCt_2$	transition t_1 is in structural causal connection with transition t_2
$t_1 SMEt_2$	transition t_1 is in structural mutual exclusion with transition t_2
$t_1 SSCt_2$	transition t_1 is in symmetric structural conflict with transition t_2
TI_i	the ith transition invariant
TRG	tangible reachability graph
TS_i	the ith transition semiflow
v_{ij}	the average number of visits to state i between two consecutive visits to sta
V_σ	the transition count vector of a T-semiflow
VLSI	very large scale integration
W	the weight function defined on transitions
$W(t)$	the weight of transition t
$W(t, M)$	the weight of transition t in marking M
w_k	the weight of transition t_k (shorthand)
$\omega_k(M_i)$	the weight of $ECS(t_k)$ in M_i

References

[AM82] Alaiwan H. and Memmi G. (March 1982) Algorithmes de recherche des solutions entieres positives d'un systeme d'equations lineaires homogeneus en nombres entieres. *Revue Technique Thomson-CSF* 14(1): 125–135. in French.

[AMBB⁺89] Ajmone Marsan M., Balbo G., Bobbio A., Chiola G., Conte G., and Cumani A. (July 1989) The effect of execution policies on the semantics and analysis of stochastic Petri nets. *IEEE Transactions on Software Engineering* 15(7): 832–846.

[AMBC84] Ajmone Marsan M., Balbo G., and Conte G. (May 1984) A class of generalized stochastic Petri nets for the performance analysis of multiprocessor systems. *ACM Transactions on Computer Systems* 2(2): 93–122.

[AMBC86] Ajmone Marsan M., Balbo G., and Conte G. (1986) *Performance Models of Multiprocessor Systems*. MIT Press, Cambridge, USA.

[AMBCC87] Ajmone Marsan M., Balbo G., Chiola G., and Conte G. (August 1987) Generalized stochastic Petri nets revisited: Random switches and priorities. In *Proc. Int. Workshop on Petri Nets and Performance Models*, pages 44–53. IEEE-CS Press, Madison, WI, USA.

[AMdDN90] Ajmone Marsan M., deMoraes L. F., Donatelli S., and Neri F. (June 1990) Analysis of symmetric nonexhaustive polling with multiple servers. In *Proc. INFOCOM '90*. San Francisco, CA, USA.

[AMDN90] Ajmone Marsan M., Donatelli S., and Neri F. (November 1990) GSPN models of markovian multiserver multiqueue systems. *Performance Evaluation* 11(4): 227–240.

[AMDN91] Ajmone Marsan M., Donatelli S., and Neri F. (April 1991) Multiserver multiqueue systems with limited service and zero walk time. In *Proc. INFOCOM '91*, pages 1178–1188. Miami, FL, USA.

[AMDNR91] Ajmone Marsan M., Donatelli S., Neri F., and Rubino U. (September 1991) GSPN models of random, cyclic, and optimal 1-limited multiserver multiqueue systems. In *Proc. SIGCOMM '91*. Zurich, Switzerland.

[AT85] Alaiwan H. and Toudic J. M. (February 1985) Research des semiflots, des verrous et des trappes dans le reseaux de Petri. *Technique et Science Informatiques* 4(1): 103–112.

[BCBC92] Balbo G., Chiola G., Bruell S., and Chen P. (March 1992) An example of modelling and evaluation of a concurrent program using coloured stochastic Petri nets: Lamport's fast mutual exclusion algorithm. *IEEE Transactions on Parallel and Distributed Systems* 3(2): 221–240.

[Ber87] Berthelot G. (February 1987) Transformations and decompositions of nets. In Brawer W., Reisig W., and Rozenberg G. (eds) *Advances on Petri Nets '86 - Part I*, volume 254 of *LNCS*, pages 359–376. Springer Verlag, Bad Honnef, West Germany.

[BF89] Balbo G. and Franceschinis G. (January 1989) Modelling flexible manufacturing systems with generalized stochestic petri nets. In *Proc. International Workshop on Modelling Techniques for Flexible Manufacturing Systems*. Siena, Italy.

[BL89] Barkaoui K. and Lemaire B. (June 1989) An effective characterization of minimal deadlocks and traps in Petri nets based on graph theory. In *Proc. 10th International Conference on Application and Theory of Petri Nets*, pages 1–21. Bonn, Germany.

[Bla89] Blakemore A. (December 1989) The cost of eliminating vanishing markings from generalized stochastic petri nets. In *Proc. Int. Workshop on Petri Nets and Performance Models*. IEEE-CS Press, Kyoto, Japan.

[BLW90] Boxma O. J., Levy H., and Weststrate J. A. (1990) Optimization of polling systems. In King P. J. B., Mitrani I., and Pooley R. J. (eds) *Proceedings of Performance 90*. North-Holland.

[CAMBC93] Chiola G., Ajmone Marsan M., Balbo G., and Conte G. (February 1993) Generalized stochastic Petri nets: A definition at the net level and its implications. *IEEE Transactions on Software Engineering* 19(2): 89–107.

[CB88] Chen C. H. and Bhuyan L. N. (March 1988) Design and analysis of multiple token ring networks. In *Proc. INFOCOM '88*. New Orleans, USA.

[CBB89] Chen P., Bruell S., and Balbo G. (December 1989) Alternative methods for incorporating non-exponential distributions into stochastic Petri nets. In *Proc. 3rd Intern. Workshop on Petri Nets and Performance Models*, pages 187–197. IEEE-CS Press, Kyoto, Japan.

[CDF91] Chiola G., Donatelli S., and Franceschinis G. (December 1991) GSPN versus SPN: what is the actual role of immediate transitions? In *Proc. 4th Intern. Workshop on Petri Nets and Performance Models*, pages 20–31. IEEE-CS Press, Melbourne, Australia.

[Chi91a] Chiola G. (February 1991) GreatSPN 1.5 software architecture. In *Proc. 5th Int. Conf. Modeling Techniques and Tools for Computer Performance Evaluation*. Torino, Italy.

[Chi91b] Chiola G. (1991) Simulation framework for timed and stochastic Petri nets. *International Journal in Computer Simulation* 1(2): 153–168.

[Cia89] Ciardo G. (1989) *Analysis of large Petri net models*. PhD thesis, Department of Computer Science, Duke University, Durham, NC, USA.

[CL93] Ciardo G. and Lindemann C. (October 1993) Analysis of deterministic and stochastic petri nets. In *Proc. 5th International Workshop on Petri Nets and Performance Models*, pages 160–169. IEEE-CS Press, Toulouse,France.

[CR85] Coolhan J. E. and Roussopoulos N. (July 1985) Timing requirements for time-driven systems using augmented Petri nets. In *Proc. Int. Workshop on Timed Petri Nets*. IEEE-CS Press, Torino, Italy.

[Cum85] Cumani A. (July 1985) Esp - a package for the evaluation of stochastic Petri nets with phase-type distributed transition times. In *Proc. Int. Workshop on Timed Petri Nets*. IEEE-CS Press, Torino, Italy.

[DB91] DeCindio F. and Botti O. (December 1991) Comparing Occam2 program placements by a GSPN model. In *Proc. 4th Intern. Workshop on Petri Nets and Performance Models*, pages 216–221. IEEE-CS Press, Melbourne, Australia.

[DCDMPS82] De Cindio F., De Michelis G., Pomello L., and Simone C. (1982) Superposed automata nets. In Girault C. and Reisig W. (eds) *Application and Theory of Petri Nets*. IFB 52, New York and London.

[Don90] Donatelli S. (February 1990) *L'uso delle reti di Petri per la valutazione e la validazione di sistemi di grandi dimensioni*. PhD thesis, Dipartimento di Informatica,

Università di Torino, Corso Svizzera 185, 10149, Torino, Italy. (in italian).

[ESB89] Esparza J., Silva M., and Best E. (1989) Minimal deadlocks in free choice nets. Technical Report 1/89, Hildesheimer Informatik Fachberichte.

[Fer89] Ferscha A. (December 1989) Modelling mappings of parallel computations onto parallel architectures with prm-net model. In *Proc. IFIP-WG 10.3 Working Conference on Decentralized Systems*. Lyon.

[FN85] Florin G. and Natkin S. (February 1985) Les reseaux de Petri stochastiques. *Technique et Science Informatiques* 4(1): 143–160.

[FN89] Florin G. and Natkin S. (December 1989) Matrix product form solution for closed synchronized queueing networks. In *Proc. 3rd Intern. Workshop on Petri Nets and Performance Models*, pages 29–39. IEEE-CS Press, Kyoto, Japan.

[GR84] Goltz U. and Reisig W. (June 1984) CSP programs as nets with individual tokens. In *Proc. 5th International Conference on Application and Theory of Petri Nets*. Aarhus, Denmark.

[Gri90] Grillo D. (1990) Polling mechanism models in communication systems – some application examples. In Takagi H. (ed) *Stochastic Analysis of Computer and Communication Systems*. North-Holland.

[Hoa78] Hoare C. A. R. (August 1978) Communicating sequential processes. *Communications of the ACM* 21(8): 666–677.

[HS86] Haas P. J. and Shedler G. S. (September 1986) Regenerative stochastic Petri nets. *Performance Evaluation* 6(3): 189–204.

[HV85] Holliday M. and Vernon M. (July 1985) A generalized timed Petri net model for performance analysis. In *Proc. Int. Workshop on Timed Petri Nets*. IEEE-CS Press, Torino, Italy.

[Hwa93] Hwang K. (1993) *Advanced Computer Architecture with Parallel Programming*. Mc Graw Hill.

[INM84] INMOS Limited, Englewood Cliffs, NJ (1984) *OCCAM Programming Manual*.

[INM89] INMOS Limited, Bristol (1989) *The Transputer Databook*.

[JR91] Jensen K. and Rozenberg G. (eds) (1991) *High-Level Petri Nets. Theory and Application*. Springer Verlag.

[KH89] Kamal A. E. and Hamacher V. C. (1989) Approximate analysis of non-exhaustive multiserver polling systems with applications to local area networks. *Computer Networks and ISDN Systems* 17.

[KL88] Kleinrock L. and Levy H. (September–October 1988) The analysis of random polling systems. *Operations Research* 36(5): 716–732.

[Kle75] Kleinrock L. (1975) *Queueing Systems Volume I: Theory*. Wiley, New York, NY.

[Kob78] Kobayashi H. (1978) *Modeling and Analysis : An Introduction to System Performance Evaluation Methodology*. Addison-Wesley Publishing Co.

[Lau87] Lautenbach K. (February 1987) Linear algebraic technique for place/transition nets. In Brawer W., Reisig W., and Rozenberg G. (eds) *Advances on Petri Nets '86 - Part I*, volume 254 of *LNCS*, pages 142–167. Springer Verlag, Bad Honnef, West Germany.

[LBR89] Legato P., Bobbio A., and Roberti L. (May 1989) The effect of failures and repairs on multiple cell production lines. In *Proc. 20th Int. Symposium on Automotive Technology and Automation*. Florence, Italy.

[LS90] Levy H. and Sidi M. (October 1990) Polling systems: Applications, modeling, and optimization. *IEEE Transactions on Communications* 38(10).

[MF76] Merlin P. M. and Farber D. J. (September 1976) Recoverability of communication protocols: Implications of a theoretical study. *IEEE Transactions on Communications* 24(9): 1036–1043.

[Mil89] Milner R. (1989) *Communication and concurrency.* Prentice Hall.

[Mol81] Molloy M. (1981) *On the Integration of Delay and Throughput Measures in Distributed Processing Models.* PhD thesis, UCLA, Los Angeles, CA. Ph.D. Thesis.

[Mol82] Molloy M. K. (September 1982) Performance analysis using stochastic Petri nets. *IEEE Transaction on Computers* 31(9): 913–917.

[MS81] Martinez J. and Silva M. (September 1981) A simple and fast algorithm to obtain all invariants of a generalized Petri net. In *Proc. 2nd European Workshop on Application and Theory of Petri Nets.* Springer Verlag, Bad Honnef, West Germany.

[Mur89] Murata T. (April 1989) Petri nets: properties, analysis, and applications. *Proceedings of the IEEE* 77(4): 541–580.

[MW84] Morris R. J. T. and Wang Y. T. (1984) Some results for multi-queue systems with multiple cyclic servers. In Rudin H. and Bux W. (eds) *Performance of Computer-Comunication Systems.* IFIP/North-Holland.

[Neu81] Neuts M. (1981) *Matrix Geometric Solutions in Stochastic Models.* Johns Hopkins University Press, Baltimore, MD.

[NN73] Noe J. D. and Nutt G. J. (August 1973) Macro e-nets representation of parallel systems. *IEEE Transactions on Computers* 31(9): 718–727.

[Pet66] Petri C. (1966) Communication with automata. Technical Report RADC-TR-65-377, Rome Air Dev. Center, New York, NY. Tech. Rep. RADC-TR-65-377.

[Pet81] Peterson J. (1981) *Petri Net Theory and the Modeling of Systems.* Prentice-Hall, Englewood Cliffs, NJ.

[Rai85] Raith T. (1985) Performance analysis of multibus interconnection networks in distributed systems. In Akiyama M. (ed) *Teletraffic Issues - Proceeding of ITC 11.* North-Holland.

[Ram74] Ramchandani C. (1974) *Analysis of Asynchronous Concurrent Systems by Timed Petri Nets.* PhD thesis, MIT, Cambridge, MA. Ph.D. Thesis.

[RH80] Ramamoorthy C. V. and Ho G. S. (September 1980) Performance evaluation of asynchronous concurrent systems using Petri nets. *IEEE Transactions on Software Engineering* 6(5): 440–449.

[SC87] Shatz S. and Cheng W. (October 1987) A Petri net framework for automated static analysis of Ada tasking. *The Journal of Systems and Software* 8: 343–359.

[Sei84] Seitz C. L. (December 1984) Concurrent VLSI architectures. *IEEE Transactions on Computers* 33(12).

[Sif78] Sifakis J. (1978) Petri nets for performance evaluation. In Beilner H. and Gelenbe E. (eds) *Proc. 3rd Intern. Symp. IFIP*, pages 75–93.

[Sil85] Silva M. (1985) *Las Redes de Petri en la Automatica y la Informatica.* Ed. AC, Madrid, Spain. in Spanish.

[SV89] Silva M. and Valette R. (1989) Petri Nets and Flexible Manufacturing Systems. In Rozenberg G. (ed) *Advances In Petri Nets 1989.* Springer Verlag.

[SW89] Shatz S. and Wang J. (1989) *Tutorial on Distributed Software Engeneering.* IEEE-CS Press.

[Sym78] Symons F. (May 1978) *Modeling and Analysis of Communication Protocols Using Numerical Petri Nets.* PhD thesis, University of Essex.

[Tak86] Takagi H. (1986) *Analysis of Polling Systems.* MIT Press, Cambridge, MA, USA.

[Tak88a] Takagi H. (December 1988) A bibliography on the analysis and applications of polling models. In *Proc. International Workshop on the Analysis of Polling Models*. Kyoto, Japan.

[Tak88b] Takagi H. (1988) A survey of queueing analysis of polling schemes. In de Moraes L. F., de Souza e Silva E., and Soares L. G. (eds) *Data Communication Systems and Their Performance*. IFIP/North-Holland.

[Tay83] Taylor R. (May 1983) A general purpose algorithm for analyzing concurrent programs. *Communications of ACM* 26: 362–376.

[Var62] Varga R. (1962) *Matrix Iterative Analysis*. Prentice-Hall, Englewood Cliffs, NJ.

[VN92] Viswanadham N. and Narahari Y. (1992) *Performance Modeling of Automated Manufacturing Systems*. Prentice Hall.

[WDF85] Wong C. Y., Dillon T. S., and Forward K. E. (July 1985) Timed Petri nets with stochastic representation of place time. In *Proc. Int. Workshop on Timed Petri Nets*. IEEE-CS Press, Torino, Italy.

[YGB86] Yang Q., Ghosal D., and Bhuyan L. N. (November 1986) Performance analysis of multiple token ring and multiple slotted ring networks. In *Proc. 1986 Computer Networking Symposium*. Washington, D.C., USA,.

[YP88] Yuk T. I. and Palais J. C. (November 1988) Analysis of multichannel token ring networks. In *Proc. ICCS 88*. Singapore.

[Zub80] Zuberek W. (May 1980) Timed Petri nets and preliminary performance evaluation. In *Proc. 7th Annual Symposium on Computer Architecture*, pages 88–96. La Baule, France.

Index